ORIENTALIZING THE JE

THE MODERN JEWISH EXPERIENCE

Deborah Dash Moore and Marsha L. Rozenblit, *editors*
Paula Hyman, *founding coeditor*

# ORIENTALIZING THE JEW

*Religion, Culture, and Imperialism in Nineteenth-Century France*

Julie Kalman

Indiana University Press

Bloomington and Indianapolis

This book is a publication of

Indiana University Press
Office of Scholarly Publishing
Herman B Wells Library 350
1320 East 10th Street
Bloomington, Indiana 47405 USA

iupress.indiana.edu

Manufactured in the United States of America

Cataloging information is available from the Library of Congress.

ISBN 978-0-253-02422-0 (cloth)
ISBN 978-0-253-02427-5 (paperback)
ISBN 978-0-253-02434-3 (ebook)

1 2 3 4 5    22 21 20 19 18 17

*To the memory of my father*

# Contents

# Acknowledgments

THIS BOOK OCCUPIED eight busy years of my life, taking in one job and then another, and a move from Sydney down the East Coast of Australia, back home to Melbourne. This book began life when I was at the University of New South Wales, in the hedonistic Eastern Suburbs of Sydney. There, my colleagues Ruth Balint, Stefania Bernini, Zora Simic, Nick Doumanis, and Martyn Lyons helped me see this project through its early stages. In 2012, I moved home to Melbourne, to take up a post at Monash University. Here, Karen Auerbach, Clare Corbould, Daniella Doron, Clare Monagle, Susie Protschky, and Christina Twomey offered insights and encouragements to see the book through to its current state. I wish, also, to thank Ian Coller, Helen Davies, Peter McPhee, Pam Pilbeam, and Maurice Samuels, for their collegiality and generosity. Eitan Bar-Yosef cast a critical, thoughtful eye over chapter 1. Elizabeth Gralton wrestled with my occasionally indulgent writing, always remaining polite, and Veronica Langberg tracked down long undisturbed documents. Daniella Doron and David Feldman both read a full draft of the manuscript. Daniella's arrival at Monash, and in Australia, has boosted the population of scholars of French-Jewish history by 100 percent, but her presence here brings benefits that cannot be quantified. David Feldman is, quite simply, scholarly generosity personified. The three anonymous readers for the press provided engaged and insightful criticisms at an important late stage. My thanks go, also, to Deborah Dash Moore, Marsha Rozenblit, and Dee Mortensen at Indiana University Press. My work is much the richer for their input. The privilege of claiming responsibility for faults and weaknesses in the text, however, remains all mine.

Being a French historian in Australia makes one heavily reliant on travel funding. Vital support came from several sources, including the Faculty of Arts and Social Sciences of the University of New South Wales, the Memorial Foundation for Jewish Culture in New York, and the Australian Research Council.

Over the last eight years, equally vital support has come from Gary Rosengarten, and my thanks go to him. Over that time, our children have grown up, through babyhood, into toddlerdom, to the almost entirely fantastic adolescents that they now are, the world at their feet. I cannot claim that they have provided support in the writing of this book, in which they have consistently demonstrated not one jot of interest, but they are a gift for which I am immeasurably grateful, every day.

This book is dedicated to the memory of my father, Arie Kalman. He survived some of the very worst of what the twentieth century had to offer, yet he never lost his great zest for life and for learning. I am still learning the significance, to me, of his example.

# ORIENTALIZING the JEW

# Introduction

THE AFTERMATH of Jewish emancipation was significant in nineteenth-century France. Jews, emancipated during the French Revolution, became central to questions of nationhood and citizenship raised by the same Revolution.[1] Jewish emancipation required the French to think about France in a radically new way, and this reconceptualization was reinforced by the new presence of Jews in public life. In nineteenth-century France, Jews were enjoying the benefits, as well as the responsibilities, of citizenship. They were moving into all areas of public life and making their way to urban centers, particularly Paris. In the nineteenth century, the Jewish population of Paris grew out of proportion to the growth of the city itself. An 1808 census counted 2,733 Jews living in the city. Thirty years later, this number had increased to 9,000, and this population was to quadruple over the next forty years.[2] The French had to get to know Jews all over again in this new context. They had to incorporate the reality of emancipated Jews into their understanding of what it meant to be French. What was a France that accorded citizenship to Jews? How did that France accord with one's own ideals? Jews could be used to elucidate questions of belonging and exclusion and thus of nationhood. Making sense of the presence of Jews in society was a fundamental part of making sense of the nineteenth century.

Elsewhere, too, could form a backdrop for these questions. Over the busy nineteenth century, punctuated by revolution, war, and regime change, many French looked to further shores to explore questions of identity and belonging. The Orient—for the purposes of this book, comprising North Africa and the Middle East—was a deeply significant elsewhere. French Catholic pilgrims, writers, and artists traveled through North Africa and part of today's Middle East. French bureaucrats were sent to these regions on diplomatic and trade missions. Many of these figures wrote lavishly and evocatively about their experiences.

But Jews were in the Orient, too. There were well-established Jewish communities, a mosaic of long-present Arabic and Berber-speaking Jews, and Jews who had fled the persecutions in Spain and Portugal.[3] These Jewish communities were living in the lands under Ottoman rule during the same period when the French were making forays into these regions. Through their pilgrimage and travel accounts, plays, novels, letters, and paintings, these French pilgrims, writers, and bureaucrats tell us that wherever they traveled in the Orient, they encountered the Jewish communities living there. *Orientalizing the Jew* brings these elements together: nineteenth-century France, Jewish emancipation, the ongoing discovery and definition of the Orient, and the concomitant discovery of Oriental Jews. *Orientalizing the Jew* places the Jew in the history of Orientalism.

As the political turmoil of the nineteenth century might suggest, the French did not necessarily agree on a model of nationhood, and this is reflected in the different ways they experienced the Orient. French Catholics went on pilgrimage to the Holy Land. In Jerusalem, they visited the Jewish community. The best known of these pilgrims was arguably the celebrated Catholic writer Viscount François-René de Chateaubriand. In 1806, he received a substantial financial gift from the Russian tsarina, which he used to fund his travels around the Mediterranean, including a visit to Palestine. For him, Palestine was the Holy Land, and he traveled there as a pilgrim. When he explored Jerusalem, he discovered that city's Jewish community. Chateaubriand was living in the years immediately following the Revolution. Jews were now his nominal equals in society, yet the Romantic Catholicism to which he adhered taught that Jews should suffer eternal punishment for the deicide. In Jerusalem, Chateaubriand could replace Jews in the space his Catholic teaching told him they should occupy. So he created a fantasy of Jews who were degraded and subjugated, just as he wished they would be. A Catholic, committed to the idea of a Catholic France, Chateaubriand felt nothing but astonishment and contempt at the continued survival of Jerusalem's Jewish community. His 1811 book, *Itinéraire de Paris à Jérusalem* (Journey from Paris to Jerusalem), was a best seller and compulsory reading for every pilgrim who followed in his footsteps.

Over the nineteenth century, an industry of Oriental travel accounts and artwork grew. Artists and writers traveled to the Orient to observe and depict it, and their guides and their hosts were most often Jews. Travelers painted the Jews they met and wrote about them. One such writer was Théophile Gautier. In mid-nineteenth century Paris, Gautier sat at the center of a wide social, artistic circle. His closest friends were among the best-known figures in the extraordinary creative world that characterizes this time and place. As a writer, he was part of this world. He also worked as a critic, and in this sense, he stood outside this movement and commented on it. Gautier was extraordinarily prolific and wide ranging in his work. He wrote novels, plays, and librettos. He produced art. He wrote as a critic of art, plays, operas, ballet, and of a wide variety of written works. Through his criticism and his social networks, Gautier lets us into the artistic world of nineteenth-century Paris. Gautier loved to travel, and he spent time in the Orient in 1845, and again in 1852. He found Jews there and wove them into his published accounts of his Oriental adventures.[4] Gautier wrote about Jews he encountered in France, too. He was a great admirer of the Jewish actress Rachel Félix and counted the composer Giacomo Meyerbeer among his friends. He wrote critical appraisals of the work of both of these figures. Gautier drew on the real Jews in his life to create the imagined Jews featured in his works. Indeed, depictions of Jews penetrate deeply into the extraordinary diversity of genres into which Gautier ventured. Gautier's work is a meeting point between fantasized and real Jews. Real and imagined, Oriental and French Jews feed into and from one another in a process of entanglement and intimacy writ large. Gautier's depictions of Jews allowed him to give voice to his ideas of Frenchness, Romanticism, and art. Many others in his circle did the same, and Gautier's life and work provide us with a way in to understanding the significance of the Orientalized Jew in artistic creation.

Sometimes very real Jews intruded into France's experiences and fantasies of the Orient. In the Regency of Algiers, French bureaucrats and traders were forced to negotiate their imperial designs and ambitions through a small Jewish trading house that acted as a political intermediary between France and Algeria for four decades. The House of Bacri and Busnach was run by two Sephardic Jewish families based in Algiers. The Bacris and Busnachs were middlemen. They provided French consuls in Algiers with loans, access to the ruling dey, help, and advice. They negotiated the purchase of enslaved citizens and cargoes from captured ships. They brokered peace. They also provided France with millions of francs' worth of wheat on credit. The debt owed by successive French regimes to the House of Bacri and Busnach, which took more than two decades to be paid, damaged relations between France and the regency so badly that it is seen by scholars as being part of the background to the 1830 French invasion of Algiers. French consuls, ministers, bureaucrats, and businessmen have left thousands of pages of correspondence that feature Bacris and Busnachs. Bacris and Busnachs were central to French ambitions and fortunes in Algiers, and they were at the center of the political relationship between the latter and France.

These are not untold stories. Most accounts of the 1830 invasion allude to the debt. Chateaubriand's work went through multiple editions and became required reading for all those who followed in his footsteps. He, as well as Gautier and his friends, including the writer Alexandre Dumas and the painter Eugène Delacroix, were all known and celebrated during their lives. They have had much scholarly space dedicated to them since. But when we bring Chateaubriand's pilgrimage together with these travel accounts and artworks and the fabled tale behind the French invasion of the Regency of Algiers, we can see that they are all linked in important ways. They are all stories about and depictions of Jews within Orientalism. They suggest how Jews could be Orientalized, whether they were found in the Orient or in France. In this book, I place Jews on the Oriental horizon as it appeared from the perspective of nineteenth-century France.

Orientalism, of course, was Edward Said's great intervention. He offered a new way of conceptualizing relations between West and East.[5] His insistence that Europe created and constantly refined itself in relation to the Muslim world brought about a shift in the way stories of empire were framed and understood. In his schema, relations between a monolithic Europe and an imagined, reified Orient were unequal, based on the notion that Western, Orientalist discourses were linked to processes of appropriation and reification and, ultimately, to the very material expression of inequality that was colonialism. This was, in the words of one admirer, a "subversive" framework that allowed scholars to think about Europe as a constant work in progress, whereby the production of knowledge served the purpose of self-legitimation as well as the legitimation of the practice of power over others.[6]

Said recognized, if somewhat obtusely, that Jews acted as a—generally unstated—referent in Orientalism, through his allusions to Orientalism as the "strange, secret sharer" of Western antisemitism or the "Islamic branch" of antisemitism.[7] Was this a straightforward recognition, as Ivan Kalmar and Derek Penslar put it, "that Jews as well as Muslims had been the target of orientalism"?[8] Or was it, according to a more cynical reading of Said's work, "a rhetorical flourish serving the strategic intent of this work to counter Zionist representation and authority"? According to this account, Said's *Orientalism* acts as a sort of palimpsest, whereby Orientalism replaces antisemitism.[9] However, Said's words might also be read as an invitation, whether intended or accidental, to explore what actually exists behind the facade of wordplay.

Jews lived throughout the Orient of Chateaubriand, Gautier, and the bureaucrats in Algiers. There is a well-established and ongoing body of work that brings to light the history of these communities. Yet a door that might, once opened, have offered an Orientalist vista in which it was possible to discern Jewish figures has remained firmly closed. Said's own engagement offers a way into understanding the extraordinary power of his edifice and thus, perhaps, the reasons behind this equally extraordinary occlusion. For as the Saidian paradigm was taken on and developed by others, Said himself came to represent victimhood in the schema of relations that he had sought to describe. It was through his own advocacy for the cause of Palestinian nationalism that the scholarship of Orientalism became attached to this, other struggle. When Orientalism was applied to the context of Israel, Jews became the victors, the colonialists. Thus, Zionism could be shackled to the sort of Orientalist ideology that enabled colonialism.[10] If it was easier to see things in black and white, then Jews could only be white and European. They could only belong to the camp of the dominating, making it impossible to create any room for them elsewhere. Jews, in scholarship such as this, have been caught in what Bryan Cheyette has called the "Manichean categories" of Eastern victim and Western, European oppressor.[11] Jews have been firmly lodged in the latter category. To allow space for them as the targets of Orientalism would be to allow for qualification in the notion that Zionism itself was a form of Orientalism, of which Arabs were the targets.[12] No place could be found in Orientalism for Jews.

Instead, theories of colonial discourse and Orientalism subsumed Jews within "a homogenous 'Western Judeo-Christian' culture," leaving no room for recognition of the "ambivalent" position of the Jew within this cultural monolith.[13]

Susannah Heschel and Jonathan Hess have both considered the possible meanings of Orientalism in German Jewish history. Both have argued that we must consider a form of Orientalism analogous to Said's framework of the European quest for intellectual authority of the Orient: an Orientalism that was internal to the West. The history of German Jews brings this to light. For example, the rise of historical theology in Germany over the nineteenth century occurred as figures such as Christian Wilhelm Dohm were exploring the possibility of Jewish emancipation.[14] In his work, Hess considers the significance of Johann David Michaelis, a biblical scholar, Orientalist, and advocate against Jewish emancipation. For Michaelis, biblical Judaism was Oriental, and contemporary Arabs were "sources of potential data for the historical study of the Hebrew Bible."[15] In order to demonstrate that Jews were not worthy of emancipation, Michaelis had to definitively separate Christianity from Oriental biblical Judaism, and this necessitated what Hess calls a process of de-Orientalization. Thus, it was necessary to know the Orient from which Judaism sprang, but this was a process of intellectual domination directed at controlling—colonizing—a population within. As Heschel argues, the logic of this Orientalist schema, "the intimacy between knowledge and power," is clear to scholars of Jewish history, familiar with "constructions of Judaism and the political uses to which they were put" in history.[16]

Jonathan Boyarin's book *The Unconverted Self* focuses on the regions making up today's Spain and brings together the Inquisition and Columbus's departure for the Indies. Boyarin argues that this medieval project of outward expansion into a New World—and the concomitant expansion of Christianity—was matched by an internal expansion that manifested itself in the expulsion of the Jews of Spain.[17] Both the persecution of Jews, "as an Other 'inside' Europe," and the conversion of American Indians, as Others "encountered as a result of a European voyage outward," were two parts of the same project of legitimizing and sustaining Christian Europe.[18] There is a significant gap in Boyarin's work, and he himself points to it. His schema neglects, as he puts it, "the existence of Jewish communities *outside* Western Christendom from the later Middle Ages through the earlier centuries of colonialism"[19] and, I would add, beyond.

*Orientalizing the Jew* builds on the insights of these scholars and brings the questions their work raises to bear on France over the late eighteenth and nineteenth centuries. In nineteenth-century France, the European project may no longer have been entirely Christian, but it was by no means a completed work. In particular, the project of defining France, and French citizenship, was intense and ongoing through the nineteenth century. Many of the travelers who discovered and depicted the Orient and its Jews also had interactions with the newly emancipated Jews around them at home in France. Jews existed both inside and outside the physical boundaries of Christian Europe and, concurrently, inside and outside the Christian European imagination. How did Orientalist creations in the nineteenth century reconcile the Jews over there, in the Orient, with the Jews at home, in France? What happened when Boyarin's "inside" and "outside" Other were one and the same? What happens when we place the Jew in Hess and Heschel's internal Orientalism, as well as in Said's external Orientalism? These questions lie at the heart of this book.

Said did not include Germany among his case studies because, as he argued, Germany was not a colonial power in the Middle East, so its Orientalism was not political.[20] France, however, an intellectually inquisitive and ultimately colonizing power, was at the core of Said's thesis. For the French, the Orient was an exotic location that could be a canvas for rehearsing questions of nationhood. When the French brought their civilization to this region, they defined precisely what that civilization meant, because this was by no means a settled matter in nineteenth-century France. In the Orient, they could practice and perfect narratives of citizenship and nationalism. Throughout the nineteenth century, in the wake of the Revolution, French society became a terrain for intensely competing discourses of nationhood, as French men and women sought to define themselves and assert a meaning for Frenchness in the postrevolutionary world. As the revolutions and regime changes that continued to punctuate this century suggest, different groups vied to impose their ideal of France on the nation in a contest that has been characterized as a culture war.[21] Whether this process was as hostile as some would have it, the project of defining France, and French citizens, was intense and ongoing through the nineteenth century. Thus, for example, Catholic pilgrims traveled to Jerusalem and depicted that city as intrinsically French and Catholic, giving their Catholicism an importance that it no longer possessed in France. Writers and artists used their travels in North Africa to make sense of rapid change in French society, including the growth of industry and capitalism. The growing popularity and frequency of depictions of Oriental encounters over the course of the nineteenth century are telling. The Orient was a significant elsewhere, a place where ideals and disgruntlement could be expressed and explored. France, therefore, provides fertile ground for a case study.

Jews were intrinsic to these processes. Jews in the Orient were very real for French visitors, who had extensive interactions with them. In Morocco, as Daniel Schroeter has shown, European social contact with local populations was almost always with the Jewish communities there.[22] Jews were their guides, their go-betweens, and often, their hosts. Jews were more likely to be able to converse with visitors; it was easier for travelers to gain access to Jews than to Muslims; Jews were familiar to, even if not always loved by, visitors; and Jews were disproportionate in the population of consular representatives and interpreters. Jews could be familiar, almost European, faces to travelers who felt themselves to be in a most foreign of lands.[23]

Yet when French observers encountered what they called Oriental Jews, they also overlaid observation with layers of agenda and interpretation. For example, writers who believed in the evils of capitalism often gave in to the temptation to overemphasize the (hidden) wealth of Oriental Jews. This allowed them to evoke tropes of rapaciousness and to explore this notion in relation to French society. Others dwelt at length on the beauty of Jewish women, allowing themselves to indulge in fantasies of sensuality and carnality that were taboo for bourgeois *moeurs*. Given the nature of such descriptions, it may be difficult to access some sort of universal truth about the way Jews in Muslim societies interacted with those French who encountered them, but what is readily available to us is the story of how these visitors fantasized them. This is important, because when French travelers, pilgrims, and bureaucrats spoke about Jews, they were speaking about the contested terrain of Frenchness.

Given the circumstances of Jewish emancipation in France, all of those who left behind accounts of the Orient that included Jews had, at the very least, some sort of contact with Jews at home in France. For example, Jews were active in the creative circles of mid-nineteenth-century Paris. The actress Rachel Félix lived a life that was the stuff of legend, enjoying a meteoric rise and wild success and suffering a tragic, early death. When she was not touring, she held a regular salon in Paris, and her busy career made her very visible and present in the city. The composer Giacomo Meyerbeer, born Jacob Meyer Beer in Berlin, came to Paris to seek his fortune. He never knew critical acclaim, but he did enjoy extraordinary popular success. Both were involved in the creative circles of Paris. Both befriended Théophile Gautier. Indeed, many of the figures in this book interacted with, and at times befriended, these and other real Jews. They could literally be known, as collaborators, fellows, and friends. Jews were still imagined figures, however, and Jewishness, for so long a trigger for fantasy, still allowed space for unreality. Jews were powerful totemic figures. They could be used to enunciate new ways of thinking and being, such as national belonging.[24] They could also be called on to reiterate older ways of explaining the world, such as Catholicism.

In one sense, the place of the Jew in Christian teaching could be generalized across Catholic Europe. At the same time, however, the place of the Jew in French society was unique, due to emancipation. The Jews' elevation to citizenship was deeply challenging to those who believed that Jews were not, and simply never could be, the same as Catholics. The true France, for them, was the eldest daughter of the church, and its citizens were Catholic. But the emancipation was just as challenging to those who did not necessarily adhere to this worldview. The figure of the Jew was used to give shape to what some saw as being unacceptable in French life. For example, Baron James de Rothschild, the youngest of the five sons sent to the capitals of Europe, was highly visible for his wealth and also for his Jewishness. For some, such as the early socialists, he became a symbol of the capitalist, materialist values that were taking root in France. They saw Jews as representative of the evils of competitive capitalism, unleashed by the Revolution. The true French citizen, in their eyes, cooperated with his fellows. For others, the figure of the Jew in French society could be read as a shining example of the inclusiveness and tolerance of the nation.

All of these opinions were based on the fact that the French *knew* Jews. For centuries, Jews had been fundamental to Christianity's own account of itself. Only Jews held a unique place in the European, Christian imagination, as the necessary precursors to Christianity and as the killers of Christ. Judaism was the pole against which Christianity defined itself: if Christianity was right and true, for example, that meant that Judaism must be inherently wrong. Christians used Jews to express the boundaries of acceptability in Christianity. Yet the continued existence of Jews in Europe provided a constant challenge to Christianity, for if the church was the natural successor to Judaism, as Christianity taught, why then did Judaism continue to survive? This could be explained by the nature of the Jew, who refused to acknowledge truth and who, therefore, was obstinate, degraded, and blind. The Jew's continued adherence to this difference also made him deceptive and untrustworthy. Jews were intrinsic to the story of Christianity and were therefore familiar figures to anyone schooled in its ideology. Jews were a significant Other within Europe. And in the significant space that was the Orient, Jews could also be Other.

French travelers came to the Orient, carrying in their baggage assumed knowledge about Jews. Yet over and over again, what the traveler, pilgrim, or bureaucrat anticipated was reshaped by the often hospitable and helpful Jews whom they found. The Jews who feature, most often secondhand, in this book, were not always passive actors. Jews also actively shaped the experience of the French in the Orient. The Bacris and Busnachs, who dictate chapter 3, might offer the clearest example of this activeness, but the Jewish guides, interpreters, silversmiths, and even hosts who are described to us served to mediate between fantasy and reality. Jews were able to get close to the French in the Orient. They were often close enough to be able to influence, mold, and shape the French experience of the Orient. At the same time, they were different enough for French travelers to seek to maintain distance between themselves and the Oriental Jew. In the French understanding of the Oriental Jew, there was interplay between this real experience and the idea of the Jew that travelers carried in their imagination. For the French traveler, the Oriental Jew was a fluid figure, both accessible and inaccessible, knowable and unknowable, and this allowed the real encounter to inspire and feed into fantasy. The figure of the Orientalized Jew allowed for the fusion of fantasy and reality in ways that are deeply significant. It allowed the French to create a space where they could speak about themselves but also speak about the Jews of France. French Jews, too, used their coreligionists in the Orient to articulate their place in the nation. This might involve real Jews, in Damascus or in Algiers, who needed saving or regenerating.[25] Or it might involve the creation of fantasies of Orientalized Jews, which allowed them to delineate their own Jewish identity.[26] The way that the French understood and described Jews in the Orient as Others gives shape to their questions of identity in nineteenth-century France. This gives us access to France's nineteenth century and to the ways that the French made use of Jews, both in France and in the Orient, to bring some order to a disordered world. How the French imagined Jews tells us much about how the French lived the busy nineteenth century, including the negotiations that took place over what France, and French identity, might be. The gap between reality and fantasy allowed space for discourses, honed both in the Orient and in France, to feed into one another. The Orientalized Jew, a fluid figure, could be imagined and constantly re-created. The fluidity of the Orientalized Jew undermines the fixity of West and East, or "here" and "there." It allows us to take apart overly simplistic categories such as colonizer and colonized. It allows us to question the category of whiteness or the identity that was French, or even European, supposedly constructed in opposition to, among other possible Others, a cleanly defined, Oriental Other.

Indeed, the figure of the Orientalized Jew allows us to question the way we understand the construction of otherness, particularly as this pertains to Jews. Recent scholarly work has sought to move beyond sweeping histories of antisemites and antisemitism and to think instead about discourses on Jews as attempts to explain the world.[27] For example, David Nirenberg has framed his recent book *Anti-Judaism: The Western Tradition* as "the history of thinking about 'Judaism.'"[28] Nirenberg argues that "Anti-Judaism," as he calls it, can be understood as "a way of critically engaging the world."[29] Yet, as his title suggests, the thinking that forms the subject of his book is thinking that casts the Jew negatively. Other recent work has explored philosemitism as a historical phenomenon, seeking to reframe a history that has focused on hatred.[30] Between these two poles, there is a vast middle space in the history of discourses on Jews that has been almost entirely ignored. When the French talked about Orientalized Jews, they assigned them attributes that were both negative and positive. If we draw on current understandings, they were both philosemitic and antisemitic at the same time. Where, on a spectrum whose two ends are antisemitism and philosemitism, would we place Théophile Gautier's description of the "Hebraic beauty" he saw in Constantine? Here, Gautier dwelt on every aspect of this woman's physical beauty, and in this complete excavation of loveliness, he locked his subject in her body. This "Hebraic beauty" was a carnal figure, and her beauty was offset by her bearing, which spoke her belonging "to a deposed and debased nation."[31] Images such as the one he drew are common in the Orientalizing of the Jew. Is this love or even tolerance? Is it hatred? In this book, I seek to conceptualize this middle space.

The Orient, of course, was not simply the stuff of fantasy. It was attached, also, to a geographic reality. France's physical Orient that takes center stage in this book is approximately contiguous with today's Syria, Lebanon, Israel, Egypt, Tunisia, Morocco, and Algeria, taking in parts of North Africa and the Middle East. To some extent, this geography has determined the book's structure. However, the main driver of this same structure is thematic, based on the forms that Orientalism took when it was directed at Jews—that is, understood through the prism of religion, fashioned in art and literature, and determined by the requirements of economics and imperialism. Chapter 1 follows French Catholic pilgrims as they made their way, in the footsteps of the Crusaders and then Chateaubriand, to the Holy Land. When these pilgrims encountered the Jewish populations there, what was the result? How did these meetings interact with efforts to recreate a Catholic France? Chapter 2 explores the Orientalized Jew as a cultural production: How was the Oriental Jew depicted in travel literature, novels, plays, and art? What dreams of domination or utopias, what expressions of opposition or desires for subversion were projected onto the Orientalized Jewish woman and the Orientalized Jewish man? What was the significance of these Orientalized Jews in the creative intensity of nineteenth-century France? And how did depictions of a fantasized Jew in Morocco, for example, or meetings with a Jewish guide or host, interact with the presence of very real Jews in the creative circles of nineteenth-century Paris? Chapter 3 explores the political face of Orientalism and the Jew through the story of the House of Bacri and Busnach. What was this trading house, and what role did these Algerian Jews play in the increasingly complicated political relationship between France and the Regency of Algiers? Through the story of France's interactions with these Sephardic trading Jews, I consider the place of the Orientalized Jew in political discourses linked to imperialism.

This process results in three large and somewhat oversimplified chapters. There was no clear delineation between the religious, the artistic, or the political in the Orientalizing of Jews, either in France or the Orient. The process of writing history, nonetheless, asks that we create meaning through the imposition of structures. In this book, my goal is twofold: first, to write Jews into a history that has neglected them and, second, to underscore the ongoing and unique relevance of Jews, both in France and in the Orient, to the history of making France, and Europe more broadly. As well as structure, I have imposed a sort of triage: the picking out of significant details from a "vast ocean of contingency."[32] This is a book about the Jew in French Orientalism. I do not seek to deny the presence of

Muslims or Christians in the Orient or their relevance to the project of making France. European Christianity might have developed, in many ways, in lockstep with Islam. However, Islam never held a place *inside* the narrative of Christianity, as Judaism did. Muslim and Christian populations in the Orient did often serve as a point of comparison with the Oriental Jew, underscoring the significance of the latter's Jewishness. In this book, therefore, while I extract the story of depictions of Jews in interactions between France and its Orient from the broader narrative, Arabs, both Muslim and Christian, "share" in it. In this book, I seek to disentangle Orientalism from the teloi of colonialism and Zionism that have governed it and to allow space for the protagonists to speak, and tell us how they configured their world. My hope is that this selective history nonetheless hints at the fertile and important messiness that lies beyond.

# 1    Pilgrimage to the Holy Land Within

IN 1806, VISCOUNT FRANÇOIS-RENÉ de Chateaubriand undertook a pilgrimage to the Holy Land. His 1811 *Itinéraire de Paris à Jérusalem* was an account of his trip. In undertaking a trip to the Orient, Chateaubriand had set out, in his words, "to complete the circle of studies" that he had always promised himself he would achieve. In the secular age of the years immediately following the Revolution, Chateaubriand alluded to his pilgrimage self-consciously:

> It may seem strange today to speak of wishes and of pilgrimages, but on this point I am not restrained by a sense of modesty, and for a long time now, I have aligned myself with the class of the superstitious and the weak. I may be the last Frenchman to leave my country to travel to the Holy Land, with the ideas, the goal, and the sentiments of an old pilgrim.[1]

With his 1802 work *Génie du Christianisme* (The genius of Christianity), Chateaubriand had announced his return to Catholicism. Terribly disillusioned, like so many others, by the extremes of the Revolution, seeking an outlet for what Paul Bénichou called his "sensitivity" and his melancholy at this great disappointment,[2] Chateaubriand found an answer in Christian teaching. The doctrine of man's fall could explain perfectly the events of recent years. With its reverse side, wherein the believer could invest hope in a better, if distant, future, it also allowed space for dreams. In Palestine, paradoxically, Chateaubriand dreamed of a glorious past. This was the Romanticism that Chateaubriand took with him. The Palestine he visited was that of history; its distant stories were of greater importance than its current reality. Thus, Chateaubriand the pilgrim walked variously in the footsteps of Jesus and of the Crusaders, both harbingers of Christianity to a site that was seen to be rightfully the property of the church. This was a direct echo of early Romanticism, which was making its first foray into France in the early nineteenth century. Early French Romantics such as Chateaubriand sought to express their literary sensibilities and indulge the Romantic self.[3] This Romanticism, as Charles Baudelaire put it, was all about the way the subject was felt and perceived.[4] In Romanticism, then, Chateaubriand could live out the Catholicism to which men like him returned in the aftermath of a Revolution that, in the words of one contemporary, had driven his spirit away from the real world, by making it "too horrible."[5]

Chateaubriand arrived in the Holy Land at Jaffa on October 1, 1806. He traveled around, visiting Bethlehem and the Dead Sea. He also spent a week in

Jerusalem. At the end of his description of his time in the city, Chateaubriand took the reader on a final, metaphorical tour. He sought to leave the reader with the image that he found "even more extraordinary" than what he called the "extraordinary desolation" of the Holy City. This was the continued existence in Jerusalem of two peoples, whose faith enabled them to "overcome so much horror and misery." First were the Christian monks, who endured "despoilment," "bad treatment," and even "death threats" to remain close to Jesus Christ's tomb. Their presence in Jerusalem was a source of comfort and protection to all: Chateaubriand described them as guardians against iniquity. Turks, Arabs, Greeks, and what he called "schismatic Christians" all sought refuge with these selfless monks, knowing that any price would be paid for their safety. These monks represented the "new" Jerusalem. And what of the "old"? This was a "little people" who lived

> apart from the rest of the city's inhabitants. The particular object of all contempt, it lowers its head without complaint; it suffers all snubs without demanding justice; it allows itself to be overcome by blows without a sigh; its head is demanded: it is presented at the cemetery. If it befalls members of this exiled society to die, their companion will bury them furtively, in the night, in the valley of Jehoshaphat, in the shadow of Solomon's temple. Enter into the homes of these people; you will find them living in dreadful squalor, making their children read a mysterious book that they, in turn, will make their children read. What they were doing five thousand years ago, this people still does. Seventeen times have they witnessed the destruction of Jerusalem, and nothing can discourage them; nothing can prevent them from turning their eyes toward Zion. You might be surprised to see the Jews spread over the earth, according to God's word: but to be struck by supernatural astonishment, you must encounter them in Jerusalem; you must see these rightful masters of Judea, slaves and strangers in their own land; you must see them, oppressed in every sense, awaiting a king who is to deliver them. Crushed by the Cross that condemns them and that has been driven into their heads, hidden near the Temple of which there is no trace, they remain in their deplorable blindness. The Persians, the Greeks, the Romans have all disappeared from the earth, and a little people, whose origin preceded that of those great peoples, still exists apart, in the debris of its homeland. If anything among the nations could be called miraculous, we think that it is this. And what could be more marvelous, even to a philosopher, than this meeting of the ancient and the new Jerusalem at the foot of Calvary: the former grieving over the sight of Jesus Christ's sepulcher arisen, the latter finding consolation by the only tomb that will have nothing to render at the end of time![6]

Chateaubriand was already an established writer when he published his *Itinéraire*. *Atala* (1801), his tragic story of a Native American woman who committed suicide rather than break her newly Christian vow of chastity, was a best seller in the early years of the nineteenth century.[7] Nonetheless, Chateaubriand would have been happy at the extraordinary success that this new publication enjoyed, since he had hoped to attract attention from his pilgrimage. His *Itinéraire* went through several editions and translations. It has also been the subject of much scholarly discussion since, and the previous passage is so widely known that it is now possible to allude to it in shorthand, as Chateaubriand's *petit peuple* (little people). But this passage must be explored fully, for it places Chateaubriand's work among an extraordinary body of self-conscious pilgrimage writings that made use of the Jews in the Holy Land to give greater meaning to the pilgrimage journey.

Pilgrims might not make predictable figures in Orientalism, just as the Holy Land does not normally figure as part of the Orient's terrain.[8] Said constructed Orientalism as an essentially secular project. However, when we bring together the Holy Land, French Catholic pilgrimage, and depictions of Jerusalemite Jews, Orientalism becomes infused with religion.[9] For this city was home to Jews, and when French Catholics undertook their pilgrimage to the Holy Land and its principal city, they encountered its Jewish community. They assigned this community a specific place in their pilgrimage narrative. This must lead us to rethink the place of religion and, specifically, of pilgrimage and the pilgrimage account in Orientalism, and the way that Jews bring this phenomenon and this concept together. Jews, of course, played a unique role in Christian theology generally. In the context of nineteenth-century France, to make space for Catholic narratives of Jews in the Holy Land is to allow an exploration of a different face of Orientalism. Insofar as French Catholics wrote themselves into a fantasized Holy Land to think through their nineteenth century, we may speak of French Catholic Orientalism. In this chapter, I explore the place and significance of Jerusalemite Jews in the broader schema of this Orientalism.

## Catholicism and Pilgrimage

The century following the Revolution was one of extraordinary challenge for the Catholic Church in France. The Catholic hierarchy was forced to find ways to bend and give without breaking, to adapt but remain steadfast to a core idea of France, as regimes continued to change. One way that Catholics maintained their attachment to the church was through pilgrimage. In the middle of the century, in particular, there was an extraordinary rise in expressions of Catholicism of this type. The role of the journey to Lourdes as a means of creating a Catholic community and ensuring the ongoing vitality of Catholicism in France has been well documented.[10] Pilgrimage to the Holy Land, while not accessible to all, was, nonetheless, also intrinsic to the process of imagining and maintaining French Catholicism.[11] Over the course of this difficult century, French Catholic pilgrims wrote the story of a Christian Holy Land that allowed them to imagine a properly Catholic France.

French Catholics had much to think about. In July 1830, the Bourbon monarchy had once again been deposed, this time in only three days, bringing to an end the reign of Charles X, the younger brother of Louis XVI and Louis XVIII. His cousin, the relatively liberal Louis-Philippe of the House of Orléans, took the throne in his place. Louis-Philippe's father had voted in 1793 for the execution of his cousin Louis XVI, and his appointment in 1830 in place of Charles X, in the eyes of many nobles, was a shameful replay of his father's ignominy. Louis-Philippe's purge of Charles X's administration was the final insult. In 1830, François-de-Sales-Marie-Joseph-Louis, Count d'Estourmel, was prefect for the department of the Manche on the northwestern coast. In July he traveled to the border of his department, received the royal family there, and accompanied them on their way into exile. Once he had left them safely in Cherbourg, he went traveling, fulfilling "a childhood dream."[12] Nobles such as Estourmel, who under the Restoration had been "Ultras," or ultraroyalists, were alienated from the new regime. They migrated to their country homes or left France and became intransigent Legitimists, so influenced by Romanticism, and perhaps by the nature of Restoration Catholicism, that they preferred to turn away from an importune present to dwell in an illustrious past.[13] Some profited from this retirement to write an overdue account of their travels. During the Restoration, Marie-Louis-Jean-André-Charles Marcellus, Count Demartin du Tyrac, had entered the diplomatic corps. He became secretary to the French ambassador in Constantinople and traveled to the Holy Land in 1820. It was only after his withdrawal from public life, however, that Marcellus took to writing. His *Souvenir de l'Orient* (Memory of the Orient) was published in 1839. (In what may have been the ultimate fit of pique, he was to refuse the inheritance of the family title after his father's death.)

In February 1848 the July Monarchy was unseated and replaced by the Second Republic. Uncertainty had in fact dominated the political scene for some two years before the reign of Louis-Philippe came to an end, and it did not finish there. In one sense, Catholicism went through a resurgence and a rapprochement with the ruling regime during the Second Republic. On the other hand, this was indicative of a shift in the position of the church on the French political landscape and an equal shifting of the battle lines. Once so blissfully beyond politics—although this did not prevent the church from engaging in highly politicized acts—the church now rolled up its metaphorical sleeves and entered the political ring. As François Furet puts it, French Catholicism had "become a party," and it threw its support behind order and property, epitomized after June 1848 by the ruling Party of Order.[14] The extended campaign over what the church termed "freedom of education" is an example of this new engagement: Clericalism was now aligned with conservatism, and secularism became "the banner" of the republican battle.[15] Schools became the terrain of a political conflict that now included the teaching of religion.

Pilgrimage can also be understood as part of the renewed expression of Catholicism. By the midcentury, pilgrimage to the Holy Land was booming. Pilgrimages now became organized, a reflection, perhaps, of the growing profile of pilgrimage within France amid the extraordinary revival of religious practice that took place in this context, spurred on by the appointment in 1846 of the charismatic Pius IX and by France's close involvement in the question of the integrity of the papal territories.[16] James McMillan describes this awakening of popular piety as one of the nineteenth century's most significant cultural movements.[17] One contemporary observer described pilgrimage, through somewhat partisan eyes, as being "destined to find its place among the most remarkable religious events of our era."[18] Pilgrimage was seconded by the rise in appointments to clerical posts and the expansion of religious orders. Through pilgrimage, as well as the veneration of local saints and holy sites and the belief in miracles, Catholics found ways to steer their faith through the modern world.[19]

In 1806, Chateaubriand may have had reason to see his pilgrimage as the closing chapter in an old tradition. This sense of an ending allowed him to look backward and indulge his nostalgia for a lost era. Pilgrims—most famously Constantin-François Volney—were still traveling to the Holy Land in the late eighteenth century. Volney published an account of his journey in 1787.[20] Chateaubriand read Volney's work, which circulated widely among what Fernande Bassan, in her exhaustive study of Chateaubriand's journey, calls the "cultured circles."[21] But Volney was one of the last to undertake a pilgrimage in his century. The momentum of the passage was interrupted by the Revolution (when to travel as a pilgrim made one suspect), as well as by Napoleon's invasion of Egypt. During the Revolution, France had also ceased to send priests to the Holy Land and had thus lost some of its influence in the region. Bonaparte's campaign in Egypt and Palestine brought about a total disruption of relations between France and the Sublime Porte. Thus, in the early nineteenth century, pilgrimage had virtually ceased. Chateaubriand was one of the first to return after this parenthesis. However, he was by no means the last. In fact, Chateaubriand's *Itinéraire* constituted a starting point for the many other self-designated pilgrims, nobles, and priests, all fervent Catholics, who were to follow in his footsteps, and all of them, just like him, wrote about their journey.

Why did so many pilgrims translate their journey into written form? What was the point of the pilgrimage account? Part of recovering the Holy Land in the Catholic imagination involved recounting and reworking the pilgrimage as a story. Thus, not only did pilgrims travel; they also published the tale of their pilgrimage.[22] They were, in Alexander Kinglake's typically pithy observation, tourists "with a journal and a theory, and a plan of writing a book."[23] One such tourist was Count Auguste de Forbin, who had been appointed director of the Musées royaux of France in 1816. Forbin was sent to the Levant in 1817 to acquire antiquities that would fill the gaps left in the Louvre after the powers of Europe had forced France to restore treasures acquired by Napoleon on his campaigns. Forbin spent two years in the region, and his *Voyage dans le Levant, en 1817 et 1818* (Voyage in the Levant in 1817 and 1818) was printed by the royal publishers in 1819. The Count d'Estourmel, who traveled in 1830, noted cheerfully that "Lamartine, Michaud and Poujoulat, the Duke de Raguse, Géramb, Marcellus, and especially Chateaubriand [were] in everyone's hands. What remains in the field," he asked, "to be collected by a weak gleaner trailing behind harvesters such as those?" Nonetheless, he published a two-volume account of his own travels.[24] The Count de Rosset de Létourville described himself as writing his notes "without any order, under a tent, during a halt by a stream or a water tank, with the help only of those authors whose work I carried pillion in my portmanteau." And he delivered the same notes "to the readers without any preparation other than having brought them together and put them in order."[25] Their journey was informed by books. As Michel Butor puts it, they were "bookish": books played a part in the genesis of their journey, books informed their travel experiences, and they produced their own book on their return.[26]

One way in which the pilgrimage became a story was in the link that pilgrims made to crusading. Pilgrimage and crusading were elided in these accounts to speak a highly specific and meaningful language of French Catholicism. The pilgrimage was French. Chateaubriand went to Jerusalem, armed not only "with the piety of a pilgrim" but also with "the courage of a crusader,"[27] and following his return, he referred to himself as an "old crusader."[28] For an early nineteenth-century Romantic such as Chateaubriand, to look back, seeking to achieve unrestrained artistic expression in the language of Catholicism, was to find the Crusades. The nature of Romanticism, of course, is elusive: a movement that placed the individual and their impulses at its center generated as many versions as it had adherents. But it can be said of early nineteenth-century Romanticism that it was mostly reactionary, and while it saw itself as progressive in that it rejected classicism, paradoxically, it also looked to the past for inspiration. It espoused royalism and Catholicism. The writer, especially the poet, became the philosopher; in Bénichou's words, "Romanticism consecrated the poet."[29] And if the individual could create his own little fiefdom of sentiment, the poet ruled over all. Exemplified by Goethe and his gift of Werther to a generation of young Germans, the poet became a medium by which others could access emotion and self-expression. In France, one such poet-god was Torquato Tasso, whose *Jerusalem Delivered*, originally published in 1581, was part of a wave of popular historical writings being printed (or in Tasso's case, reprinted) during this period. James Smith Allen has detailed how such works were strongly nationalistic, to the extent that, to quote one contemporary writer, Charlemagne and Saint Louis "were French like us."[30] They served to bring together the French Catholic nationalism and nostalgic Romanticism that Chateaubriand had packed as mental baggage in his valise. Religion and history fed into and informed one another. Little wonder, then, that the French pilgrimage narrative sought to evoke the Crusades.

For this purpose, pilgrims relied on Tasso, whose tale of the first Crusade was a very popular and significant choice. The work slipped quietly into the best-seller lists of the early nineteenth century. Between 1816 and 1845, this account of Christianity's retaking of the Holy Land went through numerous editions. For the first nine years of this period, *Jerusalem Delivered* sat in the middle of the list of what Martyn Lyons has judged to be the best sellers of publishing in early nineteenth-century France, between such works as Perrault's *Contes de fées* (Fairy tales) and Voltaire's *Oeuvres complètes* (Complete works).[31] Along with La Fontaine's *Fables*, Fénelon's *Télémaque* (Telemachus), Abbé Fleury's *Catéchisme historique* (Historical catechism), Daniel Defoe's *Robinson Crusoe*, either Molière or Racine, and Florian's and Perrault's fairy tales, it is one of only a handful of works to appear consistently on Lyons's carefully constructed lists from this period. Whence such popularity? Over the course of twenty cantos, Tasso presents a highly stylized understanding of historical events: Glorious, gallant Christian warriors fight for good against pagan, corrupt, and evil Saracens. Some of them fall in love with beautiful, if not entirely appropriate, women. His is a Crusade easily appropriated and modified to suit the needs of nostalgic Romanticism.

Thus, for example, toward the end of the poem, the Christian forces prepare to take Jerusalem, and the French, "all reverent," fall on their knees to pray and kiss the ground before they "charge on" into battle.[32] Ever the greater gentlemen, even in battle (the "sudden, horrific blows" of the Turk kill men too quickly, not even allowing them time to pray, whereas the Christians kill their foe "with less terror, and less misrule"),[33] they win what is rightfully theirs, and their first view of the Holy City is described thus:

> But when the sunlight strikes the stubble fields
> with rays now bright and rising in the sky,
> behold, they see Jerusalem appear!
> Behold, Jerusalem is drawing nigh!
> And behold, a thousand voices now acclaim
> as one the promised land—Jerusalem![34]

And the perseverant reader, reaching the end of the epic, is rewarded with an image of Godfrey de Bouillon, the French-born commander, praying at the Holy Sepulchre:

> So Godfrey has attained the victory;
> and leads, in the last light glowing in the west,

the victors into the city now set free
and to the place where Christ was laid to rest.
To the temple with the other chiefs goes he,
nor does he set aside his blood-stained vest.
He hangs his arms here: with devoted brow
adores the great tomb, and fulfils his vow.[35]

The presence of Tasso's work on the best-seller lists not only attests to the success of popular Romanticism but also reinforces, as others have suggested, that the Middle Ages were reimagined through works such as his.[36] But the story of the Crusades involved not just Christians and Muslims. The same Crusaders with whom Chateaubriand identified also massacred Jewish communities in the Rhineland as they made their way across Europe. In Jerusalem, the Jewish community was subject to the same fate as Muslims, as Christian Crusaders behaved in what one historian of Jerusalem has described as a most unchristian manner.[37] Contemporary accounts detail how Crusaders herded Jerusalem's Jews into the synagogue and then set fire to it.[38] Tasso described the blood of Saracens running in the streets of Jerusalem. The city's Jewish population did not figure in Tasso's version of events. Nonetheless, just as there had been a Jewish population in Jerusalem in 1099, there was one in 1806, when Chateaubriand visited the city. And unlike Tasso, Chateaubriand described and discussed it.

## The Holy Land

There had always been some sort of Jewish presence in the Holy Land. By the beginning of the nineteenth century, the Jewish community there was overwhelmingly urban, concentrated in the four holy cities of Jerusalem, Safed, Hebron, and Tiberius. (Some also based themselves in the coastal ports of Jaffa, Haifa, and Acre.) A lack of reliable evidence makes it almost impossible to accurately determine numbers, but it can be said with some certainty that when Chateaubriand visited Jerusalem in 1806, the city housed some two thousand Jews.[39] They lived in their own designated quarter, between the Dome of the Rock and Mount Zion. At the very beginning of the nineteenth century, the Jewish population was mostly Sephardi. There was a ban on Ashkenazi settlement, a response to the debt incurred by the group that had arrived in 1700 under the leadership of Yehudah Hasid. This was lifted only in 1816, when Sultan Mahmud II issued a *firman*, or decree, that canceled the debt. The very few Ashkenazim who sought to remain in the city in defiance of the ruling had to dress and pray as Sephardim. Many of these had come to the Holy Land to die and be buried there. They, like many others among the community, were unable to support themselves. They were able to rely on an extensive charitable system known as Halukkah, the distribution of sums collected from Jewish communities throughout the Diaspora.

This was overwhelmingly a poor community, living subject to hostility from its Muslim neighbors and buffeted by the pasha's constant demands for money. The Jews of Jerusalem enjoyed a somewhat fragile peace and security. Their presence in Jerusalem was greeted with tolerance at best. At worst, they could be subjected to outright hostility and violence. They were liable to be targeted by those who regularly revolted against Ottoman rule. Life in Jerusalem in general was hard; the city was overcrowded. Water had to be bought from villages outside and then held in underground cisterns that, when uncovered, could become receptacles for animal droppings and refuse. Jerusalem was ripe for disease, and indeed, the city's population was visited regularly by epidemics. The plague overtook Jerusalemites in 1812. Smallpox broke out in 1842–1843, and there were cholera epidemics in 1833, 1837, and again in the 1860s. This may have been a contributing factor to the high rate of infant mortality in the Jewish community. The population growth that occurred in the community over the course of the century was due as much to immigration as to any natural increase. And the population certainly did grow. In the 1870s the Jewish population of Jerusalem had reached approximately nine thousand, but already by 1839 there were more Jews than either Muslims or Christians in Jerusalem.

The parlous situation of Jews in Jerusalem was reflective of a more general anarchy and poverty across Palestine. Indeed, if pilgrims imagined themselves visiting a Holy Land, they had to negotiate this with the reality of Palestine. By the turn of the century, Jerusalem and its environs had become little more than one of many supports for court life in Istanbul. In a direct line of exploitation and impoverishment, wealth flowed out of the administrative district, or *sanjak*, of Jerusalem, first to the local administrator, who would be appointed with a short period in which to enrich himself; then to the governor in Damascus; and finally to the Ottoman capital. This meant that peasant farmers, the *fellaheen*, were subject to multiple layers of exploitation that were ultimately crippling. The countryside was reduced to abject poverty, and it stagnated. Added to these drains on the population was European economic exploitation in the form of trade concessions, known appropriately as the Capitulation Agreements, since these had been forced on the Ottoman Empire by European powers in the sixteenth and seventeenth centuries. Under the Capitulary regime, European traders received 5 percent off customs taxes, exemption from all interior taxes, and diplomatic protection for themselves and their merchandise.

All these conditions, in turn, led to virtual anarchy in the countryside, which was ruled by self-styled warriors, such as the notorious Abu Ghosh, and numerous Bedouin tribes. Travel through the region was dangerous: the foreign traveler who managed to avoid capture by pirates on the sea would face the prospect of disease and attack. No traveler would get through this countryside successfully in any form of travel other than a caravan with an armed guard. No traveler could pass without the payment of designated tolls to tribes and villages along the way. Early nineteenth-century pilgrims traveled alone at their own—considerable—risk. And assuming they reached Jerusalem, they would find an equally impoverished city, unable to rely on food sources from the surrounding countryside, subject to hunger and regular epidemics, and barely able to support its relatively small population. Neglect and mismanagement meant that the city had fallen into virtual ruin. If this were not enough, in the early decades of the nineteenth century, the Turkish authorities were not welcoming toward pilgrims, and non-Muslims were subject to strict controls on their movements and behavior. Before 1831 and the Egyptian conquest, the country attracted only a slow trickle of pilgrims, those equipped with the necessary sense of adventure.

If pilgrimage could be read as a sort of intrusion, this was fed as much by Ottoman collapse as by any imperial desire. Egypt was fighting the Turks for control of Syria and Lebanon. In 1831, Ibrahim Pasha, the son of the Egyptian ruler Mohammed Ali, marched into Palestine at the head of an invading army. Jerusalem came under Egyptian control. The Trappist monk Marie-Joseph de Géramb arrived in Palestine on his pilgrimage at the same time as the troops, and he reached Jerusalem just ahead of Ibrahim Pasha's soldiers. He was suspicious that the apparently pro-Christian measures being put in place by the new rulers were simply masking greater pain to come.[40] But he was mistaken. The pro-Western regime that ruled from 1831 made pilgrimage safer and more straightforward and thus more common. Although the Egyptian conquest was to last barely a decade, it created a momentum of travel that was not stopped. Europeans were not keen to relinquish the sense of freedom and greater power that they had enjoyed in that short decade. They began to establish consulates and patriarchies: the French consulate in Jerusalem was established in 1843, and the Latin patriarchy was restored in 1847. France set itself up to be the sole protector of Latin Christianity and its adherents in Palestine. This development coincided with the appetite for stories of elsewhere. In France, learned societies were established, journals were produced, publishers began bringing out digests of travel accounts, and a literature of the Orient took root.[41] The armchair voyage was most definitely in vogue.[42] So was history. In this context, travel accounts found an eager audience. The number of journals that reproduced such accounts attests to their popularity: travel tales were printed in the *Mercure*, the *Annales des voyages*, the *Journal des voyages*, and the *Revue des deux mondes*.

In 1853, the first of what were to become regular caravans to the Holy Land departed from Marseilles. Thirty-five such caravans, initially organized by the Society of Saint-Vincent-de-Paul, were to leave France between 1853 and 1873, taking 618 pilgrims to the Holy Land. Organized to travel twice a year, once at Easter and once in August, their goal, stated in the first article of their constitution, was to "facilitate the journey to Palestine for all Catholics."[43] (The 1858 edition of the *Bulletin de l'oeuvre des pèlerinages* noted optimistically that "one of the most tangible" results of pilgrimage to the Holy Land was "the religious good that pilgrims carry out around them" on their return to France.)[44] Jean Chelini found it easiest to divide this group into just two social categories: priests and Catholics, "belonging mostly to the aristocracy or to the grand bourgeoisie."[45] Louis Enault would have found good company in the latter group; the Legitimist writer and journalist was on the first caravan and wrote about his 1853 experience in his *La Terre sainte* (The Holy Land). In his group was also the abbé Azaïs, chaplain for a school in Nimes. Azaïs was one of several priests who took the caravan to the Holy Land and then recounted their journeys. Among them were the Jesuit father Amédée de Damas and the Marseillais abbé Daspres.[46]

The year 1853 also saw the outbreak of the Crimean War. The Ottoman authorities formed a united front with the French and British to discourage Russian ambitions in the empire. The war, fought mostly on the Crimean Peninsula, did not affect or slow the passage of pilgrims. Politically, the Ottomans knew that their victory was an allied victory, and in the wake of the war conditions for foreigners improved. For example, churches and synagogues were repaired, some new ones were built, and rules against foreigners owning property were relaxed. The war, which had ostensibly broken out over a dispute between the Latin and Orthodox Churches in the Holy Land, left French Catholics with every reason to believe that their cause in the Holy Land now had ascendancy over that of the Orthodox Church, supported by Russia.[47]

## Jerusalem

These were the circumstances in which pilgrims arrived at the walls of Jerusalem. Pilgrims generally traveled overland from Jaffa and were thus afforded their first view of the Holy City from the Mount of Olives or Mount Scopus. Most of them were overcome, sinking to their knees or remaining standing, speechless, as they imagined the glories contained within. "Here I am," Abbé Delorme told his young readers, typically describing himself walking the streets that the Holy of Holies once walked, and where his voice was heard.[48] The very ground was sacred, but it was being defiled. For as well as being the site of Jesus's death, Jerusalem, by the nineteenth century, had also been under the rule of Islam for several hundred years. The pragmatic Edouard Blondel, who described himself as a businessman rather than a pilgrim, was disappointed at the "curtain of domes and minarets" that "hid the cupola of the Holy Sepulchre" from view.[49] Félicien de Saulcy, the wealthy soldier-explorer who kept the Louvre in a steady supply of antiquities in the middle decades of the century, was more susceptible than Blondel, describing his first view of the city: "the dilapidated cupola of the Holy Sepulchre, the cupola of Omar's mosque, and the spires of the minarets."[50] Léon de Laborde spent four years traveling through the Mediterranean and the Middle East with his father,

Alexandre, between 1824 and 1828 and produced two volumes describing his travels through the Holy Land.[51] He, too, phrased his disappointment somewhat more eloquently than Blondel. Jerusalem, for him, rose

> gradually from a red and gray landscape, dotted with dusty olive trees; all in all, a rather dull outlook. At first, it is disappointing; the imagination of intense devotion has gone beyond the impossible, and reality does not even meet the expectations of the artist. . . . But the imagination is so pliable, so docile, that it lends itself to all disappointments; and, as we approach the walls, it has already had history and the misfortunes of Jerusalem fraternize with this grim, destitute landscape.
>
> "Ada El-Qods," cry the Arabs to us. A new disappointment: the great name of Jerusalem, this name that is known all over the world, which our children stammer and our elderly remember when all else is lost to their memory, this holy name is unknown in this land.[52]

For these men, almost three decades apart, the Muslim domination of Jerusalem was clearly visible in the city's skyline, blocking the Crusades from view. Islam intruded on the fantasy.

Saulcy, Laborde, Delorme, and Blondel may not have kept company; beyond the fact that they made their journeys some two decades apart, the three former figures may not have found common ground with the latter. But they and their fellow travelers did have something in common: They all knew in advance what they were going to find, for they knew this landscape. They expected it to be familiar, and indeed, it was. Eitan Bar-Yosef has described how the British involvement in the Holy Land was predicated on a Jerusalem understood as much in the context of England itself as in relation to the actual city. Palestine and Jerusalem were so intrinsic to the English understanding of themselves that, as Bar-Yosef puts it, "the accumulation of knowledge" about the region was not a precursor to imperialism and domination but, rather, the confirmation of a preexisting claim to the land.[53] As holiness, in the Christian understanding, was internal rather than focused on a fixed location, a Holy Land could be conjured within one's own consciousness. The journey to the location became a confirmation of a world already created rather than the starting point for the creation of this world. Yet the experience of travel could also enrich the imagined landscape. Maurice Halbwachs has discussed the complex relationship between concrete locality and religious memory. As he saw it, the continued existence of the Church of the Holy Sepulchre, for example, allowed Christians to maintain their belief in its "supernatural" qualities—that is, "useful virtues that fortified faith, revitalized dogmas, and embodied and illustrated them."[54]

> Although the memory of these events was at risk of disappearing, the Church replaced that same history in a made-to-measure dogmatic framework in which the most vivid beliefs of contemporary society could be expressed.[55]

The landscape was familiar because it was eternally Christian. Louis Enault, for whom Jerusalem was the theater "of all the main scenes in the religious drama,"[56] made explicit the importance of the city, not in and of itself, but precisely as a vessel:

> The Church of the Holy Sepulchre, which was not built to a consistent plan at all, or according to mature and reasoned architectural thought, does not present to the eye the great and noble lines that we admire in the religious monuments of the north and west in any way. . . . But little matter! It is hardly admirable architecture that we seek here; it is a memory and an emotion. This memory, the very stones render it to your soul; this emotion, everything contributes to its birth: the number and the layout of the sanctuaries, the mysterious twilight of the vaults, the byzantine decoration.[57]

Memory was connected to place as well as to text. Even for those travelers less imaginative than Enault, the story of Christianity was offered for the reading in Jerusalem. The city was, in the words of Laborde, a "beautiful museum of Christianity."[58] Little wonder that all pilgrims—including Blondel—carried a Bible for reference. It was their Baedeker. For it was in this region that the holy book came to life; pilgrims traveled through the Holy Land as though they were traveling through a book of Bible scenes. The writer and librarian Xavier Marmier journeyed around the world in the 1840s, and his travel writings were to earn him a chair at the Académie. In his volume on the Orient, he went so far as to state that without their faith, without what he called their "religious memories," Palestine would be nothing to its visitors: "a dry and uncultivated land, sand hills, ruined cities inhabited by poor populations."[59] A Jerusalem colored by faith was what all pilgrims wanted to find. This was how to obliterate Muslims from the city's skyline and from its history. This was how to rediscover the presence of the Crusades in the Holy Land.

And the land did offer traces of the Crusades. For Jerusalem was, of course, lost to the infidel, but the gallant Crusaders eventually won Jerusalem back, for Christianity and for France. For Léon de Laborde, in this land, truly holy, "the Old Testament, the Gospel, the Crusades, and the pilgrimages form[ed] an uninterrupted series of events."[60] As Laborde stated, whosoever wished to know the Middle Ages "perfectly" had merely to travel to the Orient, for it was there that they would "meet the image of the twelfth century at every step."[61] Chateaubriand took *Jerusalem Delivered* with him when he examined the areas outside the walls of Jerusalem, and it was this work that he used to reconstruct the taking of Jerusalem by the crusading army. He was "struck" by Tasso's accuracy; his description of events was clear, precise, and explicit.[62] In a nod to the authority of the poet, Chateaubriand noted inaccuracies as poetic license or as instances where the poet, in his wisdom, chose to "confound" the reader:[63]

Whosoever is sensitive to the beauty, the art, the interest of a poetic composition, to the wealth of detail, to the accuracy of the characters, to the generosity of feeling, should make *Jerusalem Delivered* their favorite work. It is, especially, the poem of the soldier. It breathes valor and glory, and, as I observed in *The Martyrs*, it seems to have been written on a shield in the midst of the camps.[64]

The priest Vidal de Langon reread Tasso as he explored Jerusalem and found that the author's descriptions enhanced his experience of the places he saw.[65] Henri Cornille, who befriended Géramb while he was in Jerusalem, described how he left the gates of the city, Tasso in hand, to study the positions of the crusading army and found the author's accuracy "striking."[66] And while the presence of the Crusaders was to be fleeting, nonetheless, of all influences in Jerusalem, theirs—and that of Christianity—were the most enduring for all these pilgrims. Thus, for example, for Father Amédée Damas, while Solomon's reign may have been "spectacular," it had been "surpassed" by the city's later "glory."[67] Abbé Jean-Hippolyte Michon brought together all of the possible sources of inspiration to be found in Jerusalem: "Jerusalem is an inexhaustible mine for the historian, the archaeologist, and the Christian."[68] He was not wrong to put the three categories together. Many pilgrims undertook research and wrote detailed histories. Explorers recorded their emotion upon arriving in the Holy Land. History and religion were one.

Thus it was that each and every pilgrim came to Jerusalem, armed with a full understanding and appreciation of its true nature as a Christian city, whose history was that of Christendom. It was a place where Christians could be united "in thought and experience,"[69] or they could come away with their faith more "vivid": "a firmer hope, a greater love of God, and something of a foretaste of the joys to which the true Christian will be called in the heavenly Jerusalem!"[70] Jerusalem itself resonated with Christianity, and its presence was overwhelming in the city. Abbé Vidal de Langon found Jesus Christ "everywhere." For him, "time and revolutions" had not managed to erase the traces of Christ's divinity, neither in the sites that bore witness to his life, his teachings, and his martyrdom nor in the very air, the "evangelical perfumes" that one breathed "everywhere."[71] When Xavier Marmier was taken to a mountaintop to enjoy a view, he responded, "What a panorama! What memories!"[72]

For Chateaubriand, it was indeed the past that made Palestine what it was, much more so than its present situation. He might have traveled through Palestine of the nineteenth century, but he saw the ancient land all around him. All around him, the holiness of Christianity spoke. "Everywhere" he saw "a land teeming with miracles: the burning sun, the towering eagle, the barren fig trees, all the poetry, all the images of Scripture are there":

Every name holds a mystery; every cave announces the future; every summit resounds with the accents of a prophet. God himself has spoken here; parched streams, cleaved rocks, gaping tombs testify to the wonder; the desert still seems mute with terror, as though, having heard the voice of the Eternal one, it has not dared to break the silence.[73]

Perhaps it was in part their determination to overcome the Muslim presence with a Christian Jerusalem that explains why many included a long history of the city that was overwhelmingly Christian. These histories began with descriptions of virtuous, biblical Judaism, which was then superseded by Christianity, its natural successor. And while Jerusalem may have been founded on (acceptable) biblical Judaism, nonetheless it enjoyed much more glory as a Christian city.

## Encountering the Jews

We have seen that pilgrims sought to write a story of the Holy Land that made it eternally Christian. And just as in the story of Christianity the Jews played a vital role, so their presence in Palestine was central to the re-creation of that region as essentially Christian. The Christian version of the Holy Land's history could simply not be told without them. Jews were represented in these pilgrimage accounts in their historical context, playing the role that the church had assigned them. One of the comforts of what was an otherwise uncomfortable physical journey to Jerusalem was to rediscover the historic place of the Jews in a world where any barriers separating them from Christianity had been pushed aside. More than one pilgrim sought to place the Jews firmly back into their historical context, so that historic Jews could be the very same Jews that pilgrims found in contemporary Jerusalem.[74] In his long history of the city, Vidal de Langon told the story of one episode in which Jews were reputed to have massacred Christians. In the following chapter, he described the current-day Jews of Jerusalem, still awaiting their "liberator" who would make them masters once again. These same Jews still failed to understand the enormity of their original crime and lived under the weight of their punishment: the blood of the Son of God would forever be on their children, and the "deicide city" was forever condemned to "atone for the agony of the divine victim in mourning and abandonment."[75]

This, too, was common rhetoric. For while pilgrims understood the Holy Land as timeless and eternal, at the same time, and paradoxically, it was also in decline, a mere shadow of what it had once been.[76] Some discerned the traces of Christianity both in the full flower of its glory and at the climax of its great tragedy. More than one pilgrim understood Jerusalem as a city in mourning, stained with the death of Jesus, "exhaling" the crime of his martyrdom, as Delorme put it.[77] The city had become "the shadow of what it once was; a mutilated corpse."[78] Blondel saw in Jerusalem a "desolate spectacle of impiety and superstition."[79]

Nowhere was this sense of degradation more visible than in the Jewish quarter. Almost all of the pilgrims featured here paid a visit to the Jewish quarter of Jerusalem and wrote about this and the city's other communities. In fact, the way in which the different communities of Jerusalem were described often followed a similar pattern. First the pilgrim would tour the Armenian quarter and find it to be the best maintained. If the Greek and Latin quarters were not quite as clean, this was because these two communities were so selfless: Who could keep their own home pristine when they were so occupied maintaining the homes of others? The Muslim quarter was generally found to be somewhat disorderly but inoffensive overall. This is striking, given the way that Islam intruded on the first view of the city, and underscores, perhaps, the way that Muslims were being given a specific place in a constructed narrative. For, as though at the bottom of some sort of hierarchy of acceptability, the description of the Jewish quarter, often the longest and most evocative, would come last. The enormity of Judaism's fall from grace was reflected in the way Jews in Jerusalem lived. Thus, Cornille noted that it was "especially" in Jerusalem that the Jews lived out their punishment. The Jews of Jerusalem were "only half alive; barely breathing," under the weight of the stigma of reprobation by which they had been marked.[80] Similarly, the Jewish quarter itself, in all accounts, was the dirtiest, poorest, and most dilapidated.[81] Vidal found it impossible to cross the quarter "without being asphyxiated by a foul and nauseating odor."[82] The Count de Forbin sought out the Jewish quarter first when he was in Jerusalem in 1817. There he found a street that barely merited the name; there he saw "haggard and unhealthy beings, with a strongly pronounced physiognomy, fight tooth and nail for a few coins."[83] The Jews lived separately from the other populations of the city. Their observers understood this as rightful: a consequence of their punishment for the crime committed by their forefathers in that very place, and a reflection of the place that Judaism occupied in the world of the nineteenth century. For Xavier Boniface, writing as Saintine, Moses's curse had been fulfilled in Jerusalem, more starkly than anywhere else. Where once they had been "as numerous as the stars," there now remained only a few, living as "fainthearted strangers." They were "a people with no homeland in its very homeland."[84] Jewish misery in the Holy Land served to confirm Christian truth.

Perhaps to add to this misery, the Jews lived surrounded by the vestiges of their former splendor, a constant reminder of how far they had descended. Enault could still see traces of their "native nobility" in their person: "a forehead that widens at the temples—as though to contain more abundant thoughts—delicate and supple hands, fire in the eyes, pearly teeth, and the proud curve of an aquiline nose."[85] It was also reflected in their physical environment. Vidal described them languishing in "an abyss of woe": "A short distance from the place where once they built the most beautiful temple that man had ever erected to the Lord, the children of Abraham have humble underground rooms, where light barely manages to enter through openings, for sanctuary."[86] All visitors to the synagogue stressed its dilapidation. It was reached down "a ruined staircase into cellars whose archways had caved in or were held up by pillars that once had been sculpted and covered with gold," where (as the Book of Kings described it) "their fathers worshipped the God of Israel and of Judah underneath porticos of marble and archways leaning on Lebanon cedar."[87] Forbin was drawn to the Jewish quarter to visit the synagogue, which he had long desired to see. He found it "miserable and disgusting": children in rags learned the history of the city from an old man who was, appropriately, blind.[88] Others laid stress on a metaphorical blindness. Estourmel found what he called their "constancy of error, this faith in promises whose accomplishment has been right before them for the last eighteen centuries without their realizing it," to be "extraordinary."[89] The Count de Marcellus described the Jews of Jerusalem, "seduced by the shadow of a homeland," awaiting the Messiah "a few steps away from his tomb."[90] In phrases highly reminiscent of tropes of Judaism, Géramb's "unhappy" Jew had eyes but did not see and ears but did not hear; he was intelligent, but understanding continued to elude him.[91]

Thus, Jews were "relegated to the bottom of the city,"[92] and everything about their physical situation spoke of their spiritual state. One thing that the real Jerusalem gave Christians was the sight of the Jews of Jerusalem in their degradation, so close to the tomb. The Jews were now slaves in a place that they had once possessed, weeping "over their past glory."[93] They were now little more than "remainders."[94] In this place, "where they denied their God," Marmier found it right that they should live "under the humiliating yoke of servitude." Their presence and their state were "like a decisive proof, one of the living proofs of the truth of prophets and the judgments of the Gospels."[95] Géramb, too, noted that the Jew existed "less for himself than for others" so that the decree of his own condemnation, written in the book that he preserved, "carefully but blindly," might be displayed to anyone who would read it. Géramb likened the Jew as he understood him to "a criminal who is sentenced to be taken to the ignominious place where he might have deserved to live, carrying before him the notice that he does not see and that nonetheless is noticed by all those who see it."[96]

Nowhere was their rightful punishment illustrated better than at the Western, or Wailing, Wall. Considered to be the remaining vestige of the Temple, Judaism's Holy of Holies, the Western Wall was—and indeed still is—a site of immense significance in Judaism. It was dubbed the "Wailing Wall" because every Friday afternoon the Jews of Jerusalem went to the wall, as close as they could get to the now forbidden Temple Mount, to mourn the destruction of the center of holiness in Judaism, the Temple. This ritual became an essential stop on the tourist route. While the spectacle of "men and women from all stages of life, sitting in the dust and weeping for their conquered homeland," was one that aroused pity in those who witnessed it, the sight also confirmed all that they knew. The Jesuit Damas acknowledged that his "ardent and sympathetic soul" was moved by what he saw. But his reason spoke otherwise. For the Jews' mourning was merely the result of their own actions. For Damas, the Jews' tears were calculated:

> Unfortunately, the carnal and greedy Jew is a false personification of grief. In Jerusalem, as elsewhere, interest remains their idol. Their eyes on the site of the Temple, they lament its ruin; and their heart still heavy with sighs, their eyelids still wet with tears, they go and lend money at an exorbitant rate of interest to an unhappy victim obliged to seek recourse in their funds. Usury has become their element, as their name is an outrage.[97]

If elements of a more secular expression of hostility can be discerned in Damas's writings, this was not uncommon. The Jews of Jerusalem served to confirm what pilgrims already knew about the faith that they held so dear. But these same Jews also served to confirm all that pilgrims knew about Jews and Judaism, not just within the story of Christianity but also in the context of nineteenth-century France. In this sense, their physical voyage was also a journey within. Far beyond a simple displacement, this journey provided the opportunity for definition, idealization, projection, and interchange. The physical journey allowed these pilgrims to take comfort from the satisfyingly lowly state of the Jews there and to use this as a starting point for the imagining of an ideal world. In the process of this imagining, the Jews they saw in Jerusalem and the Jews who were their fellow French citizens became one and the same, and thus the Jews of France were neatly sent back in time and back to the ghetto. The Count de Marcellus, describing his meeting with leaders of Jerusalem's Jewish community, happily quoted Montesquieu out of context: "Nothing is more like an Asian Jew than a European Jew."[98] In his 1721 *Lettres persanes* (Persian letters), Montesquieu had his protagonist, Usbek, the author of this letter, go on to describe Judaism as the "mother" of Islam and Christianity, "two daughters who have overwhelmed it with a thousand cuts."[99] But Marcellus displayed no such ambiguity. The Jews, he noted, paid him compliments. If they gave him nothing, nonetheless they offered to lend him money. And this, continued the censorious Marcellus, was "their standard politeness": "In Jerusalem, as with everywhere else, they are bankers, and they lend Christians the sums they need to buy the prerogative over the shrines from the Turks, at high rates of interest."[100] In this way, then, Jews everywhere could share similar qualities. Vidal found that the "humble and obsequious bearing" of the Jews of the Orient made them "immediately recognizable,"[101] as though they were the same everywhere. For Cornille, too, all Jews shared the same origin. In the Holy Land he saw young Jewish girls who carried this "heirloom": "an original and pure beauty, . . . like a souvenir of Solomon's daughters and Esther's triumph."[102] While the Jews of Europe had the good fortune to live in enlightened times, they themselves were "far from being rehabilitated." They still carried what he called their "inherited biases," and the enormity of their actions, and the corresponding revenge of Heaven, still prevailed over them. United as one family, alone in their exile, they remained "pure in disgrace."[103] Thus, all Jews, in the words of Marmier, were eternally damned: neither time nor different climates had managed "to erase their distinctive features and the signs of the celestial fury that has struck them."[104] Everywhere they maintained "the characteristic type that distinguishes them from all populations in the universe: that character, that mark that neither time nor nature has been able to erase."[105] Equally, they were eternally homeless: these were the children of Israel who still wandered "through the world; strangers in the land that saw their birth, in the countries where they live, rootless, and with possessions nowhere." Marmier's Jew had indeed been "cruelly treated in much of arrogant Europe."[106] But while Marmier spoke of what he saw as the Jews' misfortune, his tone was nonetheless damning. For as eternal as their damnation was their love of lucre. Gold was their consolation.[107]

And this was the quality that Jews shared above all else: that of banker. The practice of money lending was so intrinsic to their character, according to Daspres, that they had great difficulty giving it up.[108] The primary objects of their ruinous practices were Christians.[109] This was a standard feature of these depictions. Jews in Jerusalem, whether recent or more long-term inhabitants, shared these qualities with their coreligionists in Europe: they calculated, they dissembled, and they despoiled. Daspres saw a need to sound a note of warning to his readers: a gold or silver object bought at the bazaar from any of the Jews from Germany or Poland who had come to Jerusalem to die would change, after purchase, into copper.[110] If the Jew was "Jewish," for Géramb this meant that interest was his idol, and while the Jew might weep "rivers of tears for the destruction of the holy city and the dispersal of his nation," nonetheless, "his heart still heavy, his eyes still veiled with tears," he would lend at exorbitant rates.[111] Damas saw the Jews of Jerusalem not as citizens of the city but as a conquered population "full of hatred and vengeance." But just as Tasso's Muslims fought in an unchristian manner, so the Jews of Jerusalem sought to avenge themselves against the Christians they so hated with an unchristian war: "Incapable of using a sword," they conspired against Christianity with gold and money, "the most fearsome enemies of God's church."[112] This could be read as a sign of Jewish degradation. The Jews of Jerusalem could stand in for the threat to the church that Jews in France were perceived to be. Saintine cloaked his contempt in a false pity. If the "poor Jews" were unhappy in Judea, it was because the country offered them no access to their "two great consolations": commerce and usury. Yet they maintained their skill for making money, which was as great as their ability to disguise their wealth "behind a guise of poverty." Thus, if the Jews of Jerusalem appeared to be poor, in fact, "a good number of them, in their dark and unhealthy homes, have an old bag hidden in an old box, where crowns wait only for the right moment to increase and multiply."[113] Marmier observed that although most Jews in Jerusalem relied on the charity of their coreligionists to survive, some were rich, hiding their wealth "behind an exterior of poverty."[114] Géramb noted that these same rich Jews provided a much-needed source of credit for the Franciscan monks, if for some reason their own charitable payments were delayed. He felt that he "hardly need add," proceeding to do so, that these loans were "far from being free" but were paid "dearly, very dearly."[115]

This universal sameness that pilgrims such as Géramb and Marmier found so comforting could also provide comfort in a different sense: while the Jews of Jerusalem were generally evilly familiar, at times they could simply be familiar. They did not always figure at the top of the hierarchy of evils of the Orient. They could also occupy a sort of middle ground. In Jerusalem the Jew could be a conduit between the European and Oriental worlds. Their ability to straddle or occupy these two worlds was underscored by the fact that they often acted as guides, interpreters, and even hosts to these travelers.[116] Indeed, Jews were much more accessible to the foreign visitor than were Muslims. Ashkenazi Jews who had come from Europe to settle in Jerusalem could communicate with French pilgrims. Moreover, many of the European consuls and agents were Jews, as was a significant proportion of the merchant population. In contrast, Europeans had very little contact with leaders of the Muslim community. In a place so very foreign to the pilgrim, at times the Ashkenazi Jew very nearly became a fellow European to the disoriented visitor. Kerhardène, who used a Jewish guide, felt that he found "something of Europe" in the ghetto, and his walks there provided a welcome respite from the overwhelming foreignness of the city.[117] Saintine spent time in Jerusalem with a rabbi he had met on the boat. He enjoyed his time with the learned man, grateful that he had found a valuable source of information on the Jews of Jerusalem.[118] Damas proclaimed himself to have been "struck," as was Géramb, by the Jews' "deep respect" for the Old Testament: "No nation carries to a higher degree its veneration for the books that contain the dogmas, the moral laws, and the history of its religion." He found this familiar adherence reassuring.[119]

Géramb spoke approvingly, too, of the Jews' industriousness: teachers educated the children with "zealous care"; the poorest among the Jews "kept himself busy," undertaking whatever activity he could rather than experience the "shame" of holding out his hand. Géramb's own tinsmith was Jewish, and Géramb had the constant pleasure of being "surprised by his assiduity and his tireless activity." Never had Géramb seen a Jew dressed in the rags of poverty, "like one encounters among the Arabs and the Christians," and the Jews did not know "the vile love of rest that is so common to the people of the Levant, whose lazy and useless lives are the principal cause of indigence." Just as the different quarters of Jerusalem served as contrasts and comparisons with one another, Arabs, too, could be invoked to highlight some aspect of the character of the Jews. And while Géramb spoke of the unchanging nature of the Jew's physiognomy (and by extension, his character), at the same time, he noted having observed faces among Jerusalem's Jews that were "not only beautiful" but that had "remarkable character," possessing "an air of nobility," which, he avowed, he had been "far from expecting."[120] Géramb, Damas, and Saintine acknowledged the respect they felt for the religious sincerity and erudition of Judaism and of certain Jews. Yet they could not help but despise the idea of these same Jews, as Catholicism had taught them to do. Was this part of a struggle to keep hold of what they had wanted to find, in the face of the reality that they did find? Were their preconceived notions being challenged by the familiar and friendly Jewish faces they encountered along their way?

The desire to create a narrative that would allow these pilgrims to think of France as essentially and eternally Catholic was strong. Nothing demonstrates this more clearly than the popularity of the pilgrimage novel, a new and successful genre. In her 1843 novel *La Palestine, ou Une visite aux Lieux-Saints* (Palestine, or A visit to the Holy Sites), Clara Filleul de Petigny, whose work had the stamp of approval of the producers of the *Bibliothèque morale de la jeunesse* series, had her protagonist, M. Brucion, tell the reader that "the Jewish population seemed to me to be the most wretched of all; to visit its synagogue is to get a true understanding of its poverty. It is a true shack, threatening to fall into ruin! What a temple, in exchange for Solomon's magnificent monument! What abjection, in exchange for the ancient glory of the people of God!"[121] Petigny benefited, as did others, from the extraordinary popularity of the pilgrimage novel. Her work was reprinted regularly between 1843 and 1867. A drama set in the medieval period, *Bérénice, ou Le Pèlerinage à Jérusalem* (Bérénice, or The pilgrimage to Jerusalem), was first published in 1843 and went through nine editions up to 1867.[122] In this work, the young Bérénice acts as a witness to the events surrounding the siege and taking of Jerusalem. When her father, Eustache de Bouillon, eaten up by rancor, loses his way, Bérénice is his moral compass. She brings him back to Christianity and repentance at his death. Abbé Rousier's 1844 *Le Jeune voyageur dans la Terre-Sainte* (The young traveler in the Holy Land) was republished in 1856 and again in 1857 as *Voyage à la Terre-Sainte* (Journey to the Holy Land). The similarity between these fictional accounts and the writings of those who did travel is striking: these tales followed the same narrative arc, seeking to depict the Holy Land as Christian and to give the reader a lesson in Christianity. When he was a simple priest in 1852, Georges Darboy (who later became archbishop of Paris, before he was executed by members of the short-lived Paris Commune in May 1871) wrote *Jérusalem et la Terre-Sainte: Notes de voyage* (Jerusalem and the Holy Land: Travel notes) to help the reader "know" the Holy Land. To know the

Holy Land, for Darboy, who wrote his travel account at his desk in France, was to know the history of Jerusalem up to the coming of Jesus and during that city's time under Christian rule. The only value in undertaking what he described as a journey of eight hundred leagues to visit the place itself was, as Darboy put it in his introduction, because of its "great past and the memories and beliefs that are part of it."[123] These pilgrimage novels brought together dynamic Catholicism, Romanticism, nostalgia, and exoticism. They found a ready audience. The act of pilgrimage was supported by its metaphorical use as a way to learn and to think Christianity. Perhaps these authors had read Chateaubriand, like so many others. These works write the Holy Land as eternally Christian: the guidebooks they offer the reader are the Bible and Chateaubriand. They cover biblical history and the Crusades; they lead the reader through Jerusalem on a tour that includes a Jewish community that has been put firmly in its rightful place. Their success suggests that the desire to imagine modern France through these prisms was strong.

Nonetheless, both the pilgrimage accounts and the pilgrimage novels also suggest that pilgrims struggled to impose their Christian framework on Palestine, just as they struggled to reintroduce it into France. Abbé Vidal de Langon made the observation in his work, in relation to the Jews of Jerusalem, that for those who had lost everything, religion was a homeland.[124] The very same could be said of him and his fellow pilgrims. The nostalgia that these figures expressed, their desire to see in Jerusalem a Christian city, was a nostalgia that they brought with them from home. Forbin, whose work was printed by the king's own publishing house, dedicated the account of his voyage to the Bourbon Louis XVIII. "Everywhere," he noted, the pilgrim was "reassured by the sight of the fleur-de-lis, which recall the noblest notions of glory and justice."[125] Glory and justice for Forbin, of course, evoked the rule of the Bourbon kings. Similarly, a reviewer of Forbin's book was delighted that in his account of his voyage, Forbin was guided by "love of the fatherland and of national glory that make him, in the Orient, carefully seek all traces of us."[126] Forbin would have found common cause with his son-in-law, the Count de Marcellus, who by the time he traveled could no longer be a monarchist but was obliged to become a Legitimist, committed to the idea of the return of the Bourbon monarchy. Marcellus noted that one of his sadder duties was to announce the death of the Duke de Berry to the Franciscan monks in Jerusalem. For him, the assassinated Bourbon heir was an "august victim of our revolutions," and his tragic death reminded Marcellus of a passage from Tasso.[127] Estourmel also remembered. On his journey, he thought of his uncle, "driven out" of France by the Revolution. He was sustained by "his devotion to the royal family," and "gifted with a remarkable strength of character, he maintained [this devotion] in the midst of all the political vicissitudes. Religion sustained him when religion itself seemed lost."[128] Estourmel found strength, perhaps, in the memory of his uncle's fortitude and found himself in that heritage. What this suggests to us is that Estourmel had a religious experience in the Holy Land, because that was what he sought. Like their forebear in pilgrimage, Chateaubriand, who sought to find, in religion and Romanticism, a refuge from the prospect of a terrifying France, these men truly found their homeland in religion, all the more so when this was in the absence of a properly Catholic homeland.

To a significant extent, their writings were all about re-creating an ideal. Overwhelmingly, this ideal was a Catholic France. That crusading existed between the lines of pilgrimage was not indicative of a hidden imperial impulse. Rather, the inclusion of the Crusades in the pilgrimage narrative allowed these French Catholic pilgrims to better define their Catholicism as specifically French, and their Frenchness as deeply Catholic. These pilgrims were explicitly placing Catholicism at the center of their understanding of their own identity as French men. Some of the tropes that pilgrims called on in their descriptions of the Jewish community are recognizable for their universality, part of a longer, broader history of Christian depictions of Jews. However, these pilgrims set these same depictions within their own specific context. This was a French story. As he made his way through Palestine on his pilgrimage, Chateaubriand was delighted to hear French spoken. He understood France's presence in the Holy Land as rightful: "It was French chevaliers who reestablished the kingdom of Jerusalem. . . . At Calvary you can see the sword of Godfrey de Bouillon, which, in its ancient sheath, seems still to guard the Holy Sepulchre." And Chateaubriand understood himself to belong to this proud inheritance. Reflecting on receiving the order of the Holy Sepulchre, he wrote, "I am a Frenchman; Godfrey de Bouillon was a Frenchman; and his ancient weapons, in touching me, imbued me with a renewed love for the glory and honor of my fatherland." The ashes of Godfrey and Baudouin, French ashes, were the only ones to be buried "in the shadow of Jesus Christ's tomb." Chateaubriand did not doubt that they were fully deserving of this honor, and for him, this was also a "claim to honor" for France.[129] Henri Cornille described being shown the sword of Godfrey de Bouillon and having the "temerity" to place his own feet in the spurs of "this noble chevalier, the avenger of the Holy Sepulchre."[130] Abbé Delorme expressed his emotion at landing "on the same shores that were once walked on by Godfrey de Bouillon, Tancred, [and] Saint Louis."[131] Saulcy, who opened his 1882 work *Jérusalem* with an account of the crusading army's arrival at the walls of the city, followed in the spirit of their footsteps:

> On Tuesday June 7, 1099, the army of Crusader princes, coming from Ramallah and walking at night to avoid the torrid heat of the day, arrived at dawn at the walls of the Holy City. At the sight of these walls that it had come to break down, the entire army was suddenly filled with a sense of respect and

veneration, and they prostrated themselves in the dust and then arose enthusiastically, and their ardent cry of Jerusalem! rose to the heavens.

After the extreme suffering that they had experienced for two long years, the Crusaders reached the goal that they had had so much difficulty achieving. Christ's tomb was there before them, and this tomb, which they were to set free, was now no farther away than the thickness of a wall.

The following morning the laying of the siege began; on Friday July 18, the standard of the cross flew from all of Jerusalem's towers, and at the same time, all the holy sites rang with jubilant hymns.

Arriving by a different road from the one the Crusader army took, on December 23, 1850, a little before midday, I, a humble pilgrim, reached the crest of the hill that overlooks Jerusalem from the north, the hill that the ancients named Scopus. . . .

If I did not follow the example of Godfrey of Bouillon's soldiers, I was nonetheless under the spell of a strong emotion.[132]

These pilgrims sought to re-create their Catholic homeland in Jerusalem, and that city's Jewish population was available to play a central role in their story.

Not all chose to call on them. Yet absences and silences, too, could be meaningful. To write the Jews out of the pilgrimage account could be to make the statement that Judaism no longer had any role to play in the Holy Land. Louis Enault managed to dismiss Judaism as a competitor with the statement that, of all the Jews living in Jerusalem, "very few" had any actual history in the city. The vast majority, according to his reckoning, were "foreign."[133] No Jews figure in Alphonse de Lamartine's descriptions of Jerusalem. Their presence in Jaffa, as described in his work, "from all corners of the globe," served to underscore both their absence from Jerusalem and their lack of roots in the Holy Land.[134] Marcellus saw not live Jews but mostly ancient Israelites on his journey. The one meeting with representatives of the Jewish community that he records is dismissed with Montesquieu's quote. Marcellus was more concerned with the presence of members of the Greek Orthodox Church.[135]

For these pilgrims, the physical displacement of their journey was secondary to the internal world they created. The Jerusalem they encountered was informed and given meaning by their faith, their Romanticism, their patriotism. The finished image was an ideal world. And while, for a few, this utopia was all the better defined by the presence of Greek Orthodoxy, for the majority of these pilgrims, rightfully punished Jews added meaning to the pilgrimage. A world where Jews lived in deserved degradation was their ideal. This had been France before the Revolution, and this was the France to which they longed to return.

Yet longing was not reality, and pilgrims acknowledged this. Marmier alluded to the impressionistic nature of his travel description when he wrote that "the high-society traveler will no longer see those cities, once so rich, those paths so full of flowers, the biblical beauty of the Carmel and of Sauron's plain. But the pilgrim will visit this holy landscape, where blessed feet have passed, with pious emotion. Everywhere, there are the solemn images of the Bible, the miracles of the Gospels, and everywhere, also, there are legends."[136] Marmier was right to distinguish the traveler from the pilgrim. On his trip to the Dead Sea in 1850 and 1851, Félicien de Saulcy was pleased to find the signatures of his friends, the novelists Gustave Flaubert and Maxime du Camp, on a hotel register. Flaubert and du Camp did travel together through the Holy Land in 1850, and both of them, not unexpectedly, recorded their impressions. The Holy Land that they visited differed markedly from the stories I have explored to this point, and that difference is telling. Their impressions contrast with those of the pilgrims, just as Marmier predicted. For travelers such as Flaubert, du Camp, and others like them, Jews were at best a curiosity or an irritation. For the most part, they were simply peripheral to the travel experience, irrelevant. In their accounts, Jews never took on the deep significance that pilgrims such as Chateaubriand sought to give them. Their journey was nothing more than that; it was neither a pilgrimage nor a religious experience. Flaubert noted, on his third day in Jerusalem, that he still had not experienced any of the emotions he expected: "neither religious enthusiasm, nor arousal of the imagination, nor hatred of the priests, which at least is something. Before all that I see, I feel emptier than a hollow barrel."[137] Du Camp wrote, similarly, that the two friends "stayed cold, insensible, looking with curiosity but without emotion or faith." Christianity, he predicted, would soon be relegated to history.[138] Frédéric Goupil, who traveled to the Holy Land with the artist Horace Vernet in 1839, found the bickering between Roman Catholics and Orthodox Christians over the Holy Sepulchre "ridiculous."[139] When the former merchant Jean-Baptiste Morot visited the chapel, he noted that "there was no trace" left of the tombs of Godfrey de Bouillon and Baudouin. This nephew of a priest found Jerusalem itself to be nothing more than "a heap of rubble and ruins. . . . One needs nothing less than the eyes of faith to be able to bear the sight of it."[140] In stark contrast to the way pilgrims saw the city, Flaubert found "everything . . . very dirty."[141] Du Camp noted that the Jews of Jerusalem looked "*less* degraded than elsewhere."[142] And in a moment of extraordinary clarity, Morot noted that "Jerusalem becomes greater the farther away one gets from it."[143]

These accounts raise the specter of Ernest Renan, who also traveled to and famously wrote about this region in his 1863 *Vie de Jésus* (Life of Jesus). Renan's work fits within the context of the growth of travel and travel literature and the new approach to biblical studies that came about as a result. In a process parallel to that undergone by pilgrims, for Renan landscape became text, filling in an already-established framework. Renan's travels made the history he had set out to write "solid." Renan also used his work to explore questions pertaining to modernity—in particular, the idea of racial categories and nationalism.[144]

Renan's writings on Jews and Judaism do not form a cohesive whole, and his attitudes were varied and complex.[145] Renan naturally included Jews in his writing of Jesus into historical context: they were, predictably, the "haughty, audacious, and cruel" architects of Jesus's downfall.[146] However, the comparison stops there, and ultimately Renan's accounts of the region are as telling as those of Flaubert and his contemporaries in underscoring the constructed nature of the pilgrimage account. The contrast between his account and those of the pilgrims is shown clearly, for example, by his characterization of Jerusalem as the negative pole of Galilee, which he described in overwhelmingly positive terms. Renan did not need Jerusalem to be a Christian city, and the presence of the Holy Sepulchre did not color his understanding of it.

When he did discuss his travels through Palestine, in his 1864 *Mission de Phénicie* (Mission to Phoenicia), he was primarily concerned with architecture and its significance; in particular, he wanted to show that in the outward signs of their religious observance, Jews were "neither artists nor builders."[147] In Palestine, he found "a real lack of taste, and a sort of gaucherie."[148] In a thousand years, the Jews had built only three temples, of which at least two "were built under foreign influence."[149] And in a note, Renan brought this fault into the present day:

> In our times, in synagogues, the furniture, the priestly robes, the lamps, the candelabra, the chairs, have all been borrowed from the Catholic rites. The Jewish synagogue has never had original material, neither in its architecture nor in its furnishings. Even the chants, the preaching, the minor ceremonies are all quite modern.[150]

It is clearly in this sense that Renan was preoccupied with Jews. Even Saulcy, to whom Renan referred and who also traveled in the service of "science," saw a greater significance in his journey.[151]

Accounts such as these throw the tales told by self-defined, self-conscious pilgrims into stark relief. A minority of pilgrims might not have written Jews into their story. Some devoted just a few pages to the Jews they encountered. Others allotted them entire chapters. However, whether they figured prominently or little, the Jews of the Holy Land, and particularly of Jerusalem, were intrinsic to the pilgrimage account. In nineteenth-century France, many still wished for the return of Catholicism to the center of French life. Their project was hampered by the presence of Jews as equals in French society. Christian theology taught French Catholics that equal citizenship was not the rightful place of the Jew. Jews provided a constant challenge to the Christian narrative, and once they had been emancipated and the place of the church in French society undermined, this challenge became more acute than ever before.[152] Across the nineteenth century, the drama of Jewish emancipation wove its way through the intense negotiations over the nature of the nation that marked French society.[153] What was to be done?

We cannot, of course, imagine that all politically engaged Catholics of the nineteenth century understood their faith or their world in the same way.[154] However, for Catholics such as these, the Orient provided a perfect site for the re-creation of a properly French Catholic world. The consistency of these accounts across the greater part of a century is remarkable. It tells us that these pilgrims elaborated their French, Catholic identity as much within the walls of Oriental Jerusalem as they did on the hallowed soil of the eldest daughter of the church. It tells us that knowing the Jews of Jerusalem gave Catholic pilgrims the power to elaborate an ideal France. In this sense, the French Catholic Orientalism of these pilgrims was as political as were the activities of the church in France, and religion and politics combined to create a markedly nonsecular Orientalist project. In this sense, theirs was a specifically French Orientalism. Yet their accounts tell us, also, that when fantasy met reality, pilgrims struggled to make room for both in their schema. The uncertain position of a church that had much to mourn in France as a result of the Revolution was reflected in the writings of these pilgrims. Nowhere are the push and pull between confidence and loss clearer than in their depictions of the Jews of Jerusalem.

In 1850–1851, Félicien de Saulcy undertook a journey around the Dead Sea. He traveled with a party that included his son and the abbé Jean-Hippolyte Michon, whom he described as "a devoted friend." For a time, he was joined by Gustave de Rothschild, the son of Baron James. The two volumes resulting from this journey consist mostly of long, detailed accounts of monuments and local features. In this work, Saulcy assigned Jews the familiar role of historic figures. This changed when he described his experience in Safed. As he approached this city, he realized that some members of its Jewish population were waiting outside the gates for Rothschild. While "no one paid attention to us," "when our young traveling companion appeared, everyone was upstanding, all heads were uncovered, and a welcome harangue was pronounced." Saulcy saw only too well the calculation behind the "effusiveness" of this welcome. Saulcy and his fellow travelers went ahead and so were the first to announce Rothschild's arrival to those waiting at the synagogue. The role of courier was one that he accepted, "in the beginning, with good grace." But he soon lost patience with Rothschild's coreligionists, who allowed themselves to treat him "with an informality that I [was] in no mind to endure for long."[155] Saulcy described how he came to the end of his tether:

> I briskly brought the household together and made these good people understand that I am the leader of the caravan, and that since I am paying them, they will take orders from me and execute them with haste. It took no more than five minutes to set things right, and our evening passed very pleasantly. Surprised at first, our hosts became entirely attentive and polite.[156]

The game did not last long.

Saulcy's discomfort raises two issues with which to finish this chapter and look to the next. The sudden irruption of a Rothschild into his narrative speaks to the inability of travelers or pilgrims such as he to incorporate both imagined and real Jews into the story they wished to tell. Yet not only was Gustave de Roth-schild a real Jew; he was also a French Jew. The presence of Jews, not only in the Orient but also in France, was part of the baggage that pilgrims brought with them. The Jews of France are a silent presence in this chapter. In the next, I explore this aspect of the story more explicitly, through the prism of artistic and literary depictions of the Orientalized Jew. What was the interaction between depictions of Jews in France and in the Orient? How did these inform and feed into one another?

## 2  Travel and Intimacy

IN THIS CHAPTER, I explore the Orientalized Jew through the prism of the world of culture. Jews in the Orient were the objects of travel writing, and those who chose to depict them saw themselves as artists rather than as pilgrims, as exemplified by Gustave Flaubert and Maxime du Camp in chapter 1. It is this distinction that differentiates this chapter from the preceding one. Jews in the Orient were the objects, too, of art and of one particular play. But Jews in France were also the objects of, and participated in, the production of culture that featured an Orientalized Jew. Culture thus allows me to explore the place of the Jew as an inside and outside, Orientalized—and, at times, Orientalizing—Other. Many of the travelers who discovered and depicted the Orient and its Jews also had interactions with the newly emancipated Jews around them at home in France. How did Orientalist creations in the nineteenth century reconcile the Jews over "there," in the Orient, with the Jews in their "here," in France? This chapter follows the creative schema in which the Orientalized Jew was implicated: here, there, and back again, and as the schema suggests, it is divided into three parts, brought together through the person of Théophile Gautier.

Théophile Gautier was an enthusiastic traveler; he visited the Orient twice and wrote about his encounters. Gautier found Jews in the Orient, but he also counted Jews among his wide social circles and wrote about them and imaginary Jewish figures in his novels. Gautier is significant because Jews feature in all of the creative genres into which he ventured. And Jews featured in his life. Gautier had well-documented friendships with very real Jews. So how did he reconcile his depictions with his relationships? How did he bring together the Jews he knew within his own here in France and the Jews he encountered there, in the Orient? In this chapter, I explore the relationship between Gautier's depictions of Jews and his writings about the Orient. Gautier is significant, too, because he offers insights into the creative world of nineteenth-century Paris, both through observation in his criticism and through participation in terms of his own creative output. If, as one Gautier scholar would have it, Gautier sat "at the heart of his time," he was also a coruscating critic of the same.[1] Through his criticism, he interprets nineteenth-century artistic Paris for us. He also acts as a commentator on the period and its protagonists, of which he is one: in his criticism, he also gives us himself.

Gautier was born in Tarbes, in the southwest of France, in 1811. He moved with his family to Paris in 1814, when his father, a royalist, found promotion through his connection with the abbé of Montesquiou, then minister of the interior. Gautier's creative output was to include seven travel accounts, but he also wrote eight novels and five plays and ballets and produced works of art. His work stretches across all of the genres of his time. Yet although Gautier's greatest wish was to take part in the creative life of nineteenth-century Paris, and he was indeed prolific, he was also obliged to work as a critic to survive. In 1836, Gautier began writing literary criticism for the newspaper *La Presse*, the organ of journalist and editor Emile de Girardin. In 1855, he moved to *Le Moniteur*, the official government organ. Gautier's output as a critic was extraordinary. His critical opus includes more than fourteen hundred articles spanning art, literature, theater, ballet, and opera. In 1844 alone he wrote forty-six critical articles on literature, ten on art, and four others. His career as a critic was one that he pursued with ambivalence, if not reluctance. If the many articles he wrote over the course of his lifetime ensured an income, they also gave him less time to devote to his own writing, his first love and great ambition. Yet what Gautier chose to see as his hack work actually ensured his place at the center of artistic society in mid-nineteenth-century Paris. Gautier's criticism allowed him to explore his great skill as an observer, commentator, and judge. His role also gave him power: his correspondence is full of letters from supplicants, begging humbly for some attention, or others, equally humble, sending fawning thanks for a good review. A favorable word from him in *La Presse* was, in the words of one thankful recipient, "a service that can be repaid only with eternal gratitude."[2] Kind words from Gautier could ensure the happiness not only of the artist in question but also of his family.[3] Friends would regularly request introductions or favors.

Scholars of nineteenth-century French literature have devoted considerable attention to Gautier's opus.[4] But Gautier's importance goes beyond his work and extends to his person. Gautier has a central role to play in the history of this period. He lived through much of the tumult of nineteenth-century France, and he wrote about it with insight and wit. He was a caustic observer of life in France, through the decades from 1830, which were punctuated by regime change, and ending with his observations of life under siege in Paris, written at the end of his own life and in the aftermath of the Franco-Prussian War. He understood events—and people—through his adherence to Romanticism. Gautier's life and work can offer insight into the significance of the Orientalized Jew in the creative life of nineteenth-century France. This chapter begins by using Gautier to trace the contours of the web that joined France and the Orient, and French and Oriental Jews, as the objects of creation. Romanticism is the tool with which to make sense of the work of Gautier and others, and in part 1 of the chapter I explore the relationship between Romanticism, Orientalism, and the Jew through Gautier's 1846 play *La Juive de Constantine* (The Jewess of Constantine), his sole, unsuccessful foray into melodrama.

In part 2, I focus on the place of Jews in travel accounts. Travel writing saw a rise in popularity in the nineteenth century, and creative works depicting other parts of the world proliferated. The Orient featured heavily in this output, as did Oriental Jews. Artists, writers, polemicists, and bureaucrats, the French journeyed to Oriental North Africa and wrote about and depicted their travels. Much has been written about how we might conceptualize the encounter and interaction between traveler and local. Mary Louise Pratt, for example, defined what she called "contact zones" as "social spaces where disparate cultures meet, clash, and grapple with each other, often in highly asymmetrical relations of domination and subordination, like colonialism, slavery, or their aftermaths as they are lived out across the globe today."[5] Is this a helpful framework for understanding French interactions with Jews in the Orient? Were Jews, somehow, surgically "extracted" from their landscape and thus divested of agency?[6] Or were travelers mere individuals, governed by their "anxiety" at their own deficiencies?[7] Said described the travelogue as intrinsic to what he called "the great cultural archive . . . where the intellectual and aesthetic investments in overseas dominion are made."[8] This was the work of appropriation of the non-European world by cultural representation. Through seeing came mastery.[9] In the framework that he and Pratt offer, travel writing has been understood as one more form of colonial discourse, a language by which the work of imperialist expansion could be assimilated, understood, and thus owned. Its authors are portrayed as white agents of empire.[10] Yet even if the exotic Oriental creatures that these travelers found were constructed, they were not constructed out of nothing.[11] Perhaps travelers did bring imperial baggage from home, but they also brought knowledge of the Jew, whether based on church teaching, personal interaction, or both. The figure of the Orientalized Jew complicates this overly simplistic framework in important ways. If, for the pilgrim, the Jew was fluid, both familiar and unknown, then it follows that this would have been the same for the traveler. How, then, might we conceptualize this tension between closeness and distance? This is the focus of part 2.

In part 3, we return to France and to the life and creative output of Gautier. Gautier created imaginary Jews in his novels, some of whom were hateful figures. He also enjoyed friendships with Jews in his artistic circles. What was the interplay between the real and the imagined, the negative and the laudatory, in depictions of Jews, by Gautier and others? In part 3, I place these writings on Jews in the context of theories of alterity. Are writings such as Gautier's best understood in terms of antisemitism and philosemitism? Or is it possible to carve out a middle ground, where we might place Gautier's ambivalence?

## Part 1

Gautier's notoriety began with his performance in a battle that was, in retrospect, a formative event in the history of the Romantic movement. Almost thirty years after this battle, Gautier described advocates for both the Romantic and classical movements gathering in 1830 at the premiere of *Hernani*, a new play by Victor Hugo:

> It was thought that the performance would be tumultuous, and enthusiastic young people were needed to support the play. The hatreds between classicists and Romantics were as intense as those between Guelphs and Ghibellines, between Gluckists and Piccinnists. Victory was dazzling, like a storm, with whistling winds, lightning, rain, and thunder. The entire audience was aroused by the frenetic admiration of some and the opinionated anger of others! . . . At that time, I was considered to be an ardent neophyte, and I was given the command of a small squad to which I distributed red tickets. It has been said and written that in the battles of *Hernani*, I knocked out recalcitrant bourgeois with my enormous fists. I was not lacking in will but in fists. I was barely eighteen, I was frail and delicate, and I wore size seven and a quarter in gloves. Since then, I have fought in all of the great Romantic campaigns. As we left the theater, we wrote "Long live Victor Hugo!" on the walls to propagate his glory and annoy the philistines. God was never more fervently adored than Hugo.[12]

By the end of the following year he was well entrenched in a group of young artists known as the petit cénacle, renowned for their extravagant parties. One, in particular, held next door to Gautier's apartment by his friends Gérard de Nerval, Arsène Houssaye, and Camille Rogier, was to become legendary. Its aim, according to the loving recital of Gautier's life published by his son-in-law, was "to protest against *bourgeoisisme*."[13] Gautier would soon take on his own cause: the pursuit of complete artistic freedom, an ideal that would come to be known as art for art's sake. He achieved his first literary success in 1835 with the publication of *Mademoiselle de Maupin*, a work celebrated for its merits but also for its long preface, an eloquent argument for Gautier's cause.

Gautier was both a writer and a critic, and in this sense he took part in the creative life of mid-nineteenth-century France and also observed it from a distance. In this way, Gautier offers insights into the creative world in which he participated, but he also decodes and explains the creativity of others in terms of his beliefs and priorities. Gautier was an exponent of Romanticism all his life. Chateaubriand, the pilgrim crusader, might have been the "Sachem" of Romanticism in France, but he was nominated for this role by Gautier himself.[14] And it was Gautier who was to become the movement's grand old man, the final case study of Paul Bénichou's opus.[15]

Bénichou has argued that the Romanticism of Gautier and his circle can be characterized as disillusionment, which began with the events of 1830. A fellow artist, Charles Augustin Sainte-Beuve, caught the initial spirit of optimism that greeted the July Revolution of 1830. "People and poets," he wrote, "are marching together. . . . Artists are henceforth on a popular footing in the arena with the masses, side by side with tireless humanity."[16] He and his fellow artists were soon to realize that, although they had seen themselves as revolutionaries, the 1830 Revolution was not theirs. Their youthful optimism soon turned to what Béni-chou has termed "disenchanted passion" amid "ruined certitudes and hopes."[17] The Revolution of 1848 was to be the second great disappointment. Louis-Napoleon's coup d'état in 1851 marked the end of optimism and the victory of disenchantment. By the time the events of 1870 occurred, Gautier complained to Bergerat that he was "a victim of revolutions." With the 1830 Revolution, his father's fortune was lost, and Gautier, destined to be a man of leisure, now had to earn a living. Whatever he had managed to put in place for himself and his family by 1848 was brought down by the February Revolution. And then, in 1870, poised to enter the Academy, "Paf! It all buggered off with the Republic."[18]

At the heart of Gautier's Romanticism lay a fascinating and important tension between distancing and engagement. Writing his *Histoire du romantisme* (History of Romanticism), looking back at 1830 from a distance of forty-two years, in the year that was to be his last, Gautier described the group known as the petit cénacle, caught up in the excitement of youthful discovery:

> Everything was germinating, everything was about to bloom, everything burst open all at once; the air was intoxicating, and we were mad for lyricism and art. It seemed as though we had just rediscovered the great secret that had been lost, and it was true: we had rediscovered poetry.[19]

Bénichou, perhaps the greatest chronicler of the French Romantic movement, has argued that its adherents were linking thought and literary creation "in a vital and organic way": "the questions that were raised during this creative period . . . were discussed by writers rather than by philosophers."[20] Gautier scholars have made much of the ironic tone that permeates his work,[21] seeing it as Gautier's way of distancing himself from a world that he rejected. Yet it could be argued that Gautier's rejection of politics was, in itself, a political act in a life that was, after all, so influenced by the political events of his time. Gautier himself argued that his work was a direct reflection of and meditation on his world:

> We have no desire to shut ourselves away, not even in an ivory tower, away from the events of our times. Men of dreams and of action, of study and travel, having experienced life in all its changing phases, we bask fully in the midst of our times; we renounce none of it.[22]

Perhaps, as one scholar has argued, Gautier's political act was a refusal to embrace modernity and all its trappings.[23] The secular, materialist individualism of the July Monarchy in particular may have presented a challenge to Romantics. Certainly, the movement's adherents experienced this society with a sense of loss and nostalgia. Romanticism allowed them to project an ideal onto a different world, seeking traditions or myths that might reenchant the present world.[24] This idealism might draw on the past, as in the work of Chateaubriand, or it might look to other lands. It might understand the age of Godfrey de Bouillon as one of perfection.[25] Gautier's Romanticism was in many ways a search for an ideal. Gautier was obsessed with beauty. His friend the poet Charles Baudelaire, called him "the exclusive love of the Beautiful."[26] In the preface to his *Jeunes-France* (French youth), Gautier stated that he preferred "the painting to the object that it represents,"[27] and he later noted that he preferred "marble to flesh."[28] Gautier sought reenchantment, equally, in exoticism.[29] But the exotic canvas could serve a dual purpose, for Gautier and others also inscribed their great disenchantment on the exotic world. At times, this disenchantment was projected onto a closer but equally exotic target: the Jew.

Jews feature all throughout Gautier's opus. Between 1838 and 1870, their presence in his work is uninterrupted. Sometimes they were central figures, as in his 1858 *Le Roman de la momie* (The romance of a mummy). More often, however, they played bit parts: they were local color in his travels or actors in poems such as the *Vendeurs du Temple* (Sellers in the Temple, 1838) or *Tableaux de siège* (Portraits of a siege, 1871), written at the end of his life.[30] In the words of the only Gautier scholar to have considered his writings on Jews in any detail, depictions of Jews penetrate "deeply [into] the astonishing diversity of genres into which Gautier ventured."[31] And the Jews in his work are objects and clichés: Jewish women who were overwhelmingly physical creatures of almost unbearable beauty, and Jewish men whose hateful, ugly souls were written, equally powerfully, on their bodies.

Gautier's considerable opus on Jews situates the link between Orientalism, Romanticism, and the Jew. Gautier's disenchanted Romanticism needed the Jew, since the latter played the role of antithesis and, in the process, served to define Romanticism—both its inner workings and its outer limits. As Romanticism's worst enemy, the Jew was also its greatest ally.[32] It might be useful to understand Gautier's writings about Jews in the context of his Romanticism. But it might be equally useful to understand Gautier's Romanticism in the context of his writings about Jews: his reported hatred of capitalism and the systems that promoted its adoration, his great love of beauty, and his ability to objectify in the service of his credo. The Jew makes clear the outlines of Gautier's world. Gautier allows us to reconstruct a world of Romanticism, Orientalism, and creation over the middle decades of the nineteenth century in France. Gautier wrote his Romanticism and his Orientalism through Jews, both in the Orient and in France. His world gives us access to the Jew's importance in holding together the web that links Romanticism and Orientalism, and in this way, he acts as guide. This chapter offers a study of this complicated web. It begins with Gautier's play *La Juive de*

*Constantine*, a melodrama inspired by his travels in which he draws on his travel experiences to create fictionalized Jews within a fictionalized Orient. *La Juive de Constantine* allows us to begin to consider how Orientalism, Romanticism, and the figure of the Jew came together in Gautier's work.

On November 12, 1846, *La Juive de Constantine* premiered at the Théâtre des Funambules in Paris. Africa was in vogue: there was a veritable explosion of learned and travel articles on the Orient in the *Revue des deux mondes* in 1846, but playwrights such as Prosper Mérimée, Charles Nodier, and Victor Hugo had already been exploring the exotic in the theater over the previous decade. Others were bringing the Algerian conquest into the realm of culture, repackaging it for an audience at home in a way that appears to have been in line with government policy.[33] By 1846 the public was tiring of Algeria, and the grand plan to colonize and farm the land was failing to attract adherents.

Gautier had traveled to Algeria, also with some government support, in the summer of the previous year with his friend Noel Parfait, who accompanied him as his personal secretary. (It is generally accepted that Parfait set out the plot of *La Juive de Constantine*, and Gautier wrote the dialogue.)[34] Gautier reportedly loved the "local color,"[35] and this was to provide the backdrop for his play. Literal backdrops were constructed from models provided by Gautier. Inspiration for the plot came from a story Gautier had been told: In the Algerian city of Constantine, in the Jewish cemetery there were empty tombs. These tombs, complete with epitaphs, contained no bodies, since their subjects—both young women—were still alive. The women had married outside their religion, and the response of their families was to treat the marriage as a death and to mourn the lost loved one, complete with funeral. Gautier was struck by what he called the "ancient harshness of the tribe and the family, seeing any girl who had not fulfilled her duty as being dead; this strange situation where a being, full of life, has a funeral, and then, as she comes and goes, her dress might brush against her own tombstone."[36]

The play is essentially a tale of French civilization, or, as Maurice Samuels argues, the civilizing mission, thrown into sharp relief by the setting.[37] The play is set in Constantine in the first two years of French occupation and centers on the love between a young French officer and a beautiful Jewish girl. Gautier sought a setting and characters that would resonate with the audience. He chose Jews. And not just any Jews: The beautiful Jewish girl, Léa, is in love with the fine, upstanding French officer, Maurice d'Harvières.[38] Her father, Nathan, indulges in all the fanaticism of his religion. These are fairly predictable tropes. It was a commonplace of the nineteenth century for Jewish women to be considered beautiful, particularly by non-Jewish men, and there are multiple examples of similar rhetoric. Nor was the relationship between controlling father and beautiful daughter an innovation. Literary scholars trace this literary tradition back to Marlowe's *Jew of Malta*, first published in 1590, and argue that it was then developed by others, such as Shakespeare in his creation of Shylock and his daughter and Walter Scott in his portrayal of Rebecca (the object of desire of the Templar Brian de Bois-Guilbert) and her father, Isaac.[39] The novelist Honoré de Balzac, who had a long-lasting friendship with Gautier, was creating similar characters.

Gautier chose to write the play in the melodramatic style, hoping to emulate the success of others such as Dumas, who had done well in this popular genre. Classical melodrama set out four central characters: the unhappy and virtuous woman who is under the influence of a tyrant or a traitor, loaded up with all the vices; an honest man, protector of the innocent; and a fourth character who is the jester.[40] The plot would then unfold in predictable fashion, albeit with side plots and misunderstandings. But vice would always be punished and virtue rewarded, and courage would win out over cowardice. Thus Gautier, in choosing to cast the play as a melodrama, was constrained to certain conventions. And indeed, his central characters fit into the melodramatic mold.[41] The main love interest, Léa, is not only virtuous but also beautiful, but her life is to be determined by her fanatical and controlling father, Nathan. In opposition to the father is the valiant young officer Maurice d'Harvières, who offers Léa an alternative future. Around them revolve a series of secondary characters, who represent religious fanaticism and intolerance. Two Arab warrior chieftains, Ali Bou Taleb and Mohammed Ben Aïssa, are one-dimensional clichés: one is the lazy fatalist, and the other is the fanatic. A loyal but easily duped nanny shares the role of jester with Dominique. And of course, some, if not all, of these characters reach a crisis point where they are forced to betray a loved one or their own beliefs.

When the play opens, we focus, with Maurice's servant Dominique, on Nathan's shop. As Dominique waits for Nathan to open up, the former sets the scene and works his way through a litany of prejudices: The Arabs are "brigands"; Nathan, the shopkeeper, is secretly rich, hiding "bowlfuls of precious stones."[42] Ben Aïssa, the Kabyle chieftain, waits too, hoping for a glimpse of Léa. Dominique, in turn the narrator and the jester, is bigoted and angry. Nathan, the Jewish father, represents absolutist fanaticism, which is demonstrated, in the first instance, through Nathan's own statements. When he does appear, he is being chased by an angry, hostile mob, which is calling him a dog of a Jew (*chien de Juif*). He responds with this speech:

> This is the only thing that Mohammedans and Christians agree on. . . . Even though I have the face of a man! The blood that flows in my veins is purer and more ancient than yours; it is the blood of the kings of Judah. . . . My religion dates from the patriarchs, and Moses is more than two thousand years older than your prophets![43]

Nathan has been chosen to become a rabbi; he is very keen to close down his shop and begin his new life dedicated to study and religious observance. In her absence we discover Léa, too: she commands the love of both Ben Aïssa and Maurice d'Harvières, the French lieutenant whose love she returns, and they tell us that she is beautiful and that her beauty is Oriental. But her father has arranged her marriage with one Ben Rabbi, named, it would appear, so that the audience could have no doubt regarding his religious adherence. This complex love knot forms the crux of the play. Secondary characters with their own influences reinforce it: Kadidja, the sister of Ben Aïssa, is in love with Maurice. Ali Bou Taleb, the other chieftain, is in love with Kadidja.

Maurice is to escort a convoy of weapons from Constantine to Philippeville. Bou Taleb plans to ambush the convoy and steal the weapons, which will be used in an uprising against the French. Nathan, meanwhile, discovers Maurice and Léa's love and Léa's conversion to Christianity. Ruled by his fanaticism, he prepares to kill Léa. Fatherly love, however, wins out over religious absolutism, and he has her drink a drug that will make her appear dead but will not kill her. In this way, he calculates, he can clear his name and retain his daughter. As the household mourns the apparently dead Léa, Maurice visits Nathan's home for a final farewell and instead finds Léa, laid out as though dead.

The climactic fourth act brings Ben Aïssa, Kadidja, Maurice, Léa, and Nathan to the cemetery. The funeral is over, and Nathan is guiding Léa (now awake) out of the cemetery under cover of darkness. Ben Aïssa is there, brought by Kadidja, who wants to prove to him that Léa is dead. Maurice, who had been captured by Bou Taleb and Ben Aïssa, has escaped and is hiding in the cemetery. Maurice and Léa are reunited, but their joy is short-lived; Ben Aïssa tries to kidnap Léa, but Nathan appears and stabs him. Léa begs Nathan to forgive her, but he refuses— once again, his stubborn fanaticism wins out—and he departs. Maurice and Léa prepare to leave also, but Ben Aïssa reappears. He collapses, calling for help. An Algerian cavalryman arrives on the scene, and Ben Aïssa accuses Maurice of murder. Rather than implicate Nathan, Maurice chooses to admit guilt.

In the fifth and final act, Léa is left alone in the cemetery. She writes to her father to tell him of Maurice's arrest. But the vengeful Ben Aïssa, now a lover scorned, intercepts Nathan's reply. Ben Aïssa captures Léa, and when Nathan returns to free Maurice, Ben Aïssa threatens to kill Léa if Nathan tells the truth. A group of rabbis now enter the scene: they have come to the riverside to enact the ritual of transferring their sins to a scapegoat on the eve of the Day of Atonement.[44] Ben Aïssa confronts Nathan in front of his coreligionists and tells him that if he goes any further, Léa, who is being held over a ravine by Ben Aïssa's men, will be allowed to fall to her death. Nathan's internal struggle reaches its climax, but his fanaticism must win out (Gautier must also have understood

Nathan's fanaticism to be believable). Thus, to prove to the assembled rabbis that the woman in question is not his daughter and that she is truly dead, he takes a few steps. Ben Aïssa gives the word, and Léa falls. Nathan, consumed by grief and guilt, now admits the truth to the rabbis. Whereas a moment before he wished only to save face and honor, now he abandons all: "I thought myself strong," he cries; "I was only barbaric!"[45] But he grieves too soon: as Ben Aïssa gloats over his revenge, Maurice and Léa appear together, alive. Kadidja, choosing death over unrequited love, took Léa's place, and as her lifeless body is brought to her brother, now mad with grief, he tears off the bandages covering his stab wound and dies beside her, thus bringing the play to a close.

The various manuscripts of the play show that Gautier was initially fairly muted in his statements of French patriotism, but these became stronger in final drafts.[46] Gautier deliberately styled this work for an audience, and apparently he imagined that strong statements of French patriotism would be appealing to the theatergoing public.[47] So Maurice, who in initial drafts was quite tempered in his views on colonialism, makes overtly patriotic statements in the final version. To the French settler, Saint-Aubin, Maurice states, "Barbarism is in the process of disappearing off the face of the earth. . . . We are waging a civilizing and holy war!"[48] Gautier has Maurice say to his Arab captors, upon being told he would be executed, "France set foot on African soil to drive out barbarism, and in the eyes of the world, it will accomplish its noble task! You may slow its progress for a moment, but God protects it, and you will not prevent its triumph!"[49] Saint-Aubin also advertises his role:

> Even though our role is less heroic, we, too, serve the cause of humanity. Every arpent of land that I clear makes two wild beasts take one step back toward the desert: a lion . . . and a Bedouin! And I prefer that to growing peas and melons on the outskirts of Paris![50]

Nathan loses nothing of his uncompromising nature between early and later drafts. We are constantly reminded of his unbending character. Maurice comes to Nathan's shop to collect a wallet that was being repaired. In conversation, Nathan says to Maurice,

> I know that in your country, the Israelites, who have forgotten the laws of the Talmud, throw in their lot with idolaters; but here, the God of Moses has more faithful servants, and there can be no friendship between a Christian and a Jew. [Reaches out his hand.] That wallet costs three douros.[51]

To reinforce the message of Nathan's fanaticism, Gautier also has the two main characters dwell on this aspect of his personality. In act 2, scene 1, we find Léa at home, bewailing her situation to her well-meaning but ineffectual nurse,

Bethsabée. Léa complains that her father is so taken up with his study of the Bible and the Talmud that he has no affection for her. "Deprived of affection," she "suffers."[52] In act 4, scene 7, Maurice, Léa, and Nathan are reunited in the cemetery. Maurice encourages Nathan to forgive his daughter, telling him, familiarly, to "cease listening to your barbaric prejudices; obey your heart. What holds you back is the fear of a few obscure fanatics."[53] The nameless rabbis also help reinforce this image of Judaism as inflexible and intolerant.[54]

But even Nathan compromises. By the end of the play, he realizes the folly of his ways and accepts his daughter's choice of religion and marriage partner, defying the censorious rabbis. Léa, too, is not fixed. Gautier gives her beauty, as so many of his fellows were doing in their own creations. But her love for Maurice also gives her the chance to achieve civilization. Part of the complicated love knot involves the Arab woman Kadidja, who is in love with Maurice. When Maurice is being held prisoner in the cemetery, Kadidja visits Léa and proposes to free Maurice, on condition that Léa give him up. Léa refuses:

> I am a Christian; I am strong! Yes, you said it; there is something that I place above my love, and I glory in it, and I give thanks to the God that I serve, to that God whose law was revealed to me. . . . He is good. He is just. He will save the innocent man![55]

France, for Léa, is now "that homeland for free souls, where all men are equal, and where . . . love and charity mix all men into a single religion."[56]

In this sense, the Jews in the story can be redeemed. Léa and Nathan can both move between the two worlds of the play—from barbarism to civilization.[57] The Arab characters are the foil to this fluidity, or perhaps it is the role of the Jews to highlight their mix of lazy fatalism and fanaticism. Either way, they are given no such choice. Léa herself interprets Kadidja for us, describing her as "a barbaric woman who listens only to her wild instincts."[58] It is perhaps these "wild instincts" that lead to her death. Her brother Ben Aïssa, consumed with unchristian hatred, dies also. Ali Bou Taleb seeks refuge in religion. When he realizes that Kadidja does not return his love, he makes the following speech: "I was mad to believe in the love of a woman . . . to seek emotion and joy elsewhere than in the triumph of Islam! Allah is punishing me for it. . . . The punishment is merited!"[59] Their choices are thus to return to Islam or to die.

If Gautier was prepared to strengthen statements of patriotism in order to appeal to his audience, then perhaps the choice of Jews as main characters was just as deliberate. Gautier needed to find ways for the main characters to resonate with the spectators and for the audience to identify with his morality tale. Perhaps he believed that Jews would make the Arab more accessible to a French audience. It is not only Gautier's use of Jewish characters that is significant, though;

his treatment of them is equally so. Both the *juive* and the *juif* in Constantine are fluid characters: They are not entirely Oriental; nor are they French. They are not completely barbaric; nor are they civilized. The Jews in Gautier's play could move between these two worlds of the here, of French (Christian) civilization, and the there, of Oriental barbarism. Here were Jews who could, apparently, exist both within and outside Christian Europe. They could represent what lay beyond the boundaries of the acceptable in Gautier's Romanticism, but they could equally enter the circle of acceptability. They were figurative go-betweens, a reflection of the literal fact that when men such as Gautier traveled to the Orient, their interpreters and guides, often their hosts, were Jewish. Gautier, in his travels, would have had plenty of opportunities to encounter Jews on which the caricatures of Nathan and Léa may have been based. That they were not truly *of* either world was significant: this deep ambivalence about the Jew was, after all, what enabled Gautier to create a Nathan who was the epitome of unbridled religious fanaticism and a Léa who was weak, shackled as much to the men around her as she was by her beauty. Samuels reads these depictions as philosemitism.[60] I would argue, however, that rather than encase Léa and Nathan in positivity, it is important to excavate the ambivalence surrounding them. Gautier's depictions of the Jews in *La Juive de Constantine* belong not at one or the other end of the spectrum on which love and hatred form the boundaries but in a more complex middle space, where Nathan and Léa could be used to explore Gautier's views of the Orient and its populations.

Despite Gautier's compromises, the play was poorly received. On opening night the fourth act in the cemetery was greeted with hoots of derisive laughter. Gautier and Parfait dropped it after the premiere and revised and reworked the dialogue. Even so, the play closed after a relatively short and fairly undignified run of twenty performances. It was never staged again. *Constantine* was also panned by the critics, many of whom used the play's failure as a sort of tit for tat for poor reviews they had received from its author in the past. The tone of the reviews varied. For one reviewer, "The disappointment was great, and painful, especially for those who, like me, love the young, vivacious, free, and bizarre talent of Mr. Théophile Gautier. It is rare for me to read him without pleasure. I listened to him with chagrin."[61] Others, perhaps in imitation of Gautier's celebrated style, chose to adopt an ironic tone: "Like a bird that got bored with being told that it could only fly, he decided to walk."[62] Yet others were more brutal: If the literary worth of Gautier's works was generally "not great," with his *Juive de Constantine* he had reached new lows. The play was nothing more than "a well-used subject, situations that were common, poorly executed, poorly joined together, in a most vulgar and neglectful style." The reviewer concluded with a masterful blow: "The people that you flay in such cavalier fashion each week, through intuition, study, or practice, they know the *acoustics* and the *optics* of theater. You have no knowledge of any of that."[63] Indeed, so harsh was the criticism that one critic felt compelled to write, a week after his first review, to defend Gautier:

> He made a mistake with his *Juive de Constantine*. Who has not made a mistake? . . . But does that mean, that in realizing his fall, it was necessary to sting M. Gautier—a colleague!—with the sharpest of strokes? He has been literally torn apart. Irony, acerbic humor, biting mockery, all has been used. . . . One was no longer judge; one was the executioner.[64]

Perhaps a critic to the end, Gautier wrote his own review, four days after the play's opening. In it, he stated that his intention had been to show the true Algeria to the public. (This was in contrast, perhaps, to a play such as Franconi's *Mazagran*, which Gautier had reviewed six years earlier.[65] Franconi's heroic dramas, in Gautier's words, "always" consisted of "the same gunshot dialogue, the same racket, and the same smoke.")[66] Gautier's true Algeria was the "stoic barbarians, those descendants of the Carthaginians and the Numidians, draped in their Roman togas, with the gestures and poses of statues, their radiant black faces, their serene melancholy."[67] Gautier avowed his surprise at the audience's hilarity before the scene in the cemetery, which "during the rehearsal had moved the firemen on duty, and some stagehands' wives had brought their handkerchief to their eyes during the passages that were found to be the most comical."[68] But the theatergoing public was incapable of imagining Algeria the way Gautier wished them to: personified in "the Bedouin and the Kabyl who have cost us so many millions and so many heroes." The French public did not "believe in Algeria."[69]

Perhaps the lukewarm reception the play received does bear this out. Yet the one characterization that critics of the play seem to have fully accepted was Nathan. Paul Lamy, in *La Patrie*, noted that Nathan was "Israelism incarnate."[70] Another commentator, in *Le Furet de Paris*, described Nathan as "a Jew above all."[71] Whether or not they wished to understand and appreciate Algeria, these critics clearly felt that they already understood Jews. In this aspect, Gautier's judgment would appear to have been correct.

*La Juive de Constantine* may not have enjoyed popular or critical success. It warrants analysis, however, because it helps us begin to discern the web that links Romanticism, Orientalism, and Jews. The Jews of Constantine make clear the outlines of Gautier's world: his idea of beauty, personified in Léa, and his great hatred of what he saw as ugliness, represented by Nathan's greed and his adherence to religious law. It also shows us that as he was using Jews to personify tropes, he could also allow them to move away from them and be humanized. Gautier's Jew had fluidity of meaning. The Jew in Romanticism performed a parallel function to the Orient, in that the Jew helped delineate a certain idea of France. The Jew could also define the Orient. As Gautier's play suggests, North

Africa, along with its inhabitants, was a medium through which men such as Gautier could express grievances and ideals. And the Jew was just as significant to this process as to the process of making sense of a Romanticized world. The logic of this congruence, the easy way in which these factors come together, is overwhelming. And this is all the more significant since Gautier was only one of the many who wrote within and about this world. His work can offer insight into the meaning behind the work of those around him, so many of whom he knew, and who were proud to know him.

## Part 2

Gautier was inspired to write a play after hearing about two empty tombs in the Jewish cemetery of Constantine. But Gautier also wrote about the living Jews he encountered on his travels, as did others. How did they depict those Jews? And what is the place of those depictions in a broader schema of Orientalism? Colette Zytnicki has recently explored the place of the Jew in French travel writing from the Orient. She lays out writings within a framework of antisemitism and on the understanding that in France, by 1789 Jews "had practically disappeared."[72] Ronald Schechter has also underscored the relatively small number of Jews in France on the eve of the Revolution. Jews, as well as being few in number, were present in only a very few parts of France. However, as Schechter has also shown, Jews loomed large in the popular imagination.[73] This is the starting point for part 2 of this chapter: The idea of the Jew was significant for these travelers, in a way that was disproportionate to the actual number of Jews. Just one James de Rothschild, or one Rachel, was sufficient.

A voyage to the Orient was no small undertaking. As Jean-Claude Berchet wrote, the journey required "leisure, a fortune, and diplomatic support."[74] Gautier was able to travel thanks to government funding and financial help from his publisher and great friend Pierre-Jules Hetzel. Even so, he ran out of funds and was obliged—according to one biographer—to write his work *Constantinople* (1853) to raise the necessary money for his ticket home.[75] Others in Gautier's wide-ranging and overlapping circles traveled also. Genevan-born Charles Didier arrived in Paris late in 1830, one of many young men who made their way to the creative center in the wake of the 1830 Revolution, full of hope for the future of the arts and their own impending glory. He traveled to Morocco during a trip to Spain in the 1830s and published accounts of his journey in the *Revue des deux mondes*. While Didier never reached great heights of success (his one biographer described him as living "in the wake of Romanticism"),[76] he moved with many who did. He and the novelist George Sand were lovers for a short period. Among his friends, he counted Catholic priest Félicité de Lamennais, Chateaubriand, and for a time the literary critic Charles Augustin Sainte-Beuve. He moved in the same circles as

Gautier. Didier may not have counted among Gautier's closest, but Gautier's great friend, the writer Gérard de Nerval, published an account of his journey in 1851.[77] In 1846, another friend, the artist Théodore Chassériau, was invited to visit by the caliph of Constantine. Author Alexandre Dumas toured Spain and North Africa during the autumn and winter of 1846–1847, sent as part of a government project to inspire enthusiasm for the new colony. A Dumas-authored travel account, it was thought, should have just that effect. In the previous decade, another painter and friend, Eugène Delacroix, had traveled to Morocco with the diplomatic mission of the Count de Mornay.

It was not only those who moved in Gautier's circles who traveled. Others, fresh from their pilgrimage to the Holy Land, now transformed as travelers, also made their way around the Mediterranean, and here we pick up some familiar figures at a different stage of their journey. And there were many others, besides: writers and artists but also journalists, bureaucrats, and amateur collectors. If some, such as Delacroix and Dumas, enjoyed a guarantee of financial and diplomatic security on their voyage, others chose to depart with a great deal less backing, hoping that the journey itself would be the source of wealth to come. Indeed, Berchet may have exaggerated slightly: the market for travel accounts was such that the writer could go in the hope of recouping costs through publication of a travel account. Writers did travel to the Orient, and works with titles that were variations on *Voyage en Orient* (Journey to the Orient) were appearing regularly. They encountered an eager market. The late eighteenth century had seen a marked increase in the number of books on travel, accompanied by a rise in coverage of such works in the press.[78] This popularity continued unabated through the nineteenth century. The extraordinary success of Chateaubriand's *Itinéraire* would certainly suggest that this work reached a receptive audience. It also inspired many others to follow in his footsteps, and throughout the nineteenth century—transcending, or perhaps because of, regime changes—the literature of travel thrived in France. All of this meant that by the time Gautier published his opportunistic *Constantinople* in 1853, that city was well and truly "à la mode," and travel writing itself had truly become a genre.[79]

Political instability was not a feature of life only in France. Following the invasion of Algeria, France experienced tensions with Morocco over poorly defined borders. Tensions were exacerbated by the execution of two Moroccan subjects in Oran by French military forces, who accused them of seeking to incite violence. At the same time, Moroccan authorities were holding three French ships—the *Albine*, the *Marie-Joseph*, and the *Amitié*, captured during the invasion—in one of their ports. These events created a difficult diplomatic situation, and in this context, King Louis-Philippe's government decided to send a mission to Morocco to obtain a guarantee of Moroccan neutrality along the new frontier created by the French occupation of Algeria. This was to be led by a young diplomat, Count

Charles de Mornay. Mornay's brief was to negotiate the restitution of the three French brigs, settle outstanding commercial problems, and establish an acceptable frontier between the new French colony and its neighbors. He was accompanied in his mission by a bureaucrat, Antoine Desgranges, and an official painter, Eugène Delacroix, whose responsibility it was to record any memorable diplomatic moments in art for posterity.[80] The mission did indeed achieve its aims to a point: if after twelve days of negotiation, de Mornay was not able to extract any promise from the sultan that he would stay out of Franco-Algerian affairs, he did manage to have the imprisoned boats released. Whatever the vagaries of diplomacy, however, from the point of view of artistic creativity, Delacroix's time in North Africa was most certainly successful. In the six months he spent there between January and July 1832, Delacroix produced more than one hundred paintings. Artistic creation took place against a backdrop in which France's political relationship with these near neighbors was being renegotiated and France was renewing its sense of itself as a colonial power. Delacroix's context—and his success—set the tone for much of the work representing this part of the world to be produced over that decade and into the next.

Travelers would normally set out by boat from Marseilles to a port such as Beirut or Alexandria, with at least one stop at another Mediterranean port, most commonly Sicily, Athens, Malta, or Rhodes. The travel route might start in Cairo and make its way to Syria, or it might follow the same path in the opposite direction. Typically, travelers would take a boat up the Nile from Cairo to Thebes and back again, and a route to the Holy Land via Suez and the Sinai Peninsula. Generally they would travel by boat between what today are Israel and Lebanon or between the ports of Akko or Jaffa and Beirut or Tripoli. In Syria they would visit Baalbek and Damascus. Travel became easier as the century progressed. By the time the Count de Pardieu traveled in 1851, the would-be voyager needed only "a few months of freedom, a few thousand francs in savings to spend; and with that," he noted, "you cover the universe without the least difficulty."[81] Pardieu's triumphalism may have been a trifle optimistic, if not exclusive. But the steamship certainly made journeys more rapid and straightforward. In the words of two other travelers, it had "made sailing the Mediterranean a promenade."[82]

The French were not the only Europeans to undertake a Mediterranean promenade. Indeed, travelers from all over the world met and interacted in the Orient. However, the unsettled nature of French political life perhaps provides some clue to the particular popularity of the travel account in France. "Elsewhere" became a canvas for imagining the nation. This might entail writing Palestine as Christian, as discussed in chapter 1. It might lead to references to the ills of modern French society, placed against an Algerian backdrop, as with Gautier's ill-fated *Juive de Constantine*. Or it might involve the articulation of France as a bastion of Enlightenment, as demonstrated by the contrast between it and the formerly great civilizations of the Mediterranean but also by the dissemination of light: the bringing of French values to degraded societies, such as the newly occupied space of Algeria. For Gautier, travel accounts were part of his own project of imagining himself elsewhere.[83] Before his first trip to Spain, Gautier described how he had "dreamed" this "poetic and wild land" through poetry, such as Alfred de Musset's 1830 *Contes d'Espagne et d'Italie* (Tales of Spain and Italy) and Victor Hugo's 1829 *Les Orientales* (Orientalia).[84] In a letter to his close friend Gérard de Nerval, Gautier suggested a game: to place well-known figures in the country and the century "where their true existence should have taken place." Gautier himself, he explained, was Turkish, "not from Constantinople but from Egypt." "It seems to me," he went on, "that I have lived in the Orient, and when, during Carnival, I dress up in an authentic caftan or *tarbouch*, I feel as though I am putting on my true clothes. It has always surprised me not to be able to understand Arabic properly. I must have forgotten it."[85] The Jewish actress Judith reported him as explaining, one evening over dinner, that he had "a Muslim soul." "The proof is," he stated, picking up on a recurring stereotype, "that I am very lazy. I would like to spend my days on my heels, smoking a hookah. . . . Our civilization of factories and coal disgusts me. I need blue sky. . . . I will go to the Orient and make myself into a Turk!"[86] For the better-loved and more devoted of his two sons-in-law, Ernest Bergerat, Gautier was already quite naturally, an "Oriental."[87]

Gautier got the opportunity to explore his imagined roots in June 1852 when he traveled to Constantinople. He was also able to reap some pecuniary benefit from this journey, since the outcome of the trip in 1853 included his work named after the city. In one particular passage in this book, Gautier described a stroll he took through the city. On this day, he told the reader, while wandering the streets, he became lost and found himself in what he called "a strange quarter."[88] Gautier took the reader on a walk through this quarter, gradually building to a crescendo of decrepitude. The houses were sick men: "dilapidated, poor, and dirty. Their facades, sour-faced, gummy, wild-eyed, were peeling away, lopsided, breaking apart, ready to fall into putrefaction. The roofs appeared to have tinea, and the walls, leprosy; the flakes of graying coating were coming away like the layers of a skin covered in sores."[89] Illness was contagious; the quarter's dogs were equally unwell: "reduced to a skeletal state, eaten away by vermin and bites," sleeping in "fetid black mud."[90] And predictably, the district's inhabitants suffered the same ill health as its buildings and animals. As he passed before the houses, Gautier looked in through their "wild-eyed" windows and made out "bizarre faces of sickly lividness, between wax and lemon, . . . fitted with small, slight, flat-chested bodies, held in by a shimmering fabric, like the leaves of a wet umbrella; doleful, lifeless eyes, with an overwhelmed look, which in these yellow faces looked like coals that had fallen into an omelet."[91] This, Gautier then announced to the reader, was Balat, the Jewish quarter of Constantinople. On display was "the residue of four centuries of oppression and snubs, the manure under which this people, exiled everywhere, huddles."[92]

Gautier waded into Balat leaving all uncertainty behind: his evocations were created with all the tools of artifice that a writer could call on. The images that Gautier drew—in bilious greens and yellows—were truly damning metaphors for the depravity of the Jew's soul.[93] Furthermore, not only had the Jew earned his situation, but he also chose to maintain it in the cause of his greed. The Jews of Balat lived consciously and deliberately in mire, as they had always done. The avarice of Gautier's Jew was so extreme that he would knowingly eat poisoned food if it were free. This community hoped, explained Gautier, "to save itself" by inspiring disgust. And indeed, Gautier found it difficult to imagine "anything more hideous, foul, and purulent." So consumed were these Jews by avarice that they allowed themselves to be devoured by "scrofulous, scabies, leprosy, and all the biblical impurities, which [they have] carried since Moses's day." They did not even pay heed to the plague, if there was a chance of making a little profit on the clothing of the dead.[94] All that the Jew was, and all that surrounded the Jew, was a result of Jewishness. Thus, Jewish homes, and even Jewish districts, were necessarily degraded. How could they be otherwise, when this was the state of Judaism itself? Gautier's Balat was a sickness.

Gautier sought to have the reader accompany him on a journey of discovery. But Gautier knew very well where he was. Why, then, did he choose to wait before revealing this knowledge to the reader? Did the "false delay" of the moment of revelation give the account a ring of authenticity? For if Gautier's voice was authentic, then what readers had before them was no more than any other straightforward travel account, what one scholar has called a "documentary observation," which was therefore also original and objective.[95] In *Constantinople*, Gautier self-consciously endowed himself with the authoritative voice of the dispassionate observer: he introduced the passage on Balat with the admission that he preferred to give "a rough sketch of things in their natural state, an honest impression, given with sincerity" rather than to attempt to appear especially knowledgeable.[96]

In Gautier's work, there was tension between his emotional perceptions of what he saw and experienced and his desire to present this as distanced, and thus, authoritative: a balance between witnessing and fantasy.[97] The nineteenth-century travel narrative was commonly influenced by Romanticism.[98] This meant that, just as Romanticism put the individual and their emotions at the center of the movement, so the author would place their own responses to their voyage and their process of self-discovery at the center of their narrative.[99] This was hardly, as much literary analysis would have it, a process of exotification, commodification, or objectification, helping the reader digest "the exercise of empire."[100] This was a highly self-absorbed process. Gautier drew on meaning around him to construct a new story that would be meaningful to him and also, presumably, to readers. Jews made the narrative meaningful because they were already known. For example, in his description of the houses, Gautier may have been drawing on discourses of disease that were circulating in France, taking up notions from home and applying them in this other context. The cholera epidemic of 1832 had killed eighteen thousand people in Paris. Official concerns came to focus on the idea that disease was linked to character and environment—that is, the "insalubrious" dwelling produced disease and acted as an indicator of morality.[101] Gautier used disease, in this context, to condemn the Jews of Balat as immoral. Gautier's work was meant to be a simple traveler's tale, yet he manipulated the setting to fabricate the Jew. In this way, the Jew's situation came across all the more strongly as predetermined.

Gautier's description of Balat was bookended by equally telling symbolism: he took the reader into the Jewish quarter, through "the marble turbans and the fragments of tombstones that were scattered over the slippery hillsides,"[102] and he led them out through the same type of gate: the Jewish cemetery on a "dry, bald and dusty hillside," which absorbed "their unhealthy generations." Their tombstones were "shapeless," burned by the sun; nothing grew, and there were no trees to offer shade.[103] The state of the Jewish cemetery was, he told us, the fault of the Turks, who had "made a point of maintaining the look of a rubbish dump." The Jews were "barely allowed to engrave some mysterious Hebrew characters on the cubes that coarsen this desolate and cursed hill."[104] Was Gautier moved by pity at this late stage? Was it, as one scholar would have it, "corrective concern;" the rectification of a "destructive cliché"?[105] Gautier did not complete a tour that recorded the Jewish quarter in all its disgust-inspiring splendor only to be overcome by an equal disgust with himself. There was no pity in Gautier's writing, only censure. To include the heartless brutality of the Turks was to put Gautier's voice in perspective; the reader could then understand fully that Gautier's viewpoint belonged to one who was part of a greatly superior culture. And thus the final seal of legitimacy was placed on his accounts.

As much as he poured condemnation on the inhabitants of Balat, Gautier waxed lyrical about their female coreligionists in Algeria. Seven years earlier in Constantine, Gautier had shown enthusiasm for a "Hebraic beauty" that he had encountered in the streets of the Algerian city. He was "dazzled": "Raphael's Madonnas did not have a more demurely elongated face, a more delicate and noble cut to the nose, eyebrows more purely curved." Where the eyes of the Jews of Balat were coals in an omelet, hers were "like black diamonds," swimming "in pearly corneas of incomparable radiance and softness, with that sun-filled melancholy and azure sadness that make every Oriental eye a poem."[106] For Gautier, however, the subject of his admiration was as much a carnal creature as the poor specimens of manhood that Gautier found in Constantinople. For example, he dwelt on the Jewish woman's arms. They "sprang, bare and sturdy," from her tunic. "Athletic," with small hands at their end, these arms were "a distinctive characteristic of the Jewish race." Gautier had never seen a Jewess with thin arms.[107] If her body betrayed her carnality, her bearing spoke her debasement just as loudly; her lips had a "fearful half-smile" that was common to what Gautier called "oppressed races." Her great beauty was a mistake. Gautier could see beyond the beautiful lily to the manure that had helped it grow.[108] "Each one of her perfections had the imprint of a pleading grace; she seemed to beg pardon for being so radiantly beautiful, even though she belonged to a deposed and debased nation."[109]

All that the Jew was, and all that surrounded the Jew, was a result of Jewishness. Thus, Jewish homes, and even Jewish districts, were necessarily degraded. How could they be otherwise, when this was the state of Judaism itself? Others, who would not have shared Gautier's outlook nonetheless shared his perceptions. In the late 1820s, Baron Renoüard de Bussière, who spent two years in Constantinople in the late 1820s as secretary to the ambassador under the deeply conservative government of the Bourbon Charles X, made several visits to the Jewish district. He, too, found a city that was run down and diseased, its air "thick and foul."[110] The Legitimist writer and journalist Louis Enault, who went as a pilgrim to the Holy Land, found the mud of Balat "blacker and more fetid" than that elsewhere. Like Gautier, for Enault the very dwellings denoted illness. He, too, described "leprous" walls coming away in flakes.[111] For these observers, just as for Gautier, the district's inhabitants matched the environment. For Abbé Azaïs, the school chaplain who had shared a caravan with Enault, the "hovels" in which the Jews lived told all about the "abjection" of the race itself. Balat contained the "ruins" of a people.[112] For Bussièrre, the inhabitants of Balat were "sickly and blind." Their district was enclosed like a prison.[113] The notion that the Jews were suffering a deserved punishment was expressed in a variety of ways. Enault told the reader that the "miserable hovels" of Balat hid millionaires. But, he continued, if the Jews had once enjoyed some importance in the city as bankers, "modern progress" had left them behind in a deserved state of abjection.[114] Jews in France might personify a type of progress that made France less than ideal. In the Orient, it was possible to rewrite this schema so that the notion of progress melded with a more comforting narrative, such as that of the deicide and subsequent punishment of the Jews. In this narrative, Jews were left behind.[115]

Such descriptions extended beyond Constantinople and beyond Gautier, and were repeated in travel writings across time and the space that was North Africa. In Morocco in the 1840s, for example, the writer Charles Didier told a similar story. From the rooftop of a house in the Jewish quarter of Tétouan he saw "a city within a city, a true emblem in its isolation of the people who live within, a nation alone in the midst of nations."[116] "Alone," the Jew of the Orient was fearful. Fear, according to Charles Didier, was the Jew's "first instinct."[117] This made him deceptive and untrustworthy:

> If you follow the Jews from the shop to the synagogue, you find them true to themselves: enslaved by practices whose spirit is dead and whose meaning is lost, they mix up everything, Moses and the cabala, the prophets and the rabbis. The maddest of the superstitions are observed the most closely, and the sublime canticles of the psalmist are translated into such a monstrous clamor that one wonders, upon hearing them, if they are not drunken savages bellowing around their idol.[118]

Jews deceived because they were driven by hatred, and this made them vengeful and vindictive. Joseph-François Michaud, traveling through the region in preparation for a work on the Crusades and whose correspondence with another traveler, the Legitimist writer Jean-Joseph-François Poujoulat, was published in no fewer than seven volumes, accused the "fanatical" Jews of Constantinople of harboring a "violent antipathy," heartily returned by the Greek population.[119] Didier's Moroccan Jew avenged himself on the non-Jewish population by duping them "without mercy."[120] But while the Jew might on occasion have targeted Greeks or Moors, his greatest foe remained the Christian. Raoul de Malherbe observed that the Orthodox Christians needed the Jews; in "their financial operations and as bankers," they were "all powerful." But this did not temper their hatred. Malherbe described, in biblical terms, how the Jews had taken up arms with the Muslims against the Greeks in Salonika: "On the bodies of the martyrs they exhausted all the refinements of the most odious cruelty. Bathing in Christian blood, they asked only to plunge themselves in it again; they hoped to exhaust its source by exterminating an entire people, which had dared to make a sign forever abhorred shine in their eyes."[121] The Viscount de Basterot also placed Jewish vindictiveness in its historic context. In a passage leading up to a discussion of the Damascus Blood Libel of 1840,[122] Basterot described how, throughout the history of the city, the Jewish community had been persecuted, first by the Romans and then by the Christians, so that when Muslim forces came to take over Damascus, they were welcomed by the Jews "with joy." The events of 1840 served only to show that the Jews had "always remained the enemies of the Christians."[123]

None of these descriptions diverged from what has been shown elsewhere to be standard discourse.[124] All the qualities of the Jew were a package: his situation, morality, and physicality were all a result of the fault of being Jewish; they were all a reflection of a Judaism that signified power, avarice, deceptiveness, and vindictiveness. Whatever the Jew was, whatever his qualities, he had brought these on himself. In this sense, for travelers to the Orient, the Jew was always instantly recognizable, just as he was for those pilgrims in Jerusalem who wrote Jews into their tale of a Catholic Holy Land. Those who knew the Jew knew that these features would be written on him. The Jews stood out, as Count d'Estourmel put it, "from among a thousand Christians";[125] their physiognomy distinguished them "from all the other inhabitants of the capital." None of the other populations of the Orient could be recognized as easily as the Jews.[126] For the veterinarian Pierre-Nicolas Hamont, who had been sent to Egypt to establish a veterinary school and who normally wrote about horse breeds, the Jews were like a fast-flowing stream that could cross a lake yet maintain its original color. In ancient Egypt, despite a stay of many centuries, the Jews "maintained their original traits and manners intact." In the Egypt that he now visited, "as elsewhere," the Jews remained distinct; they were easily recognized thanks to their "unchanging physiognomy."[127] Just as for pilgrims the holy landscape was fixed in time, for many travelers, so were the Jews. They were the signs of the ancient, and this could denote purity, but it could also be indicative of the failure to properly understand civilization. Charles Marcotte de Quivières, another noble bureaucrat, was taken back in time as he surveyed the countryside from outside the city of Constantine. He "saw migrations of Jews," and he "distinctly recognized Rachel, Judith, Rebecca, and so many others." The contemporary Jewish women he saw around him were a true copy of these "antique" specimens.[128] When Alexandre Dumas in Tunis knocked at the door of his guide, David Azencot, he described how "a woman of thirty came to the door; on her head she wore a turban, like a woman from the Bible." This was Azencot's wife.[129] Jean-Joseph Poujoulat's brother Baptistin, also a writer, was an observer at a Jewish wedding on his travels and understood himself to be witnessing a rite that had not changed since the days of the Kingdom of Israel.[130]

Rites such as these, which remained unchanged, also served to maintain separation. Michaud and Poujoulat observed that the Jews of Constantinople lived as a separate nation, governing itself with its own laws "as though it were still in the city of David and Solomon."[131] Didier observed continuing separation in an embarrassing scene at the home of his host, where the assembled Jews were forced to admit that they were prohibited from drinking wine poured by Christians, even if that wine had been brought as a gift by Didier and his fellow travelers.[132] Hamont saw Jews as strangers everywhere, in whoever's midst they might find themselves. In Egypt, the Jews were "a white people in the midst of black races," while in Germany and northern France, Jews stood out because of "the olive tone of their skin and the darkness of their hair." In other words, they stood out in the Orient "because of the contrast that is entirely the opposite of what is generally the case in certain parts of Europe."[133] And thus, the Jew was never truly of the place where he was. Like the stream that rushed through the lake and left nothing of itself behind, the Jew did not plant roots anywhere.

If the Jew was distinctive, all travelers found, as Gautier did, that this was generally not because of an excess of beauty. Basterot took exception to the "extreme ugliness" of the Jews in the Orient, "like a stain in the midst of the picturesque populations that surround them."[134] For Malherbe, the Jew was "always revolting." Malherbe summarized in a short paragraph what countless others had also written:

> A filthy fez, wound up in a dirty black serge rag, a haggard and cadaverous complexion, deep-set eyes rolling around in their sockets, a tangled and disgusting beard, dirty clothing that is in rags, excessive thinness, and a back that is half stooped from the habit of humiliation, and that is the exterior; as for the morals, a proverbial cowardice, a sordid avarice, a voracious cupidity, a remarkable deceitfulness, a hereditary disloyalty, unequaled shrewdness, a marvelous business sense, groveling humility, blind hatred for Christians . . . an inviolable attachment to the religion of his fathers and to the monstrous errors introduced by unworthy commentators who have made the religion established by Moses into an antisocial religion that destroys all that it is not.[135]

And yet, following Gautier's lead again, almost all found a striking contrast between the Jewish man and his female counterpart. Women could be literal color in the Jewish quarter, a landscape that distinguished itself in shades of dirty gray.[136] Charles Didier gave detailed descriptions of the costume worn by the Jewish women of Morocco. They consisted of "gaudy" colors and precious jewels, making a "picturesque" whole. Didier's host had two daughters "who brought to life all the poetry of the Song of Songs and the image of whom has since come to serve for me the young Queen Esther and Ruth, the pretty gleaner."[137] Marcotte de Quivières, watching a group of Jewish women attempting to cross a river without lifting their skirts but without getting them wet, became so involved in "this interesting scene" that he forgot his horse and was almost thrown. The prettiest of all the women was "a veritable Rebecca."[138] Similarly, Eugène Delacroix described the Jewish women to a friend as "pearls from Eden."[139] If on one occasion in Tangiers Dumas had knocked on David Azencot's door to have it opened by his wife, on another, he encountered "an adorable Jewish girl, resplendent with youth, dazzlingly beautiful, and sparkling with rubies, sapphires, and diamonds."[140] This was Azencot's cousin, Molly. Gérard de Nerval, the great friend of Gautier, also studied the physiognomy of Jewish women, this time in Constantinople. He found "delicate regularity" but also a "resigned softness" that distinguished the Constantinople Jew. Like the Jewess of his friend's imagination, Nerval's subject wore her beauty apologetically, as though she did not deserve a face that did not comply with the status of her people.[141] And this beauty was fragile. Dumas suggested as much when he noted that Molly's beauty was, in part, due to the precious stones that she wore. Didier was less subtle. The daughters of his host were beautiful for their youth; at twenty-five, Didier informed the reader, they would look fifty.[142] Michaud and Poujoulat, however, were not deceived by any exterior charm. They saw through to the corruption of the Jewess's soul: Jewish women, they informed the reader, went into harems, "where they provide for all tastes, involve themselves in all intrigues, and go along with all sorts of services."[143] Maxime du Camp, another friend of Gautier who had been unimpressed by Jerusalem, responded similarly to the "white Jewesses" he encountered in Damascus. They were sickly, right through: the puffiness of their faces was revealing of the fact that there was "more pus in their veins than blood."[144] If beauty was fleeting or deceptive, this was perhaps a sign that the observer enjoyed a superior culture. Jewish beauty was weak, corruptible by Judaism itself. Jews themselves, therefore, were weak and corruptible, too. Here is the fluidity of the Jew: if in the *Juive de Constantine* Nathan and Léa could be saved, they could also be damned, an interesting contrast to Arabs, whose place and character were always fixed and a reflection, perhaps, of feelings of ambivalence toward Jews in French society.

Nowhere was weakness manifested more clearly than in Jewish greed. It was greed that all saw as the fundamental building block of Jewishness. Azaïs's Jew, with his curved nose and shaved head, was a metaphorical vulture; Azaïs described him "bustling about," doing business in the bazaars.[145] Pierre-Nicolas Hamont described the sickly Jews of Cairo as maliciously cheating Christians.[146] Didier's host in Tétouan, "although a Jew," did not fleece him too much.[147] Didier most probably felt he should point this out because, in his eyes, Samuel Bendelacq's conduct was an exception to the rule. Once again, all of these qualities were inscribed on the Jew's house. The doors of his home, in Didier's imagery, were "built by terror": "They are made of enormous beams, three or four inches thick, completely covered in big iron strips, and protected by triple locks; this is the fence of a prison or a fortress, and in effect, the Jewish houses are both one and the other. This first door, which opens on to the street, not being enough to calm the anxieties of Israelite avarice, there is a second that opens on to the courtyard and is built in the same way as its twin."[148] The desire to protect was matched by a will to deceive, for what from the outside appeared to be a decrepit hovel became a "veritable palace" upon entry: "golden, sculpted, all a-shimmer with mirrors and paintings."[149] Didier made a telling comparison between these Jewish houses and Moorish ones: Moorish homes, he noted, were like Jewish homes. The Jews were not the only ones to be exploited by the authorities: the Moors, too, were particular targets of avarice. Thus, the Moorish population, about whom Didier generally had nothing good to say, built homes whose facades spoke poverty in order to protect the riches within.[150] In Didier's version, Moorish homes told a tale of cause and effect, offsetting the less innocent nature of Jewish homes, which, built in the same style, told of Jewish greed and deception. Didier echoes the work of early socialist commentators such as Pierre Leroux and Alphonse

Toussenel. In their worldview, Jews personified the cynical individualism that caused the deep inequalities of wealth in French society that they perceived and abhorred. Didier wrote that wealth was power, and where Jews were concerned, such power was a danger. Money, for the Jews, was "their god, . . . their religion." And in a sudden leap back to July Monarchy France, Didier stated that in the Jews, "one could not imagine a more perfect personification of this material society that is presented to us every day as the ideal for humankind."[151]

Didier, of course, was referring to the liberal materialism of the regime under which he lived. A decade after he arrived in the capital, in 1841, Didier published *Nationalité française* (French nationality), a work in which he exhorted France to awake, to shake off the bonds of materialism that had held it back from its true destiny as a beacon of democracy in Europe. In a confusion of discourses that included references to Crusades and destiny but also Toussenelian language of feudalism (of the peasants) and tyranny (of the Jews), Didier excoriated the "antihuman and antisocial doctrines"—the "political materialism" that had ruled France since the Revolution of 1830.[152] By this time, the world of the bourgeoisie gave Didier "nervous twitches," and the mere sight of King Louis-Philippe's carriage in the street would ruin his walk.[153] Didier's greatest wish for France was to see democracy prevail. It is clear from his writing that he adhered to the beliefs of George Sand and those of her good friend Pierre Leroux. Leroux was known for his 1849 anticapitalist work *Malthus et les économistes, ou Y aura-t-il toujours des pauvres?* (Malthus and the economists, or Will there always be poor people?). This was a work in which he combined what we in retrospect would call a socialist ideology with a strong Christian morality and blamed Jews for the individualism that was the key evil of his time.[154] Sand, too, wrote greedy capitalist Jews into her work.[155] For Sand, Leroux, and others like them, the Revolution had unleashed individualism, and Jews, as they saw it, had benefited disproportionately from this new system. This was the competitive individualism that so horrified Didier. Given the striking visibility of a figure such as the enormously wealthy Jewish Baron James de Rothschild, Jews could be an easy scapegoat for those who were disgruntled by the state of affairs. Didier, it would seem, was simply drawing on these notions in a different context, using the very real Jews he encountered in Morocco to generate a fantasy, which he might use as a vehicle for his anticapitalist idealism.The early socialists also drew on the theological stigmatization of the Jew in their outrage, and it may be that this, too, informed Didier's censure.[156]

Dumas also understood the Jew as representative of the era, and the era as characterized by gold. The Jew had "understood,"

> that he, the foul thing, which could not be touched by commodities or by women without them being burned; he who was slapped in the face three times each year in Toulouse, for having given the city up to the Saracens; he

who was chased by stone throwers in the streets of Beziers, the whole of holy week; he, the scapegoat of outrage that everyone spat on; he who could be sold as a slave . . . he understood that with gold he would win back all he had lost and that on his obscure, patient, and progressive path, he would climb higher than the point from which he had fallen.[157]

Thus it was that in Dumas's age, the Jews had ascended to "the throne of gold." Thus it was, Dumas told his readers, that the much-respected historian Jules Michelet could report reading, in an English newspaper dated October 1834, that there had been little activity at the Stock Exchange since it was a Jewish holiday. However, the Jew's ascension, in Dumas's assessment, was "justice done, for this throne of gold, they conquered it with a battle that lasted eighteen centuries; patient and inflexible, they were bound to get there." Indeed, he stated, in what might safely be called a backhanded compliment, if a Jew would "always fleece you," at least he would never cheat or steal. His conditions were "set in advance, inexorable but they are clear: to take or to leave." The Christians, on the other hand, who had their debtors thrown into Clichy (debtors' prison), took more from those who owed them money than Shylock's pound of flesh. They took "all of their flesh."[158] If this was an era of gold, it was the Jew who had understood it properly.

However commentators might characterize the place of the Jew in their time, they all wrote of their times in disapproving tones. Didier's despair at his failed love affair with Sand, the breakup of his marriage, and his inability to follow up on his early writing success was combined with his great disappointment in a regime that he felt had failed its people. Didier was a proud believer in French Republican enlightenment. He believed in the benefit of bringing this enlightenment to "fanatical" Islam.[159] However, he was, equally, staunchly opposed to the liberal materialism of the July Monarchy under which he lived. Both of these viewpoints were imposed on the Oriental canvas.

In February 1848, Louis-Philippe's regime was overthrown, and a new attempt was made to find the *juste milieu*, Louis-Philippe's compromise between "the excesses of popular power and the abuses of royal power."[160] Four years of unsteady government were brought to a close by a coup d'état in December 1851, when Louis-Napoleon, emulating his uncle, took power. For Romantics, this marked the end of optimism and the victory of disenchantment.

Gautier, like Didier, sat at the heart of his times. Bénichou notes congruence between Gautier's disenchantment and the years surrounding 1848, the second great disappointment following the Revolution of 1830, which marked a dramatic "rupture with the humanitarian spirit in the young generation of French Romanticism."[161] Yet Gautier also understood himself to be placed outside his times; as a critic, he aspired to observe and analyze his own world with a dispassionate eye.

His descriptions of the Jews he encountered in Constantinople and elsewhere suggest that his observation was more subjective than he might have cared to acknowledge. Indeed, Gautier was as strident a critic as Didier and his friends were of what one Gautier scholar has called the "mercantile evolution" of his era.[162] And as was the case for so many of his contemporaries, capitalism could come to be identified with very visible Jews such as James de Rothschild and, through them, with the entire Jewish community. For those who used the Orient as a space for elaborating grievances, what could be more satisfying than to find that the Jews there were the embodiment of the evils of their world at home? Little wonder that anticapitalists such as Didier and Gautier found greedy Jews on their travels. In a sense, the Jew, as so many travelers found him, *had* to be wealthy. So committed were these travelers to the refusal of an era that the Jew embodied, that to find that the Jews of the Orient were wealthy, and deceptively so, was a stunning confirmation of their position. In this context, it comes as no surprise to find Michaud and Poujoulat reporting that "several" of the Jews of Constantinople were supposed to have amassed "great treasures."[163]

However, just as pilgrims were obliged to adapt the stories they wished to tell in order to make room for their encounters with real Jews in the Holy Land, so for travelers, reality could also cut through these fantasies. Many travelers stayed in the homes of Jews, and the intimacy of this arrangement came to trouble the waters of neat stereotypes. In Morocco, Charles Didier was a guest in the home of Samuel Bendelacq, and Delacroix made his home in that of Abraham ben Chimol.[164] Ben Chimol ran a tannery and had the monopoly on the export of leather to Marseilles. He was also the interpreter to the French Consulate and would, according to one Delacroix scholar, "explain all the Moroccan customs to newly arrived Europeans."[165] Delacroix spent time in Abraham ben Chimol's home, as well as in those of his brothers, Jacob, Isaac, David, and Haim, and with their sister, Guimol Azencot, mother of David, the auxiliary dragoman and supplier to the Moroccan Royal Navy. The only homes that Delacroix entered were those of Jews. Moorish homes were, as he put it, "forbidden."[166] In the homes of ben Chimol's extended family, Delacroix painted portraits of Leditia, Abraham's niece, as well as of his wife, Saada, along with Preciada and Rachel, his daughters.[167] For Delacroix, the women were "goddesses," and if their male counterparts were not quite as attractive, their "air of obsequious assiduity, combined with a sort of deceitful look," served as a reminder of just how limited and unhappy their existence was under Islam. They were effectively slaves, and yet, under oppression, they were nonetheless able to maintain the powerful ties that united them, that made them a nation, "still so alive in the midst of the ruins of its tyrants and its persecutors."[168] This is what close proximity allowed Delacroix to see. In Tangiers, David Azencot, recommended to Dumas by the French consul, was not only a host and guide to Dumas and his fellow travelers but was able to provide for their every desire.[169] In the Orient, the Jew was not only host but also interpreter, middleman, banker, and guide to the *dépaysé* European.

This was the fluid place of the Jew: fanatical and enlightened, degraded and civilized, European and Oriental. The Jew could be like the traveler in morality and even, at times, in beauty. The Baron de Bussièrre was astonished to find in Balat, "in this horrible place and in the midst of these disgusting beings," the occasional "noble and well-defined figure," which "had exactly the august character that the greatest artists have given to the head of Christ."[170] But Bussièrre also noted that the Jews of Constantinople had qualities worth mentioning. They were scrupulous observers of the practices of their religion. They had a strict morality, and scandals emanating from within the Jewish community were rare.[171]

At the same time, however, the Jew was not like the traveler: the Jew was a go-between. Jews were commonly employed by consular officials: in Tangiers, Morocco, in 1832, Salomon de Judah Aboudarham was interpreter for the Spanish Consulate, and in a similar capacity, Isaac Abensour served Britain; Jacob Ben Selloum served Sweden; Abraham Bendellac, the Netherlands; Isaac Sicsu, Austria; and David Hassan, Sardinia. Bussièrre noted that in Turkey, the Jews had made themselves indispensable; through their "extreme activeness," they had become "the general agents to the Levant." "Groveling" and "scorned," they were known to be untrustworthy, yet what Bussièrre called "other nations" had all become "dependent on their savoir-faire."[172] In Morocco, the Count de Mornay, Delacroix's diplomatic companion, described to his superiors in France how he was forbidden from addressing the sultan directly but, rather, had to "speak in the name of France" through a Jew.[173] This was a deliberate choice on the sultan's part: Muslims might seek to gain wealth and power through relations with Europeans and challenge his authority; Christians, in his eyes, were likely to side with their coreligionists from across the Mediterranean. Jews, however, had no such loyalty and were already subordinate figures in Muslim society. The sultan believed that Jewish interpreters would be easily controlled and could therefore be trusted to convey his will.[174] Thus, European diplomatic officials were forced to rely on the agency of Jews. But Jews also were the windows onto this Oriental world in other ways: Schroeter claims that "practically the only social contact" that most Europeans had with local populations, "everywhere in Morocco," was with the Jewish communities there. This is borne out, not only for Morocco but also for Egypt and Algiers, in travel accounts. Not only were travelers welcomed into Jewish homes and invited to take part in festivals and celebrations; they were also given access to the world of Jewish women. This was significant, given that the Muslim world was largely closed to them, and their experience of the harem remained in the realm of invention.[175]

Travelers brought desires, anxieties, resentments, and assumptions with them from home. Packed in this baggage was what their culture knew about Jews, combined with their own experience of newly emancipated Jews. Much of this knowledge and experience could be transposed onto the Jews they encountered, and it was. The Jew in the Orient was the perfect counterimage of the European, practiced and perfected at home. Thus, the Jews of Morocco became, for the anticapitalist Didier, a Dorian Gray–like portrait of Rothschild. In this sense, encounters with the Jew in the Orient do not fit theories of contact, or of middle ground. The Jew was ever so familiar, even if discovered in an utterly unfamiliar setting. Delacroix called Morocco "an unknown land, about which we were given the most bizarre and contradictory notions."[176] Yet if Gautier could allow himself to become "lost" in the Jewish quarter of Balat, it was only because he knew precisely what he had found. This was a complex relationship. For while Didier, Gautier, and others could use the Jew to neatly encapsulate all that was wrong at home, at the same time the Oriental Jew could force the traveler onto a common ground of mutual need. For the Jew, the traveler might have been a source of income or prestige or, at times, of safety. For the traveler, the Jew could be a lifeline: one who made Delacroix's "unknown land" literally comprehensible, who offered comfort, refuge, familiarity.

When Alexandre Dumas visited Tangiers, he met David Azencot, a man he described as being of indeterminate age and medium height, with eyes that were "lively and intelligent." His accent had a hint of Italian. "The Oriental Jew was finally revealed" to him.[177] Dumas went to David's home, where he was able to purchase all the local goods that he had hoped to be able to take back to France. Dumas asked that his friend and fellow traveler Boulanger be allowed to paint David's sister-in-law Rachel, whose portrait had been painted fifteen years earlier by Delacroix. David organized instead for Boulanger to paint David's young cousin Molly, who was the age Rachel had been when she had sat for Delacroix.

David Azencot was, to a significant extent, Dumas's experience of Tangiers. For Dumas, Arabs were a different species from the French. "We," he stated, had been bringing liberty to this Orient since the fourteenth century.[178] Nonetheless, the Arabs they encountered there remained indelibly foreign, from the behavior of their children, to their sense of honor and pleasure, to their enjoyment of culture. Frenchmen and Arabs stood poles apart.[179] Dumas's understanding of David Azencot must be placed against this backdrop. When David's brother took Dumas to find Giraud and Boulanger, who were sketching in the marketplace, Dumas encountered a Moroccan woman complaining that her people must have offended their god for "Christian dogs" to be allowed to draw the palace. If this suggested a lack of politeness on her part, Dumas was not concerned. The Moroccans, he noted, had never been known for their hospitality. "Five minutes later," he went on to state, allowing the contrast to speak for itself, "we returned to David's home."[180] Dumas's Orient was a place of foreignness and difference. It accentuated his own Frenchness. The only thing that was not foreign in Tangiers was that city's Jews. If Jews, "fanaticism's pariahs," had "always gained something from extending their hand to us,"[181] David Azencot was a perfect example of how a French traveler could also benefit from this rapprochement. David was

> the unique, universal man; with David you need no other; with David you will want for nothing; on the contrary, you will live in luxury; . . . with David you will have more than reality, you will have dreams, and you will be able to believe you are a sultan in his harem, a king or an emperor on his throne.[182]

Dumas described how, when he and his fellow travelers came to settle their accounts with David for food and goods that he had supplied them, he refused to take any money. This was consistent with what Dumas called his "humble air."[183] Dumas concluded his chapter named after his Tangiers host on a high note. He reflected that in the course of his travels, he had had particular dealings with what he referred to as "two Israelites." One was David Azencot; the other was Soual in Algiers. Dumas wished that "the most honest Christians" he knew might have "their politeness, their probity, and their unselfishness."[184] Thus, he concluded a chapter that took the reader on a journey through Tangiers, led by David Azencot, with a side trip back to France, and its era of gold, reigned over by Jews. This was a chapter in which the Jews' ambiguous place was given full expression and where, just as for those who traveled as pilgrims, the desire of Dumas and others to read these Oriental Jews through the prism of their anti-capitalism was tempered by the reality of the Jews they met. This is no clear tale of the Jew as Other. Dumas's description of his time with David Azencot shows how the Orientalized Jew breaks down neat schemas of us and them, here and there, real and imagined. It shows how these categories overlap and intertwine, not least in terms of the ways in which the Orientalized Jew could be one and the other, and often both at once.

One of the best examples of the lack of fixity in the Jew and his place was in the pasha's vizier and chief banker in Damascus, Haim Farhi.[185] It was common for visitors to Syria to pay a visit to Farhi; he was the pasha's representative, and as a Spanish speaker he could communicate with European visitors in a European tongue. Farhi was an example of what "talent and skill" could achieve; he had risen through the ranks, as Marcellus saw it, "from the depths of the most despised class in Turkey to the honors given the most important ministry."[186] Those who visited Farhi wondered at his extraordinary wealth and power.[187] Yet Farhi, whose home (as many travelers took care to write) was a study in luxury, made a point of receiving his visitors in a small, simply furnished room. The British socialite and adventurer Lady Hester Stanhope described her experience thus:

> Haym's [sic] street door opened, and we went down two or three steps into a stone entry about fifteen or twenty feet square, to the left of which was a dirty

alcove, with a carpet on the floor and cushions against the wall, and opposite to it a small filthy room. . . . Any stranger, and in particular a Turk, enters thus far, and whether he comes for the business of the moment or for a few days, it is here that the master of the house sees him.[188]

Farhi, the Jew whose wealth was "overflowing,"[189] and "incalculable,"[190] sought to deceive the visitor. Count Auguste de Forbin, an early pilgrim we encountered in chapter 1 as he made his way through the Holy Land to Jerusalem, knew of Farhi's "sumptuous palace" in Damascus. Forbin wrote of how he was received by this "flexible and shrewd man" in a "rather mediocre house."[191] Marcellus, who described Farhi as "more a pasha than the pasha himself," was similarly received, in "a simple house, with no luxury at all, and [Marcellus] saw only a studied mediocrity there." The host became the "respectful slave" to his honored guest.[192] In Farhi was all the ambiguity of the place of the Jew in the schema that visitors such as Forbin and Marcellus sought to establish. He was powerful: The scion of Syria's most influential and wealthy Jewish family, he controlled financial affairs in the governates of both Damascus and Sidon. He played a role "in all of Syria's commercial enterprises."[193] His wealth and influence were such that he could weave a web of deception around himself. Yet despite the extraordinary trappings (of which both Forbin and Marcellus professed to be aware, but which neither actually saw), he remained a "humble Jew,"[194] held in "the deepest contempt" by those who were able to endure "the misappropriations, the snubs, the tyranny" of the government of which he was an intrinsic part.[195] This was the Jewish go-between, apparently at ease in both worlds but never entirely of either.

Farhi's great wealth afforded him some level of dignity, as did Azencot's enormous usefulness to Dumas. For other travelers, the average Jewish go-between was a figure of ridicule who had reckoned without the superiority of his supposed victim. A contemptuous Baptistin Poujoulat recounted his encounter with one Moses in Izmir:

> This child of Jacob is always there, watching for travelers, approaching those who seem to have a lot of money to spend. He suggests himself to them as politely as he can, as one who can accompany them in the town and show them its curiosities. Moses has the advantage of being able to offer his services to travelers of all nations, for he finds a way to make himself understood in almost all living languages. This guide from the banks of the Mélès is not unaware that the Occidental traveler in Asian lands seeks monuments, the relics of the past; he does not forget to propose that they go and visit the ancient remains on Mount Pagus. But there is something else entirely that preoccupies him in his conversations with travelers, and this is to be their guide in the bazaars and to be present for their purchases. Moses knows the price of everything; he will say that he knows the bazaars, and he will not allow a foreigner to be tricked! As could be expected, desire has not always spared such a character: at times

he is accused of forgetting the interest of the travelers with the merchants and to do better deals in the bazaars than in the Oriental ruins. If you saw Moses, I am certain that you would not take him for a broker, even less for a servant; with his brimless hat wrapped in a blue scarf, with his long brown robe tightened with a black belt, his red bootees, and his carefully combed beard, you might think you were looking at a young rabbi. One last trait will complete your knowledge of our Israelite guide: he knew that we sought an official interpreter for our voyage to Anatolia; he offered us his services for this undertaking. Moses requested one hundred francs per month, with the condition that he would rest on Saturdays; he made it known to us that if we required him to work on that day, he would need fifty francs extra. "These gentlemen will surely understand, he said to us, that a sin such as violating the Sabbath must be paid for!" This is how Moses understood religious scruples, and from there, you can judge for the rest.[196]

Didier also described his encounter with Jewish go-betweens from a perspective of superiority. It was common for Jews to act as consular representatives for the European powers in Morocco. These posts, offering some protection from the vagaries of Turkish rule, were highly sought after. Didier watched the arrival of the diplomatic body in Tétouan; the sight of Jewish consular representatives wearing European clothing, "as a badge of their dignity" and their status, was "the most grotesque scene" he had ever witnessed.[197] They wore "priest's trousers" or "seaman's pants"; one, who was four feet tall by Didier's estimation, wore clothing that was too big and dragged on the ground; another, strikingly tall, wore a tailcoat that went only "as far as his kidneys." One little old man wore a necktie so elaborately knotted that it condemned his head "to a majestic immobility," ironically giving him "an attitude that was entirely in line with the classic dress of the diplomat."[198] When the Oriental Jew tried to ape the European, he could not rise above ridicule.

The fluidity and uncertainty of the Jew's place manifested itself also in the drawing up of boundaries. Were the Jews of the Orient representative of their European coreligionists? To some, there was no doubt that Jews were the same everywhere. In Constantinople, Michaud and his traveling companion Jean-Joseph Poujoulat observed that the Israelites there did "what they did in every country": they speculated, they practiced usury, they were middlemen—brokers to merchants, bankers to the wealthy, and peddlers—they peddled and resold "all sorts of merchandise."[199] For Bussière, the Jews of Turkey encouraged disdain, just as did their coreligionists in Poland.[200] The Viscount Basterot wrote the East into the West in this passage, where he brought all Jews together:

The scourge of the bazaars, here [in Smyrna] as in Constantinople, are the Jewish ruffians and go-betweens. This intelligent and unhappy race, which strives to rise again in the Occident, practices all the vile professions in the Orient, if there is such a thing as vile professions.[201]

Others, however, sought to differentiate between the Jews of the Orient and the Jews in France. After one of his many diatribes, Pierre-Nicolas Hamont noted that he was speaking of what he called the Jews of the Orient; "the others" were "mixed in with Europeans."[202] Nerval saw a physical distinction; regarding a Jewish woman he observed in Constantinople, he found:

> Her physiognomy, of a resigned softness and a delicate regularity, represented the particular type of the Constantinople Jew, but it did not in any way resemble the types that we are familiar with. Her nose did not have that pronounced curve that, at home, signs the face with the name Rebecca or Rachel.[203]

Others saw a difference in character. Malherbe noted that in Europe, what he called "Israelite resistance" did not exhibit "a character of ferocious hostility at all."[204] Indeed, Malherbe would have been horrified to think that any of his discussion might "upset" the Israelites. They, "spread throughout the civilized nations of Europe," lived among "us" as citizens. They were "the children of the same fatherland; the enlightenment of this century and of education have established indissoluble ties between us."[205] For Dumas, too, the Jew in France had "blended in with society. Nothing distinguishes him from other men," he stated, "neither his language, nor his turns of phrase, nor his clothing." In France, the Jew could be an officer of the Legion of Honor, a member of the Académie française, or even a baron, a prince, or a king.[206] Basterot wrote of "Europe's great Jewish families, so enlightened, so above a fanaticism that no longer exists." If they allowed themselves to believe, at the time of the Damascus Blood Libel of 1840, that their wealth might have some influence in the Orient, Basterot sought to generalize their conduct to all the "small confessions": "When one is relatively small in number, solidarity becomes tighter and less reasoned. This is an excellent thing from the point of view of business, but it can blind the eyes in the search for truth. The Jews have not entirely escaped this tendency, and the most distinguished minds among them are uncompromising when these types of questions are raised."[207] Thus, difference, and with it civilization, were tempered; in times of crisis, the civilized Jews of Europe might well revert to their true nature, exemplified by the Jews of the Orient. Civilization, of the type that characterized French society, made the Jew civilized. It followed that "the farther one [got] from the center of civilization," as Dumas explained, the Jew descended, "step by step, from his commercial throne." "Once again" he became "humble, submissive, fearful."[208]

For some travelers, the fact of knowing Jews meant that their presence in the Orient could be dismissed. Victor Fontanier was a naturalist, a chevalier of the Legion of Honor who was sent to Constantinople in 1821 by Count Siméon. He was instructed to explore the Black Sea and the Ottoman Empire. He found himself in the midst of the Greek uprisings and chose to write three volumes covering his experiences. Fontanier believed that it would never be possible to make space for Muslims in the European family.[209] Fontanier's Orient was one where downtrodden Christians sought to live as best they could among wicked Mohammedans. The Jews had no place in this panorama of iniquity. Fontanier was aware of Jewish communities in the Orient, and he made passing reference to them. But his sense of their place in his tale is summed up in a discussion of the non-Muslim communities in Turkey: "Because I know nothing about the position of the Jews," he tells the reader, "I will not attend to them."[210] And thus, the Jews were written out of Fontanier's volumes. When Abbé Azaïs went from being a pilgrim in the Holy Land to being a self-nominated tourist in other parts of the Ottoman Empire, Jews diminished in importance in his tale. The references he made to the Jews he encountered in places like Constantinople were short and fleeting, as though a shorthand of stereotypes sufficed to communicate to the reader. This was a far cry from the long paragraph that described the hopelessness of the Jews at the Wailing Wall. Similarly, for the career traveler Baron Taylor, Jerusalem contained Jews, but Egypt did not.[211] Jews are also absent from the two volumes produced by the writer Alphonse de Lamartine, who traveled throughout North Africa and the Middle East and met many fellow travelers on the way. There were Jewish women in Lamartine's catalogues of beauty,[212] but in his description of the wondrous and the exotic, it is almost as though Jews did not make the grade.

Not every traveler had need of Jews in their narrative, therefore, but Jews could be called on to play a distinct role. The currency of these creations—the ease with which they could be understood by a French audience—is underscored, for example, by the fact that Delacroix, anticipating the demand for his 1839 *Noce juive au Maroc* (Jewish wedding in Morocco), made a gravure of the painting so that he could then make copies. Frédéric Goupil, who traveled through the Orient with his friend the artist Horace Vernet, made little or no room for the Jews he encountered. We know, nonetheless, that he did encounter Jews: he found them in Alexandria, "busying themselves with trade and illegal speculation."[213] But at the very end of his trip, he went looking for photographic images to complete his tour of Damascus. He had his (Arab) guide take him to the home of a Jew whose house was situated on one of the highest locations in the city. There, on the roof, he unexpectedly found himself in the midst of a "truly Oriental" scene, "surrounded by the most delightful faces of young women," "the desert of surrounding roofs blooming with envious women."[214] This was the Orient, peopled by figures who were exotic enough to stand in as artists' models but who were also accessible, comprehensible, its women uncovered, like Chassériau's 1849 *Juives d'Alger au balcon* (Jewish women on a balcony, Algeria) (figure 2.1).

Figure 2.1 *Jewish Women on a Balcony, Algeria*, by Théodore Chassériau, 1849. Musée du Louvre. © RMN-Grand Palais/Art Resource, NY.

These were the figures who could be written into familiar scripts: the enemies of Christianity, the exemplars of cupidity or of great beauty. They were perfect fodder for the travel account, for the work of art, for the melodrama. Yet while authors such as those whose work is discussed in this chapter constructed exotically familiar or familiarly exotic Jews, they also worked, interacted with, and at times befriended Jews in France. How did they reconcile the stereotypical Jews of their travelogues with the very real Jews present in their lives? How did their understanding of "civilized" French Jews and ambiguous Oriental Jews inform one another? In part 3, I return to Gautier to take up and explore these questions.

## Part 3

One of the best known of Delacroix's paintings from his 1832 trip to Morocco was his *Noce juive au Maroc*. In his review of the painting, Gautier noted that the Jews, among the Arabs, were recognizable "by their sidelong glance, their servile nature, and their apologetic attitude."[215] This, of course, recalls his descriptions from his own trips to Algeria and Constantinople, where he saw Jews who "begged pardon."[216] As we have seen, when he was creating unknown or fictional Jews in far-flung, exotic places, Gautier apparently allowed himself poetic license and created stereotypes. Yet back home in Paris, Gautier's circle included Rachel Félix and Giacomo Meyerbeer. He worked and interacted with both of them and published their praises privately, in his correspondence, but also publicly, in his reviews. How did Gautier reconcile the stereotypical Jews of his travelogues with the real Jews present in his Paris life? What part did Rachel or Meyerbeer play in this story of France, Jews, and the Orient? In part 3, I explore this intersection between the distant and impersonal Oriental Jew and the Jews in the intimacy of the Gautier circle. Thus, I pick up the echoes of Gautier's travelogues back in France. What was the interplay between his depictions of Oriental Jews and the Jews who made up part of his close circles in Paris? How did his neat dichotomies (Jews and non-Jews, Jewish man and woman), play out when confronted with the frank intimacy of his relationships? The path into this web begins with Gautier's own schema: the figure of the Jewish woman and the contrasting image of the Jewish man.

Over the nineteenth century, Paris became the center of French Jewry. It was here that a group of Jews, keen to rise socially, established themselves in banking and finance. This group gained, as Graetz puts it, "an importance far beyond its numbers."[217] The sense of opportunity that brought bankers such as James de Rothschild to Paris was equally attractive to Jews who sought to make their way in the arts. Paris in the mid-nineteenth century was a highly attractive destination for Jews who wished to practice their creativity freely. One such individual was Giacomo Meyerbeer. Meyerbeer was born Jacob Meyer Beer, the eldest son of the enormously wealthy Jewish Berlin banker Jacob Beer. Jacob the elder and his wife, Amalie, lived at a pivotal time in Berlin Jewish society. They were at the forefront in the forging of a new space for Jews between baptism and tradition, a space that Deborah Hertz has called "harmonious modernization."[218] However, for the young Jacob, a talented musician, Germany still placed too many conditions on his chosen path. He wished to remain a Jew, a desire that would have restricted his choices in Germany, where Jews could rise only to a certain level in administration and the arts and then had to convert in order to go further. Meyerbeer created his own family name by merging his middle and family names. He changed the Jewish-sounding Jacob to the Italian Giacomo, and he set off to seek his fortune in Paris. He was to achieve enormous popular success.

In the mid-nineteenth century, Jewish women were popular for what was perceived as their great beauty, particularly from the 1830s and over the following decade, during which Jewish women were prominent among artists' models.[219] Perhaps the best known was Joséphine Marix (also spelled Maryx), born Joséphine Bloch. Her beauty was celebrated, but the fairy-tale nature of her story, whereby she married a Danish nobleman, made her the stuff of legend. Scattered references to her can be found in contemporary descriptions of Paris life.[220] Writer Albert de la Fizelière introduced Joséphine, a new model, who threatened "to break many hearts before the end of the summer."[221] For Alexandre Privat d'Anglemont, she was "the most beautiful Jewish type that can be seen, . . . the Oriental type in all its purity."[222] Gautier, visiting the painter Fernand Boissard in mid-1849, found Marix lying on the sofa,

> half stretched out, her elbow on a cushion, with that immobility that had become her habit through posing, Maryx, in a white dress, bizarrely dotted with red spots like drops of blood, listened vaguely to Baudelaire's paradoxes, without allowing the least surprise to show on her mask, of the purest Oriental type, and passed the rings of her left hand to the fingers of her right, hands as perfect as her body, its beauty preserved by molding.[223]

The little we know about Marix comes to us from the painstaking research of Jean Ziegler. It is Gautier who provides much of the detail of her life, and Ziegler concludes that Gautier maintained an affectionate friendship with the woman he referred to as "Tonton."[224] Gautier visited Marix in her castle in Schleswig-Holstein, bearing the invitation that the hostess had issued years earlier in Paris. From there he wrote to his partner, the singer Ernesta Grisi, with the message that the baroness asked him to send her best wishes and to let Ernesta know that he was being well cared for.[225] The following year, when Ernesta made her own visit to the baroness, Gautier wrote to his partner, sending "much love" and remembering Tonton's "charming hospitality" fondly.[226] In another letter, hoping that Tonton's anger at a canceled visit had subsided, he lamented the fact that he was "tied up" in Paris and could not accompany Ernesta on her visit.[227] And when the baroness visited Paris, she dined with Gautier and Ernesta, and Gautier wrote to his friend and publisher Jules Hetzel on Marix's behalf when Hetzel did not respond to a letter she had written him.[228]

Gautier maintained an equally warm friendship with Jewish actresses. His correspondence reveals the existence of a protégée, Siona Lévy, the stage name of Amélie Ernst.[229] Another actress, known as Judith (Julie Bernat), has left us more evidence of her life. Judith debuted at fourteen. She was a distant relative of Rachel Félix and competed with her. In her autobiography, the story of a self-styled "great actress," Judith dwelt at length on her relationship with her better-known cousin.[230] Gautier, however, was equally generous with both actresses.

He published reviews of Judith's performances that were consistently positive.[231] In her own memoir, she described her friendship with both Théophile and Ernesta and boasted of having lent Ernesta money. For Gautier, the "young and charming Israelite"[232] enjoyed great beauty, including "large, dark and velvety eyes."[233] "Impossible," he wrote of her debut, "to dream of features that are more regular and delicate, a darker eye, a redder lip, a more elegant shape."[234] Arguably, though, the best-known Jewish woman in midcentury Paris was Judith's nemesis, the actress Rachel Félix, known commonly as Rachel, the celebrated tragedienne, perhaps as famous for her brilliant life and tragic death as for her skill on the stage.

Rachel was born Elisa-Rachel Félix in a village inn in Switzerland in February 1821. She grew up on the road; her parents, Jacob (Jacques) and Thérèse-Esther-Chaya Félix, were itinerant Jewish peddlers, and the wagon from which they sold used clothes served as both shop and home. Rachel was the second child. Sophie-Sarah had been born in 1819, and four more children were to follow: Raphaël (1826), Rébecca (1828), Adelaïde-Lia (1830), and Mélanie-Dinah (1836). All of the siblings were talented performers, but it was Rachel and Sarah who, performing on the streets of Lyons, were discovered by the Parisian musician and educator Etienne Choron. They were ten and eight. Two years later, in 1831, the family moved to Paris, and the two girls attended Choron's school, where they were trained in acting and music. In June 1838, aged seventeen, Rachel debuted at the Comédie-Française in the role of Camille in Corneille's *Horace*. She rapidly gained renown. Among her admirers was Gautier. Indeed, her career spanned, more or less, Gautier's critical career at *La Presse*, and Gautier devoted more columns to her than to any other actor. Gautier's enthusiasm should not be taken for granted: In performing the French tragedies of Racine and Corneille, Rachel was seen as reviving classicism. Gautier the Romantic might well have chosen to disdain or criticize her work. Privately, he described playing tragedy as "consisting principally in the art of placing curtains around one's shoulders."[235] He did take time to come around.[236] Ultimately, however, for Gautier Rachel represented an ideal: "She was born antique, and her pale flesh seemed made of Greek marble." She was "admirably beautiful,"[237] "incredible perfection,"[238] and an "incomparable magician."[239]

He never stopped wishing—publicly—that Rachel would go "straight into modern drama,"[240] with a play by Hugo, Lamartine, or Dumas. Drama was a genre that Rachel was "born to play."[241] When she did take on Hugo, playing Thisbe in his 1835 *Angelo, tyran de Padoue* (Angelo, tyrant of Padua), Gautier made a point of celebrating her choice, writing that she now "reigned over the Romantic empire."[242] Whatever her choice of play, however, he remained a faithful admirer. Even when he was less than happy about the tragedy, it was of little consequence "as long as there was the *tragedienne*!"[243]

Gautier was a deep admirer of Rachel's ability to achieve what he saw as perfection. This perfection was that of a sculpture. Gautier, who had declared that he preferred "marble to flesh,"[244] could give no higher praise than to state that Rachel had "a deep feeling for statuary."[245] Similar references are rife in his reviews. Gautier would watch her "like a sculptor studying all the angles of a statue."[246] Her Electra was "sculpted from pure, sparkling marble," one more beautiful statue in the museum of antiquities, already populated with Mademoiselle Rachel's creations, "so pure and noble."[247] For Rachel, a role was a statue that she "sculpted from thick alexandrine block." The secret of her art was that she moved like an artist's model. Thus, her "supple, energetic body moves harmoniously with the rhythms known to sculptors and poets of long ago."[248] In Racine's *Phèdre* (Phaedra) she became a Greek princess, and in *Angelo* she was an Italian courtesan of the sixteenth century. "Sculptors and painters could not do better." When she played tragedy, "she seemed to step out of one of Phidias's bas-reliefs onto the stage." In 1848, when she famously recited the "Marseillaise," "it was flesh like marble."[249] When she played drama, it looked as though she had descended from a framed Bronzino or Titian. She could be pale marble, an antique statue, and then take on all the warm colors of a Venetian Renaissance painting.[250]

Yet she was real. Rachel and Gautier crossed paths regularly and maintained a friendly and at times affectionate correspondence. Gautier and Rachel's friendship was possibly established in the salon of Gautier's great friend Delphine de Girardin. (Girardin and Rachel had met in late 1838.) In 1843, Rachel wrote to issue a standing invitation to Gautier; she would be "flattered" if he chose to join the few people who honored her by coming to her home on a Thursday evening.[251] When he was traveling though Belgium in 1846, Gautier described to his mother how he had met Rachel in Liège and how she gave him a box, invited him to dinner, and "embraced" him "like bread."[252] A month later, he wrote to Rachel from London to state his regret at the news that her illness would prevent him from experiencing "the pleasure of witnessing [her] effect on the English."[253] At the end of that year, she wrote to promise an explanation regarding her decision to quit the Comédie-Française.[254] Clearly the matter did not have any lasting effect on their friendship. Some years later, possibly in 1854, Rachel was inviting her "cher Gautier" to dinner, exhorting him not to forget the place he occupied in her heart.[255] When Rachel was grievously ill and shortly to die of tuberculosis, Gautier traveled with his friend Arsène Houssaye, another writer and administrator of the Théâtre français, to make a surprise visit as she attempted convalescence in Montpellier.

For Gautier, then, Rachel was art, and in the name of his credo, art for art's sake, he idealized her. What role did her Jewishness play in their relationship? In fact, in his public discussion of her, there is little or no mention of her religion, and therefore any mention of her Jewishness becomes all the more significant. If his writings on her are a true record of his understanding of her, it would appear that, for Gautier, Rachel became Jewish only when she was Oriental or ancient.[256] In his words, her Jewishness "bound her to the Orient and the primitive world."[257] Gautier's language of beauty, when it came to the Jewish women in his life, had a striking consistency, whether these women were real or imagined. Marix's mask was pure Oriental. Judith's large eyes and "regular and delicate features"[258] echo Gautier's language from an 1839 review of *Suzanne in the Bath*, a work by Théodore Chassériau, whom Gautier saw regularly at the salon of Delphine de Girardin. Suzanne, the subject of the painting, was "a great beauty; she is the Hebraic type in all its Oriental purity: large almond eyes, slender nose, a long oval face, a mouth both full and delicate, barely prominent cheekbones, a pale amber tone, tawny hair—all signs of race."[259] Nine years later, he reviewed the *Sabbath of the Jews of Constantine* by the same artist. Here, the Jewish women had "chaste ovals, nobly elongated" and "large gazelle's eyes," reminiscent of the eyes, "like black diamonds," of the Jewish woman Gautier had encountered in Constantine. Their breasts, unsurprisingly, were marble.[260] This was language practiced and developed over time by means of a number of subjects, including actresses, a model, and works of art. Gautier, as we have seen, did not distinguish: art was beauty, and beauty was art. Jewishness, in this form, became one means for communicating this notion. The Oriental, the ancient, the perfect, was Jewish.

Jewishness as a religious identity appears to have been irrelevant to Gautier. Perhaps this was in line with his well-documented detachment. Overwhelmingly, narrators of Gautier's life detail his refusal to descend into politics. The Goncourt brothers, novelists and diarists Edmond and Jules, might have described him "raging against civilization, the engineers who destroyed the landscapes with their railways, the municipal minded."[261] In general, though, both scholars and his peers talk of him in terms of detachment. Any authority he had among proponents of the arts was due to his ability to immerse himself with expertise in each of them.[262] Yet while he observed this world with great insight, he also refused much of it. Literary historians have made much of the dissociation, manifested as irony, that permeates Gautier's work:

> Skepticism and mockery are constant correctives of the lyrical. In Gautier the self-parody, the deliberate dissociation, the affectation of impassivity constitute a defense mechanism against deception and vulnerability, a recognition, too, of the ambivalence of reality. An innate emotionalism is constantly dogged by a lucid, analytical approach, what Banville called Gautier's "saine ironie."[263]

Françoise Court-Perez, who titled her book on Gautier *An Ironic Romantic*, argues that it is precisely for this reason that Gautier's work is difficult to grasp as a whole: while his criticism put him at the heart of his time, his disgust at the materialism he saw as characteristic of it made him dream himself elsewhere.[264]

All his life, in fact, Gautier was the puny, long-haired youth in the red waist-coat, battling classicists in the stalls and delightedly annoying the bourgeois while Hugo's play *Hernani* was being performed. The deep irony that so many see as characteristic of his work is equally manifested in his life. Gautier may have railed against the straw men of modernity. However, he was not above buying shares in one of the Jewish Péreire brothers' banking ventures.[265] Even his documented refusal to engage with the politics of his time could also be seen as a different, yet equally significant, form of engagement with his world. Gautier may have professed to take no interest in passing political regimes. Yet if, as Richardson argues, it was only with the siege of Paris at the end of his life that Gautier finally became a patriot, he had, nonetheless, much to say about his times, and there are striking echoes of early socialism in his words. Richardson calls him "the least materialistic of men,"[266] yet he understood his era as one in which arts, letters, religion, and arms had all crumbled, leaving only the ingot standing. The "fever for gold" had invaded society "from its depths to its heights."[267] The idea that his age was one of cynical individualism was a theme in Gautier's writing.[268] In his schema, even the Orient risked falling victim to shallow materialism. Gautier's review of Chassériau's *Sabbath of the Jews of Constantine* was a plaintive statement. The "beautiful unknown races" of the Orient that Chassériau had re-created so wonderfully were under threat. They were soon to disappear, invaded, as Gautier put it, "by our false civilization." Constantine would be filled "with dreadful shopkeepers, abominable bourgeois, and women dressed in the latest fashion."[269] The beautiful truth of the Orient would be replaced by the falseness of modern life. Even Jews, so often the carriers of modernity, could be threatened by it. The beautiful Jewish women of the painting told this story. In their eyes, "deep" and "set" was "the sense of their future death."[270] Gautier enlarged on this notion in France, too. In an 1862 review, he wrote that where once the standard theater plot was a variation on the human struggle between passion and duty, in his time, plots centered around money: "To give money . . . is the greatest act of modern heroism, and the character who is capable of such devotion is sure to provoke the bravos of admirers who, perhaps, would not imitate him." Gautier credits Balzac as being the first to realize "that the ideal of our time was no longer happiness through love but happiness through fortune." His era, therefore, was characterized by "the religion of money."[271] It was, as he had written earlier, in strikingly reminiscent language, "the century of the Rothschilds."[272] Was Gautier borrowing from his contemporary, the early socialist Alphonse Toussenel? This is certainly possible. Toussenel's *Les Juifs: Rois de l'époque* (The Jews: Kings of the era) had been published in 1845, and the two men knew one another well enough to correspond.[273]

Toussenel's Rothschild was pure metaphor: he stood in for all that Tous-senel deemed evil about society.[274] Perhaps, for Gautier, too, Jewishness was a metaphorical quality. Rachel was Jewish when she was Oriental or ancient, "bibli-cal." But when she was a Jewish tragic actress in mid-nineteenth-century Paris, her Jewishness had no relevance. Rachel's importance as representing the an-cient grew with Gautier's own move from an obsession with beauty that saw this quality as progressive to an idea of beauty that looked to the distant past.[275] Ra-chel, like Rothschild, could stand in for an idea or even an ideal. In this case, for Gautier Jewishness was ancient, and it was Oriental. The fact that Rachel played Greek heroines served to emphasize this notion.

Rachel was a prominent figure in the Paris artistic world of the midcentury. Perhaps her extraordinary presence contributed to the idea of the Jewish Rachel. For, in midcentury Paris, it might just have been possible to imagine that all Jewish women carried this name. The heroine of Eugène Scribe and Fromental Halévy's enormously popular 1835 opera *La Juive* (The Jewess) was Rachel, and the aria dedicated to her—"Rachel quand du Seigneur" (Rachel when from the Lord)—was sufficiently known that at the beginning of the following century, Proust could bestow the title as a nickname on one of his characters. As one contemporary author said of a Jewish model, "Like so many others, she said her name was Rachel."[276] Jewish Rachels loomed large for Gautier, too, and this is borne out by another of Gautier's works of fiction, published late in Rachel Félix's life. If the real Rachel re-created herself as a series of characters, Gautier bor-rowed from this to create a highly stylized figure, the "beautiful Jewess,"[277] in his *Roman de la momie*.

Gautier's *Roman* was first published in the *Moniteur universel* as a serial, running from March 1857. Hachette published the novel in 1858. The *Roman* was the culmination of years of fascination and planning. Gautier was able to bring this to fruition through a meeting with Ernest Feydeau, whose book on ancient Egypt Gautier had reviewed for the *Moniteur universel*. It was Feydeau who made documents available, gave advice, and recommended reference works. Feydeau, to whom the *Roman* was dedicated, described how what he called the "psycho-logical part of the work" presented Gautier with serious difficulties:[278]

> For a mind of the caliber of Gautier, it was as easy to understand and describe external things: monuments, landscapes, costumes, ceremonies, etc., as it was difficult to discover how Egyptians living in the city of Thebes a thousand years before Jesus Christ might have felt and thought.[279]

The enormity of the task he had set himself caused him to almost abandon the project more than once. Feydeau described the book as requiring "the as-sembled knowledge of an Egyptologist, a historian, an archaeologist, and the ge-nius of a great writer."[280] If Gautier was able to surmount these difficulties, it was perhaps, in part, because he resorted to tropes to create living characters: Jews. As in *La Juive de Constantine*, Gautier created a love knot. Tahoser, the beautiful high-caste Egyptian, falls in love with the Jew, Poëri, although she is loved by the pharaoh. Poëri does not return her love. Rather, he loves—and is loved by—the equally beautiful, Jewish Ra'hel. The balance is thus established between two strikingly handsome men and two women, beautiful beyond description, two couples diametrically opposed in terms of their societal position. In his creation of these relationships, Gautier falls back on his own well-used formulae. For example, as Tahoser follows Poëri to discover the destination of his nighttime peregrinations,

> after a quarter of an hour's walking, the palaces, the temples, and the rich houses all disappeared, making room for more humble dwellings; granite, limestone, and sandstone gave way to unbaked brick and silt kneaded into straw. Architectural forms faded; huts sprung up, through some sort of farming, like blisters or warts on deserted land, borrowing hideous shapes from the night; pieces of wood and molded bricks, piled up, blocked the way. Out of the silence came strange and worrying noises; an owl cut through the air with his silent wings; thin dogs, lifting their long pointed muzzles, followed the erratic flight of a bat with plaintive barking; frightened beetles and reptiles fled, making the dry grass rustle.[281]

Readers are taken into the Jewish quarter through a description of the houses that brings them to life. The idea of the Jew's alterity is already established in the text. Drawing no doubt on the high-profile Damascus Affair of 1840, in which members of the Jewish community of that city were accused of having ritually murdered a Capuchin monk and his assistant, Gautier includes an anachronistic reference.[282] He has a servant in Poëri's house say to Tahoser that the master most probably goes out at night "to attend the sacrifices of children that the Hebrews perform in deserted places."[283] So the reader is not surprised, and indeed, the blow is in some sense softened, when they discover that the greatest crime committed here is merely that the poverty of the hovels is a lie. The Jews in the story are merely deceptive rather than infanticidal. Gautier describes in some detail the "hidden luxury" of the interior of Ra'hel's hut: vases of gold and silver were scattered about; jewels "glittered" in their coffers, half open; flowers—rare—bloomed in a vase.[284] Their beauty, however, was eclipsed by Ra'hel's:

> She was paler than any daughter of Egypt, as white as milk or lilies, as white as the flock of sheep that has just been washed. Her eyebrows stretched like ebony arcs and met at the root of a slender, aquiline nose, whose nostrils were colored in pink shades, like the inside of a shell. Her eyes were like those of a turtledove, at once both lively and languorous. Her lips were two thin strips of crimson that, when undone, showed flashes of pearl. Her hair hung on

either side of her pomegranate cheeks in black, shiny tufts, like two bunches of ripe grapes. Pendants trembled in her ears, and gold necklaces, with plates encrusted with silver, sparkled around her round neck, polished like an alabaster column.[285]

Gautier could find no greater expression of perfect beauty than immobility. No neck could be lovelier than one that resembled alabaster.

Gautier borrowed liberally for the novel, seeking to create an authentic setting.[286] So concerned was he with presenting ancient Egypt to the reader that even his characters were created to serve the landscape. Gautier imagined ancient Egypt to be mysterious and fantastic, where the gods had the heads of animals. This Egypt was also "sumptuous and colossal."[287] All of this greatness was reflected in the men of ancient Egypt, who were "superior." Gautier's pharaoh was the main symbol of a people that was "stronger and more beautiful than life."[288] Against all this grandness, Gautier placed Jews. Gautier's "Hebrews" bore witness, as one scholar has put it, to the "civilization of giants" that was Egypt. Thus, all of Gautier's literary difficulties were solved by the use of Jewish stereotypes. In the *Roman de la momie*, the Jew served to humanize the "superhuman."[289] Gautier created tropes of primitive Jews at their point of origin, in the ancient Orient. Yet if Gautier's Jewish characters in the *Roman* were primitive, they were also timeless and eternal, and in this way they were accessible to the reader. Was it a coincidence that Gautier gave the beautiful Jewess the supposed ancient Hebrew form of the name Rachel? Just as in the *Juive de Constantine*, the Jews in the cast serve as the familiar, the recognizable.

The critical reception of the *Roman* focused in particular on Gautier's rather one-dimensional characterization.[290] Poëri and Ra'hel certainly did not have any depth as characters, but neither did any of the Jews that Gautier created in his work. To him, it would seem, they served as concepts, far removed yet so close to Rachel's sculptural perfection. Gautier's Jews were not concrete beings. They were ideas. Their power came from the fact that they were anchored in some sort of perceived reality. Ra'hel reached forward to Rachel herself. Gautier used Jewishness as a quality. At the same time, his own relationships came through in his work. Distance and intimacy were deeply entangled.

Gautier created one more Jewish character in his *Roman*. Thamar, the devoted servant of Ra'hel, was a stark contrast to the latter, both physically and morally. She was the one who, driven by love of her mistress and blind hatred for Egyptians, betrayed Tahoser's love for Poëri to Pharaoh. Her instincts were "vulgar," her reactions "bestial,"[291] and in every transaction in which she was involved, Gautier took care to remind the reader of her animal-like appearance. Her nose was like a vulture's beak, and her curved fingers were like vulture's claws; she "huddled in a corner of the room like a bat" and lowered and lifted her eyelids "like a bat's wing."[292] Returning from her betrayal, she "slid into the hut like a reptile" and climbed toward Pharaoh's throne to reclaim her reward "like a half-crushed insect."[293]

Thamar was a unique figure in Gautier's writings on Jews: an antiheroine, although arguably so much more bestial than human that her gender had little relevance. Perhaps only the plot required her to be female, since Ra'hel would not have had a male servant. Thamar seems to disturb any notion of a neat male-female dichotomy, although perhaps she is an exception in that schema, and it is the virulence with which she is drawn that is important. Whence such fury? This was not the only time that hatred was to manifest itself in Gautier's writings on Jews. The trope of Thamar, the barely human, greedy, grasping Jew, was for Gautier to be confirmed by reality and the irruption into his life of an unwanted Jew, Gautier's son-in-law, the writer Catulle Mendès. Mendès, or "Crapule m'embête," as his embittered father-in-law named him, was born in Bordeaux in 1841 to a Catholic mother and a father who came from an old Sephardic Jewish family.[294] He sought to become a writer, and at the age of nineteen set out for Paris. As one of a new group of poets, the Parnassians, renown came quickly to him. He dedicated his first book of poems, *Philoméla*, to Gautier, "with boundless admiration and profound respect."[295] *Philoméla* was published in 1863, the year that Mendès met and fell in love with the eldest and best loved of Gautier's two daughters, the writer Judith. However, all the dedications in the world could not make Mendès a suitable son-in-law in Gautier's eyes. Gautier did his best to prevent a marriage that he did not wish for and a son-in-law whom he did not want. When, in 1863, Mendès announced his engagement to Judith in the press, Gautier responded by ordering him to retract the announcement. In February 1866 he asked his editor, Julien Turgan, to make inquiries about Mendès "to find out if the person who is trying to force an entrance into the family is or is not a young scoundrel, as everyone says he is."[296] So opposed was he to the union that when he found out that Ernesta Grisi, his partner of twenty years and Judith's mother, had invited Mendès into their home, he ended their relationship, accusing her of trampling on his heart "with terrifying tranquility."[297] However, in 1866, Judith was to turn twenty-one, and Gautier would no longer be able to prevent the marriage. In April 1866, four months before Judith's birthday, he relented and gave his permission for the two to marry, his hand "trembling" as he signed the paper.[298] The wedding, in the eyes of Gautier "an act of lunacy from every point of view,"[299] took place on April 17. Gautier's former mistress Eugénie Fort, the mother of his son Toto, described him as "stricken, furious, humiliated."[300] Very early on Gautier's worst fears were realized. The marriage was unhappy.

The Goncourts maintain that Gautier rejected Mendès because of his Jewish ancestry. (The Goncourts themselves, in characteristic language, referred to him as the "blond Portuguese Jew.")[301] Gautier's biographers, when they engage with this issue, deny it.[302] They argue that Gautier was more likely concerned about Mendès's infidelity and, in particular, his prolonged affair with the singer Augusta Holmès. Yet as concern turned to dismay, and then to despair as the two were married, Gautier's bitterness toward his new son-in-law became more pronounced. In early April 1866, believing that the wedding had already taken place, Gautier wrote to the dancer Carlotta Grisi, one of his dearest friends and the sister of his long-term partner Ernesta:

> The contract is signed today. The irreparable misfortune will be settled. This marriage, an act of rebellion, madness, and indecency, must take place. For the past week and more, this wretched Jew has been filling the popular press, and the odd papers to which he can have access, with pompous announcements of his alliance with the daughter of the illustrious poet.[303]

Sometime later, in another of his letters to Carlotta, Gautier called Mendès "Master Catulle Abraham Mendès," a unique inclusion of his second, manifestly Jewish name.[304] But even before the marriage, in a letter to Turgan from early in 1866, Gautier described Mendès as "an Israelite of letters."[305] When Mendès became the truly hated object, the upstart robber of his beloved daughter, then he was a Jew, and this was an epithet used with all the visceral anger with which Gautier had constructed Thamar. However, Mendès was not the only target of this epithet. Gautier was perhaps most open and honest in his correspondence with Carlotta Grisi. Over the course of 1865, the two became closer (some assert that they were lovers), and their letters became longer and more regular. At one point, in the early months of that year, Gautier was trying to sell a porcelain washbasin for Carlotta. (In their correspondence they referred to it as Sèvres, but the voice of the editor of the correspondence overrules this in a note, stating that the washbasin's authenticity was "dubious.")[306] Potential buyers appear to have been in agreement, to the mounting frustration of both correspondents. In mid-February 1865, Gautier reported to Carlotta that the antique dealer, Manheim, had come to see the washbasin, which he had examined "with all the meticulous attention of one of Balzac's fantasy Jews."[307] In June, still trying to sell the washbasin, Gautier reported that James de Rothschild had come to see it. Rothschild, a famous collector of Sèvres porcelain, ultimately rejected the pot as inauthentic. This may be what led Gautier to belittle the wealthy, powerful baron as "that old Jew."[308]

Gautier was referring to Honoré de Balzac's creations in his *Comédie humaine* (Human comedy), his multivolume collection of interlinked novels. Gautier's Orientalized Jews can be understood as part of a series of similar depictions being produced by those in the network of creation of which he was a part. For Balzac, for example, as for Gautier, the Jewess's beauty could be understood as Oriental. His Esther, of his 1838 *Splendeurs et misères des courtisanes* (Splendors and miseries of courtesans), "would have won the prize in the harem." "The

Orient" shone in her eyes "and in her face."[309] Indeed, beautiful Oriental Jew-esses were, arguably, everywhere, from Rachel, the heroine of Scribe and Halévy's highly successful opera *La Juive*; to Balzac's Esther; to the Jewish women in Vic-tor Hugo's collections of poetry *Orientales*; to Walter Scott's Rebecca, in the wildly successful *Ivanhoe*.[310] *La Juive* was the tale of a beautiful Jewish woman in love with a Christian. The Jewish Rachel, the tragic heroine who is revealed after her martyrdom to have been born a Christian, embodied the type of fluidity that Gautier projected onto Léa.[311] The composer Fromental Halévy was Jewish, and his Judaism constituted "a vigorous source" in his life and works.[312] So, too, was the novelist Eugénie Foa, who published a series of fictional works about Jews through the 1830s and 1840s. Maurice Samuels has detailed how the Jewish figures in Foa's works were Orientalized. The titles of two of her works—*Rachel*, a group of short stories (1833), and *La Juive* (1835)—were presumably chosen for their cultural currency. Foa used exoticized—and sometimes historic—Jews as a way to reflect on questions of belonging and identity facing Jews in her con-temporary France. In the words of Samuels, Foa surrounded the heroine of *La Juive*, Midiane, "with a profusion of oriental luxury."[313] Foa even counterbalanced Midiane with a fanatical, tyrannical (Jewish) father, another trope of this period. The tension between Léa and Nathan that Gautier sought to create in his *Juive de Constantine* was a commonplace in literature and the arts. As Lisa Leff has shown, the use of the notion of racial distinctiveness by Jews themselves could be an assertion "that Jewish difference was legitimate and dignified" and that Jewish specificity contained a "distinctive morality" that would facilitate their incorpo-ration into France.[314] For Jewish authors and composers, too, the Orientalized Jew could provide a means to reflect on and articulate ideas of the nation: in this case, a France that could make space for its Jewish population.

Gautier was just as capable an inventor as Balzac. "Fantasy Jews" could express all of Gautier's outrage before the great tragedy in his life that was his daughter Judith's marriage, as well as another: the siege of Paris. Gautier stayed in Paris during the Franco-Prussian War and ensuing occupation, as well as dur-ing the Paris Commune of 1870. Along with the other residents of the city, he and his family endured great privations. It was at this time, with all the cultural life of Paris on hold, that he wrote what was to be his last work, *Tableaux de siège*.[315] This was a series of sketches of loss and destruction. Here Gautier let loose all his rage at a topsy-turvy world and perhaps also at his own *crapule*. In "Saint-Cloud," Gautier described his visit in March 1871 to the park in that area of Paris, from which the occupying Prussian army had retreated. Before him lay a vista of brutal, meaningless destruction. His discovery of the palace was a sad experi-ence: this place was now "tragic and solemn," filled with "memories of splendor and celebration."[316] Nature wept. The buildings, largely destroyed by fire, became human, stand-ins, perhaps, for a desolate Paris. Piping was like "veins in the body of the edifice"; statues in the courtyard were "decapitated, limping, arm-less, blinded, wounded with shocking gashes."[317] Once again, using a practiced methodology, Gautier made the humanness of the buildings contrast with the inhumanness of the people he encountered. On his way out of the ruins of the palace, he noticed

> at the windows of the former service buildings, faces of German Jews, sordidly and cruelly mean, with greasy hair, forked beards, a rancid color, descendants of Judas Iscariot and of Shylock, capable of taking their pound of flesh on the date of payment, receivers of stolen goods, and concealers of murder, second-hand dealers of pillage, removing, with their dirty claws, the ingots of molten metal from the piles of embers; they had that air of stupefied bliss that you see in vultures that are stuffed to the beak with carrion.[318]

It would have required only a small stretch to find Thamar among these barely human Jews. As in his travelogues, Gautier underscored his point as he left the scene. As he left the palace, Gautier described how the houses on the streets leading up to the church, "disemboweled," stood valiantly "like brave soldiers who have been struck a fatal blow but do not want to fall."[319] And from the other side of the Seine, looking back at Saint-Cloud, Gautier saw "a great cemetery, dominated by its mournful chapel. The church, alone in being spared, watched over this cadaver of a city."[320] Thus, Jewish vultures, complete with claws, picked over the dead body of Paris. Gautier may well have seen real "German" Jews loot-ing. Under his pen, though, they became metaphors, clichés. Here again was Na-than, greedy, grasping, fanatical, and cold. Here were the Jews of Balat, barely human. Here the division between the Jew as literary figure and the Jew in reality was blurred. In his works, Gautier was capable of creating extraordinarily vitu-perative descriptions of Jews. Yet in his private life, Gautier had close and affec-tionate contact with well-known Jewish figures, not simply a variety of Rachels but also Jewish men: Giacomo Meyerbeer and Fromental Halévy, among others. In 1839, Gautier was signing letters to Meyerbeer as his "very devoted and very respectful admirer," a tone of admiration not standard in Gautier's language.[321] The real friendship between Gautier and Meyerbeer began with collaboration. In 1853, Meyerbeer approached Gautier to rewrite in French the libretto of the lyrical drama *Struensee*. Gautier agreed. He ended up writing only the prologue, but the friendship was established and remained steadfast for twenty years.

Gautier's willingness to collaborate with Meyerbeer is unsurprising. He had been writing favorable reviews of Meyerbeer's work for some time, during a pe-riod when much of the critical reception of Meyerbeer's work was negative. Much of this criticism incorporated Meyerbeer's Jewishness.[322] Thus, in one review of his 1836 opera *Les Huguenots* (The Huguenots), the reviewer wrote that Catholi-cism was sacrificed to the appetite of a Jewish musician for "vulgar sensation."[323]

And in what was to become a familiar trope, reviewers made much of Meyerbeer's lack of originality. As a composer, he was "far more talented than inspired."[324] He might have lacked his own melodic ideas, according to Louis Desnoyers, but as Desnoyers pursued it, managing to throw in another hateful stereotype, Meyerbeer made up for this in his skill as a jeweler, making the most "of others' melodic gems."[325] If Meyerbeer had any genius, it was in his ability to make people believe that he was a true genius. His critics knew better. Underneath all the show was a "diligent and tenacious worker."[326] (Meyerbeer was known for his capacity for hard work and endless rehearsal.) Rootless—another popular trope—he borrowed, like a magpie, building legitimacy. But critics such as Gustave Planche and François-Henri-Joseph Castil-Blaze could see past the effects: Meyerbeer himself had no ancestors.[327] The contrast between these and Gautier's review of the same opera is striking. For Gautier, Meyerbeer's Jewishness was relevant only in the sense that, in Gautier's eyes, it allowed him to be impartial in this tale of violence between Huguenots and Catholics. For Gautier, as for his other critics, Meyerbeer might not have merited the label of genius. However, where Gautier was concerned, a lack of inspiration in Meyerbeer's work was positive, since it allowed the composer to make the most of his "extraordinary patience":

> Inspiration, as much as it is needed, is not lacking here; but in its alliance with erudition, it has taken on a more abstract, strict, and deeper character, which serves as the distinctive mark of this great composer of whom we speak.[328]

Writing in the *Presse* in 1849 on Meyerbeer's new opera *Le Prophète* (The prophet), Gautier was happy to welcome the composer back. This opera "breathed the supreme serenity of art," surely the highest praise that Gautier, that great believer in art for art's sake, could give. With this opera, Meyerbeer had reached the highest point of human genius.[329] This was no small praise, considering that the libretto for the opera had been written by Gautier's great nemesis, Eugène Scribe, a writer considered by Gautier as the worst exponent of bourgeois mediocrity. Meyerbeer, for Gautier, was a friend.[330]

What comes through clearly from these stories is that Gautier did not distinguish between stereotype and experience. His day-to-day relationships could be writ large as the imagined Jews of his fantasy. The Jews he created in works such as the *Roman de la momie* and the Jews he encountered on his travels could feed into the way he understood his relationships, and vice versa. Thus, for example, the beautiful Oriental Marix on the couch recalled the Jewish women of Algiers and Constantine in the works of Delacroix and Chassériau. Rachel, her perfection set in stone, was as distant and unattainable as Ra'hel. Nathan, the fanatical, greedy father of poor Léa, could well have lived in the ghetto of Constantinople, so close was he to the strange, foreign figures that Gautier supposedly encountered there. And perhaps all of them fed into Gautier's angry, bitter repudiations of Catulle Mendès.[331] Thamar, the greedy servant, barely human, could well have been in league with the vulturelike "German" Jews of Saint-Cloud. And could the much-admired Meyerbeer have been a starting point for the perfect Poëri? Perhaps. The point to be made here is that the possibility for this multiple cross-referencing tells us that we must understand the story of Gautier and the Orientalized Jew in artistic creation as one of entanglement. There was no clean break between French and Oriental Jew, or between real and imagined Jew. Gautier's reviews of Rachel and his vulturelike Jews of *Tableaux de siège* must be set side by side. If he created both, then should we seek to divide and categorize? Rather, we must ask why Gautier and his circle could understand the Orientalized Jew in such apparently differing ways. Jews were indeed "good to think" about bigger issues, such as, for example, the meaning of the nation or of citizenship.[332] But this thinking could take different forms according to the needs of the thinker. In these writings, the Jew acts as a totemic figure for the object of the author's desires or disgruntlements. The Jew serves as a means for expressing a particular view of the author's world. The Jew could stand in for greed or power, for capitalism or individualism. Jews could denote an ideal of ancient art or a longed-for steadfastness in faith. They could be one and the other within the same work.

Just as Gautier brought together a web of sociability in Paris, he brings together the Oriental, the French, and the Jew. In his book, essentially told and held together by Gautier, Ziegler writes of the "world of Gautier."[333] This world was one of sociability. It was a world in which he was deeply embedded. It was also one of creation, and the two intersected in complex and significant ways. Gautier's creations fed from and into the creativity of his many friends and acquaintances. The Jews in Gautier's wide circle of friends and acquaintances fed his creativity. Part 3 brings the creative and social lives of Théophile Gautier together to explore one in the context of the other, and vice versa. Gautier tells us that Jews, while not always central, were nonetheless intrinsic to his Orient, just as they were intrinsic to the entirety of his body of work and, arguably, his life.

Gautier had a wonderful gift for language. At his best, he wrote with wit and verve. Yet his relationship to the process of writing, and particularly reviewing, was ambivalent. Friends of his later life, the Goncourt brothers told how they encountered him "at the offices of the *Artiste* . . . heavy-faced, features fallen into its thickened lines, a lassitude of the face, its physiognomy asleep."[334] Gautier himself expressed this ambivalence thus:

> What wakes me up in the morning is that I dream I'm hungry. I see red meat, huge tables of food. . . . Meat wakes me up. Once I have breakfasted, I smoke. . . . Then I pull up a chair; I put paper on the table, quills, ink, the torturer's rack, and that bores me; writing has always bored me, and then, it is so

useless!—Then, I write calmly, like a public writer. I don't write quickly. . . . I never think about what I am going to write. I take my quill and I write. I am man of letters; I have to know my trade. Before paper, I am like a clown on a springboard. . . . I throw my sentences into the air. . . . Like cats, I am sure that they will fall on their feet. It's very simple; all you need is good syntax.[335]

At times, Gautier's practice of throwing his sentences "into the air" seems to have resulted in the creation of stereotypes that are entirely predictable. More often than not, the Jews he created were one-dimensional caricatures or perhaps metaphors for one of Gautier's many passionately held beliefs. Yet these flat figures drew on something concrete, either copied or twisted. This is perhaps what speaks to their power. It speaks also to an understanding of the role of the Orientalized Jew, and the idea of the Orient, that draws on notions of entanglement and intimacy. Gautier provides us with a way to understand the significance of the Jew in this schema, reproduced by so many others.

Chapter 3 further explores the relationship between the concrete and the imagined, Orientalized Jew. Political exigency weaves its way through this book. It takes the form of Catholics seeking to rethink the nation and Romantics seeking to rail against the same. Yet what was the place of the Orientalized Jew when the relationship between France and the Orient was political, as in the case of Algiers? What happened when the nation itself was the actor? These questions drive the story of chapter 3.

# 3   The Kings of Algiers

THE HISTORY OF FRENCH relations with the Regency of Algiers is a history of efforts by France to establish and maintain diplomatic and economic influence. It is a relationship that may be understood as imperial. In this chapter, I bring a cultural analysis to this history through the figure of the Orientalized Jew. I place these imperial relations in a setting of culturally generated understandings. This chapter focuses on a significant intermediary in this imperial relationship: a Sephardic Jewish trading house run by two families and based in the port of Algiers. This trading house, the House of Bacri and Busnach, was central to France's relationship with the regency, from the years of the Revolution to the invasion of 1830 and beyond. In the words of one chronicler, the Bacris and Busnachs were "the Kings of Algiers," "political intermediaries" between Europe and the regency.[1] Who were the Bacris and Busnachs? And if they truly were political intermediaries, then what does their story tell us about the role Jews played in France's imperial relationship with the regency? More broadly, what might their story tell us about the role Jews played in Orientalism and this, its political face? There has been renewed scholarly focus on the Jewish community in colonial Algeria. Joshua Schreier has explored the role of Algerian Jews as agents in French efforts to civilize them. Lisa Leff and Colette Zytnicki have detailed efforts by French Jews, and particularly Isaac-Jacques Altaras and Joseph Cohen, to insert themselves into this civilizing mission.[2] This chapter turns its focus on precolonial Algiers. It brings together, on the one hand, French ideas of Jews and of the Orient, with, on the other, their sense of the nation and of France's imperial trajectory.

In the early-modern and modern world of the Mediterranean, Jewish merchants were intermediaries par excellence. David Azencot, Abraham ben Chimol, and Haim Farhi were not isolated figures. They were part of a network of Jews throughout Mediterranean Europe and Africa who drew on their peripheral position in Mediterranean societies, their mobility, and their networks of trust to assert their centrality in mediation. In a sense, their business was the material exemplification of this book's driving argument, that Jews were central figures in the history of European relations with North Africa and the Middle East. This is the context in which we should understand the Bacris and Busnachs.

Chapters 1 and 2 of this book are based on sources standard to the cultural historian, including creative works of all kinds. This chapter draws largely on a very different type of source: decades of diplomatic correspondence, comprising hundreds of letters between diplomats in Algiers and ministers in France, in which the House of Bacri and Busnach figures consistently and prominently. The nature of the sources means that part of the work of this chapter involves reconstructing the story and the characters contained within this correspondence. This story allows us to consider the interaction between imperialism (both diplomatic and economic), nationalism, and understandings of Jews as seen through the lens of Orientalism.

But I begin at a beginning that will be, as it turns out, more of a precursor to an end. On April 29, 1827, the French consul at the time, Pierre Deval, paid a formal visit to the dey of Algiers, Hussein, according to the protocol. The occasion was the feast to end the fasts of Ramadan. However, Hussein was not in a festive mood. He was angry with the French regime and with its consular representative. The dey believed that Deval was deliberately withholding a copy of Foreign Minister Damas's response to his letters demanding payment of an outstanding debt. In fact, Damas had chosen not to respond; rather, he instructed his consul to reiterate France's position that they could not pay an immediate lump sum to the dey. The only witness accounts that we have from this meeting are from the two interested parties: Deval and the dey. The day after the meeting, Deval wrote a report to his minister, describing how, "with no provocation," the dey had struck him three times with the fan he used to keep away flies.[3] (The fan, according to one who had seen it, was "fairly massive.")[4] The dey did not deny that he had struck Deval but maintained that he had done so only because the consul's insolence had become unbearable. (The dey's version of events was filtered through the British consul, perhaps not the most disinterested of parties.) Either way, this insult generated a list of French demands, which included an apology, punishment of the pirates who had been plaguing French ships, the right to bear arms in Algeria, a statement that France would enjoy a most-favored-nation treatment in Algerian commerce, and a declaration from the dey that the French government had completely liquidated the debts still owed to the House of Bacri and Busnach. Hussein responded with a list of his own grievances. The first among these was that he had still not seen a penny of the seven million paid by the French government for the settling of the Bacri and Busnach debt. With his response, tantamount to a refusal of France's conditions, French warships commenced a blockade of the Algerian coast on June 12.

Central to this tale is this debt, a disputed sum owed by France for more than two decades to a Jewish trading house and, through them, to the dey of the Regency of Algiers. How did the money become, in the words of the Duke de Talleyrand, then foreign minister, "an affair of state" and, ultimately, of war?[5] The trading house was the House of Bacri and Busnach, owned by the Sephardic Jewish families of the same name.[6] Every story that sets out to recount these events mentions the House of Bacri and Busnach in passing and the debt owed to them by the French, which enraged the dey enough to insult the consul. In this chapter, I trace the deeper story of the trading house and its dealings with France.

Michel Cohen Bacri was a businessman who had come from Livorno to establish himself in Algiers in the second half of the eighteenth century. He may have been among Francesca Trivellato's "middle ranks" of Jewish merchants, who focused on trade routes between Mediterranean ports.[7] He was a so-called *Juif franc*, a Jew who, through his membership in the Livorno community, enjoyed privileges in Algiers. These included the right to choose his place of domicile and exemption from the sartorial laws, which limited Jews to dark-colored clothing.[8] In the previous century, Jews had established trade links between Tunis, Livorno, and Marseilles.[9] Now merchants such as Michel Bacri sought to bring Algiers into those routes. Around 1770, Michel established a trading house in the city.[10] In 1782, with the business now prospering, four of Michel's five sons joined the partnership, including the eldest, Joseph, and his brothers Mordechai, Salomon, and Jacob. Salomon moved to Livorno to run the company's operations there. A fifth son, Abraham, acted as an associate in their business dealings. Joseph's own son, David Bacri, also joined. Then, in 1797, Naphtali Busnach, another Jew of Livornese origin and a leading figure in Algiers, joined the company, which now changed its name to "Bacri Brothers and Busnach."[11] At the same time, David Bacri married Naphtali's sister Aziza, and the links between the two families were cemented.[12] In 1800, Naphtali Busnach became *mokadem*, or head of the Jewish community. This was a position of considerable potential power. The *mokadem*, an official position that provided an income, represented the Jewish community to the dey. The *mokadem* also had authority within the Jewish community "to enforce rabbinic judgments and local or imperial leaders' decrees." Finally, and significantly, the *mokadem* was given the power to tax the Jewish community.[13]

It is difficult to discern, exactly, what the designs of the Bacri and Busnach families might have been. Their own voices are notably marginal in this story, and, for the most part, they are presented to us through the medium of commentators who are not entirely impartial. Given their context, however, it can be safely said that their goal, essentially, was to run a business and that they took advantage of the resources available to them and sought ways around the impediments in their path. Thus, for example, they forged relationships with ruling deys; they established a network of correspondents in major trading ports; they drew on their local knowledge and their intermediary position to make themselves useful to consuls; and they petitioned foreign authorities when they deemed it necessary. They also calculated, seemingly, that if they supplied grain to the French on credit, this would make them desirable trading partners. Their story, insofar as it is told within the bounds of this chapter, is largely about their efforts to recover the money owed to them and to their business partner, the dey.

It is striking in this context that the French understood the Bacris and Busnachs to be powerful. For example, an apocryphal story circulated—and continues to circulate—in the literature about the families' rise to wealth and power. It is rendered all the more mythical since it is not dated. According to this story, the bey of Constantine came to Algiers. He wished to purchase a gift to offer the dey's wife, and he asked Naphtali Busnach to find him a valuable jewel. Busnach presented him with a tiara decorated with diamonds, valued at sixty thousand piasters (three hundred thousand francs). The bey bought the tiara and paid in measures of wheat, each weighing forty kilos and worth approximately four francs. The Bacris then sold the same wheat in France for fifty francs per measure, thus making a considerable profit. The jewel had apparently been bought in Paris for thirty thousand francs. Thus, so the legend goes, the House of Bacri and Busnach was able to rise rapidly to a position of wealth and power.[14] Clearly, French observers found the idea that the Bacris and Busnachs were immensely wealthy easy to believe. In 1812, Consul Dubois-Thainville reported to his foreign minister, the Duke de Bassano, that the fortune of the Livorno Bacris consisted of precious stones, which they hid in the walls of their homes. Bassano reported this in turn as fact.[15] Whereas in chapter 2, those travelers who discovered the secret wealth of the Jews they visited related this to the rise of capitalism, their predecessors, discussed in this chapter, read the wealth they, too, "discovered" as a mark of power. Perhaps because they saw the comfort of Jewish intermediaries in this very foreign world, the notion of their power was easy to access. For ideas of power and deceptiveness became fundamental to the way these families were understood. The history of their dealings with France brings together fantasy and reality once again. French representatives in Algiers and in France were dealing directly with the House of Bacri and Busnach, but they were also telling stories about it to make sense of these very dealings. The myth of power could be a way to explain France's inability to control events and people in Algiers as the French might have wished. Yet also running through this relationship was the wish to deny and negate that very same power.

The backdrop to this tale is the commercial relationship between France and the regency, reaching back into the sixteenth century. In Bona, Collo, and la Calle, first trading houses and later the Compagnie d'Afrique paid a license fee to the dey of Algiers and the bey of Constantine for the so-called concessions. These gave the French rights to coral fishing and the grain trade.[16] The French were able to establish corporations and businesses in Algeria and to fortify and defend these. They also enjoyed a commercial monopoly over a vast spread of coastline. For the chronicler of Marseilles, Paul Masson, particularly enamored of the concessions, they constituted "the permanent symbol and safest guarantee of good relations between France and the regency." It proved to the Algerians that "we were their oldest and most loyal friends." It also accustomed "our ministers and diplomats" to understand France as having a predominant and unique role to play in the regency.[17] Both the concessions and the regency were certainly important to France. As the French republic was established and struggled through its first years, the regency provided recognition and aid, both financial and material. African wheat was vital to the food supply of the southern departments of France, the Midi. When the Compagnie royale d'Afrique stopped trading in January 1794, the government ensured the continuation of the concessions with the immediate creation of another trading company, the Agence d'Afrique, with headquarters in Marseilles.[18] The agence functioned for four years until 1798, when relations between France and the Porte were ruptured by Napoleon's invasion of Egypt. (Napoleon reestablished, under a new name, the Compagnie d'Afrique in 1801.) Thus, the wheat coming from the regency was of enormous importance to France through the uncertain decades at the end of the eighteenth century and the beginning of the nineteenth. It served to feed the south of France, as well as Napoleon's armies.

If Algiers was significant in French reckoning, this was due to more than economic considerations. In the eighteenth and early nineteenth centuries, France and England were competing for influence in the Mediterranean. Each was obsessed with the other, and events and actions were interpreted through the prism of this competitiveness. Algerian grain was equally important to Britain in provisioning its Mediterranean colonies, Gibraltar and Minorca. The respective consuls of France and Britain to the Regency of Algiers bore responsibility for protecting their nation's interests and its citizens, while maintaining good relations with the regency's ruling dey. In the context of this competition, both took this delicate balancing act as a test of national honor and prestige. From the late eighteenth century until the French invasion of Algiers in 1830, both powers competed for favor in Algiers, and this competition reflected their broader struggle for dominance in the Mediterranean. French and British consuls in Algiers were both convinced that the dey favored the other power. Both, at the same time, were obliged to go through various members of the two families for the majority of their dealings with the dey.

This is the background to French outrage in the face of the perceived takeover by the House of Bacri and Busnach of the grain trade. The French consul at the time, Jean Bon Saint-André, put his perception of the state of affairs in rather dramatic terms:

> Would one have believed that all the commerce of the Mediterranean would fall into the hands of two Jews of Algiers? Nothing, however, is truer. . . . Where is there an important place where you will not find agents of Bacri and Busnach? Cartagena, Marseilles, Genoa, Livorno, Naples, Smyrna, Alexandria, Tunis, and others have them.[19]

Here, again, is another meeting point between reality and fantasy, between France's very real need of Bacri and Busnach and its covalent desire to explain this need to itself. By 1798 the Agence d'Afrique had had to close its doors. Its agent in Algiers, Astoin Sielve, blamed the "utter ruin of the concessions" on a lack of funds and the "gigantic credit" of the Jews, "who sought to supplant the French everywhere in the kingdom."[20] The agent in la Calle, Granet, wrote in May of the same year that he could not fight the competition of Bacri and Busnach. Thus, "naturally," as Masson would have it, the Bacris became the masters of a trade that had once belonged to the French.[21] The complaint that the House of Bacri and Busnach was at the center of the loss of the concessions and thus of the grain trade was repeated over the years. When he wrote about the invasion a century after its occurrence, Masson still saw the house at the root of France's troubles. Bacri and Busnach were, in his indignant words, "able to establish relationships with the representatives of the convention on missions in the Midi and to gain their confidence."[22] In his eyes, the Bacris were supple and adaptable, able to take advantage of change to serve different deys and beys and to destroy the Agence d'Afrique. With the exception of the province of Constantine, Charles-André Julien tells us, Bacri and Busnach controlled two-thirds of external trade, "arbitrarily fixing rates."[23]

The impact, in real terms, of Bacri and Busnach in the grain market is difficult to discern. We know that they exported Algerian grain to various points on the Mediterranean, changing destination according to demand and price.[24] Their trade extended beyond the limits of that body of water, taking in northern France as well as New York.[25] Whether or not they did hold the monopoly over the grain trade, we know that it was not only their access to goods that made them an attractive trading partner. Even more attractive to the cash-strapped directory, perhaps, was the fact that Bacri and Busnach were ultimately prepared to supply their grain on credit. In 1796, after Bacri and Busnach had first complained about slowing payments and then offered to supply grain from their warehouse in Marseilles in exchange for a partial payment of what was owed to them, the finance minister wrote to the foreign minister that more than two million livres were already owed to "these Algerians," and "even though they made huge profits on their deals, it had to be acknowledged, nonetheless, that they were not the most demanding of suppliers."[26] Based on this grudging acceptance, then, between 1793 and 1798 Bacri and Busnach shipped large amounts of grain to France, supplying the south and the revolutionary armies in Italy and Egypt. These efforts to explain success in terms of unfair advantage serve to underscore the fact that this is not simply a story about real events and actions. The lack of clear evidence leaves space for perceptions and, as the previous chapters demonstrate, the French were only too able to produce scripts.

It was not only wheat in Bacri boats that crossed from south to north at this time. In 1795 Jacob Bacri, one of the four brothers, established himself in Marseilles to aid in running the family's dealings with France.[27] Jacob came armed with a letter of recommendation from the dey of Algiers, Hassan Pasha, to the Committee for Public Safety. Jacob Bacri was "a person to whom [the dey was] greatly attached."[28] The dey expected that Jacob would be "assisted and protected at all opportunities," and he requested that the committee "assist him whenever he is in need of help." He ended by assuring the committee that "the marks of attention and love that you show him will strengthen the foundations of our friendship all the more."[29] Jacob himself also wrote to the Committee for Public Safety. His was a confident letter. He let the members of the committee know that his agent, Simon Aboucaya, would be presenting a letter from the dey (Jacob himself was too busy to deliver it).[30] Jacob requested that the representative citizens give him protection and expedite his plans to bring all the wheat possible into France. The quantities that had already arrived in Marseilles constituted "tangible proof," he believed, of his intentions.[31] Jacob's letter established what was to be, in his eyes, the basis of the relationship between his trading house and the French regime: service for protection. Jacob was inserting himself as an intermediary between two regimes, he was a fluid figure who was at home in both contexts, the living, active version of Gautier's Léa, the heroine of *La Juive de Constantine*. This notion, that Bacri and Busnach would offer service and request protection in exchange, was a relatively simple one. It was to lead, however, to deep entanglement.

When Jacob settled in Marseilles, that city had only recently opened its doors to Jews.[32] If Julien is to be believed, Jacob was part of "a whole Jewish colony" that had settled in Marseilles "during the Revolution in order to traffic with Algiers in liaison with Livorno."[33] As a Mediterranean port and a gateway to France, Marseilles was a perfect site for the expansion of the family business. The Bacris and Busnachs were able to take advantage of their nationality, the neutrality of their boats, and their relationship with the dey of Algiers, as well as their correspondents around the Mediterranean.[34] The timing was equally perfect. A peace treaty was signed with Spain in July 1795, reopening trade in the Mediterranean. The port of Livorno had already been reopened in February of the same year. Moreover, the fact that Bacri and Busnach were prepared to give credit to a cash-strapped French government meant that their business had leverage in a time and place where business was slow and Jews were generally unwelcome. The city's economy had been significantly affected by the Revolution. Many of its most prominent businessmen had fallen victim to the Terror, and many of those who had survived had done so by leaving the city. The port's exemption from customs duties had been abolished, as were the customs barriers that had separated Marseilles from the rest of France. For the city of Marseilles, both the Revolution and the empire were years, as one commentator has put it, "of ordeals and suffering."[35] The establishment of a Bacri in that city was, if contemporary observers as well as some more recent commentators are to be believed, a source of further misery. On July 20, 1804, the Marseilles Chamber of Commerce wrote that "when the company existed, the Jews of Algiers did not trade. Since then, that is almost all they do, because they are supported by the dey and because they take advantage of the protection he has granted them."[36] Once again, commentators defaulted to an understanding of Bacri and Busnach as powerful. Nonetheless, in times of crisis, authorities could draw on the in-betweenness, or fluidity, of these same Jews. In 1806, Marseilles police were reporting on an "influx" of forty-two Algerian Jews into the city, following anti-Jewish violence in Algiers. They "spread through the city," according to the police report, and it was not long before an official complaint was made. Seeking advice, the author of the police report described how a Mr. Famin, the agent for foreign affairs in Marseilles, counseled the police, most probably on the basis of the complaint, to "advise Bousnack [sic], Constantini, and another Jew that they will have to remove these forty-two individuals from Marseilles."[37]

Bacris and Busnachs were extending their role as go-betweens in Algiers as well. Members of both families enjoyed a healthy income from loans made to consuls for various reasons, including the redemption of slaves and gifts for the dey.[38] The House of Bacri and Busnach made money out of piracy in this corsairing port, buying captured ships and their cargoes.[39] And a consular report tells us that under the auspices of the patriarch, Michel Bacri, peace was concluded in 1794 between Holland and the regency.[40] Indeed, from the mid-1790s, Bacris and Busnachs feature regularly and continually in the consular correspondence. In terms of their prominence and the attention they are given, they have no equal, neither Jewish nor Muslim. The letters therein, from French consuls, French government officials, and occasionally from Bacris and Busnachs themselves, are revealing of the way in which a relationship, initially based on a simple premise, was becoming ever more complex. For one thing, Joseph Bacri and Naphtali Busnach were referred to in increasingly familiar terms. By 1796, Consul Jean Bon Saint-André wrote to his minister concerning Bacri and Busnach, supplying no more than their last names. Theirs was a relationship of deep reliance on both sides and barely concealed revulsion on the part of Saint-André:

> They promise the small states of Europe peace and make it; if they are discontented, they declare war on them. A question of the redemption of slaves? They are the mediators in it. A European merchant offends them? They chase him out. . . . The cause of our loss of influence in Barbary is the growth in credit of the Jews.[41]

During his time as consul in Algiers, Saint-André sought to balance the reality of his situation against the way he desired it to be, and the House of Bacri and

Busnach was central to this. During 1796 and 1797, Saint-André was particularly concerned with English efforts to muscle in on Mediterranean trade. Whether or not Bacri and Busnach were aiding the English, and to what extent, forms the basis of much of his discussion of them. Were they truly British "agents"?[42] Were they fully involved in negotiations between England and the dey?[43] How might France contain them? Their power was dangerous. For example, Saint-André reported in December 1796 that Bacri's brother "enjoyed the government's protection" in Marseilles and that Busnach's brother in Livorno "held the French national till."[44] These two members of the families "had almost been deified" by France, yet they were the "enemies" of French trade who sought "to crush us under the weight of the authority that we have granted them."[45] However, this very interest in money was the weak spot of the two families, as Saint-André saw it. Once again, Saint-André sought to create a story of French dominance and Jewish weakness. "The republic," Saint-André went on to claim, had "[Bacri and Busnach] under its thumb." If the regime were the focus of their pecuniary interests, then "it could be assured of their submission."[46] It would be a good thing for French trade, he told Foreign Minister Charles-François Delacroix in a further letter, "to humiliate these Jews a little and to make them dependent on you."[47] Two days later he wrote to his minister again, complaining that Bacri and Busnach sought to "add to French gold that of England, without thinking about the gratitude that they owe to the former." The "enterprising cupidity" of the Jews had to be stopped.[48] This, according to Saint-André, was a moment of crisis, a moment when France had to make the choice that would affect its future influence in Africa. This involved the English, of course, as the eternal competitor, but it also required mastery over Bacri and Busnach. If France did not "push the English aside and crush the Jews," then its chance would be lost forever. Saint-André was nothing if not a strategist. As long as France owed Bacri and Busnach a large sum, then, "fearing the consequences of our resentment," "they would not dare to invest with full confidence in their own schemes."[49]

Yet Saint-André also struggled to bring the two worlds of France and the regency together into a satisfactory schema. Naphtali Busnach had clearly made the dey aware of French complaints, since Sidi Hassan wrote to the Directory himself on the matter. The report, he wrote, that the trading house was acting as intermediary in the dey's granting of the trade of the Compagnie d'Afrique to the English was "ill founded." The dey took the opportunity to remind the Directory of Bacri and Busnach's "incorruptible faithfulness" and their attachment "to all that had to do with the interests of the French nation."[50] The conversations that led to the letter must have involved Saint-André, since he, too, wrote to Paris, reporting that the French had been discredited in the eyes of the dey by none other than Naphtali Busnach and Joseph Bacri, who were "triumphant" at their humiliation.[51] The dey was not the master in Algiers. It was Bacri and Busnach who reigned.[52] They were his confidants, and no one else could gain access to him.[53]

Saint-André's opinion of Bacri and Busnach was clear: they had no under-standing of their proper place. His obsession with their power, and with the ways to undermine it, is revealing of his belief that it was indeed a topsy-turvy world when Jews sought to negotiate as the equals of the republic. For Bacri and Bus-nach did negotiate and interact with Saint-André on a regular basis. As he was reporting on their power, Saint-André was also relaying accounts of his interac-tions with these two figures. On December 30, 1796, he wrote to his minister that "Bacri had the impudence to come to my home this morning, accompanied by Busnach, in order to tell me that considerable sums were owed to the house in Marseilles and to urge me to write to the minister."[54] Yet when Bacri and Bus-nach presented themselves to Saint-André as victims—not of France but of the English—he was inclined to look upon them more favorably. France's place in the regency in these years, after all, was entirely bound up with England. When Bacri and Busnach came to him early in 1797 to request that he pass on their claim for the return of the cargo of the ship *Good Hoffnung*, which had been captured by the English and then retaken by the French, Saint-André's perception was that their claim was "entirely just."[55] Once again, he makes clear how he understood the rightful way of the world. For on this occasion, France held all the power, and Saint-André was clearly feeling gracious.

Saint-André sought other ways to reclaim from Bacri and Busnach the power he felt was rightly his as the republic's representative. When Busnach came to see him, complaining that government letters were accusing him and Bacri of favoring the English, Saint André reported to his minister that he took advantage of the opportunity to let Busnach know that he, too, had made a complaint about the conduct of Bacri and Busnach, that he had told all to the government, and that "France did not intend to ruin them or to neglect its financial engagements to-ward them but that its goodwill would be in proportion to the efforts they made to deserve it." When Busnach asked Saint-André what he should do, the latter replied that he and Bacri should "serve France faithfully in the mercantile op-erations it entrusts them with, and they must, above all, not get involved in its political affairs."[56] Saint-André may have been counseling Busnach to model his behavior on that of Saint-André himself. He was a true reflection of the greatness of his nation. "In spite of the numerous and powerful friends they have around you," he reported confidently to his minister in September 1797, "[the Jews] know that the truth finds its way to you. They are fearful of managing, only imperfectly, to stifle the voice of this consul, whom their gold has not been able to corrupt."[57] Woven throughout all of the consular correspondence is the unspoken desire to maintain Bacri and Busnach in what was deemed to be their rightful place.

This was complicated, of course, by their ongoing importance to the dey. Indeed, Bacri and Busnach appear to have been important to the office of the dey, beyond any specific personality. For this was an office that changed regularly and normally in violent circumstances. In 1798, Sidi Hassan was replaced by Mustapha. Soon after he came to power, Mustapha wrote to the Directory to remind them of the centrality, in his eyes, of Bacri and Busnach and that debt, to the relationship between his regency and France. Jacob Bacri and Simon Aboucaya were "old and faithful servants" of his government. Laying out the services that these servants had performed for the republic in striking detail, Mustapha asked, as had done his predecessor, that the money owed by France be repaid, since "affairs of this nature" were "the subject of coldness and deterioration between us."[58] Receiving no response, Mustapha wrote once again, in September of the same year, that as proof of friendship and partiality between France and Algiers, he required the return of the cargo of the *Good Hoffnung* and the repayment of the debts owed to Bacri and Busnach.[59] If the dey appeared to have become the spokesperson for the House of Bacri and Busnach, this was, in part, because some of the money owed to the house was in fact his. However, it also suggests that reports of Naphtali Busnach's power might not have been entirely unfounded. Mustapha, widely reported to have been under Busnach's control, certainly understood the debt to be entangled with the diplomacy between France and the regency.[60]

The regime in Paris, too, understood the debt to be central to good relations with the regency. French bureaucrats always sought the position of power in this relationship. For them, the debt was best used as a tool in managing the regency and the House of Bacri and Busnach. In April 1798 Foreign Minister Delacroix wrote to Saint-André, telling him to arrange for Bacri and Busnach to send badly needed provisions to Malta. "Incite their enthusiasm," Delacroix instructed his consul, "with the guarantee of a prompt and faithful reimbursement."[61] Later the same month, Delacroix wrote to a colleague in finance that "in holding back the sums owed to these Jews, we prevent them from being distracted away from our interests, and we will force them to be more circumspect in their helpful dealings with the English, whom they serve with such zeal only because their presence in Barbary offers the hope of new profits."[62] When the lie of power was less easy to maintain, French bureaucrats directed their frustration at these Jews they could not control. On September 30, 1798, the foreign minister, now Charles-Maurice, Duke de Talleyrand-Périgord, wrote instructions to Charles-François Dubois-Thainville, incumbent consul in Algiers. Talleyrand sent detailed information that took up almost half of this first letter. Talleyrand highlighted two specific issues. First, a Danish ship that had been chartered by the house to bring merchandise to Algiers from London was taken, first by the English and then by the French. This was the *Good Hoffnung*. Bacri and Busnach were devoting considerable energy to the return of their cargo, as was the dey. The best way to proceed, as Talleyrand saw it, was to seek to dissuade the dey from making claims that would not be fulfilled, by apprising him of the role of "the Jews" in this affair, "fully exposing their dishonesty, without asking that they be punished."[63] Yet even Talleyrand's desire to put Bacri and Busnach in their place was hamstrung by the requirements of diplomacy. He went on, perhaps venting his frustration at this restriction:

> These men, who are held in the lowest possible esteem in the whole of the Levant, enjoy the prince's respect in Algiers; the extent of their trade, in which he often takes part and which, as a result, brings him great financial benefits, means that he values them. They have correspondents in London, Hamburg, Amsterdam, Paris, Marseilles, and Livorno, so that, promptly informed of all that happens in Europe, they are not strangers to the political resolutions of the regency. Under Hassan Pasha, they had a great deal of influence; Citizen Jean Bon Saint-André often complained about this, and, through steadfastness and firmness, he succeeded in reducing their role to that of merchant, where the republic was concerned. We believed, at the beginning of Mustapha's reign, that they had lost their credit, but we were wrong. . . . Citizen Moltedo . . . informed me that they display great attentiveness to anything that is linked to serving the republic. It is not to be believed that they are attached to it, but they fear it because it is powerful, and because they are its creditors, they must take care with it. Considerable sums have been owing to them for some time. This is, for certain, the thread that attaches them to us. We must keep them hoping that they will receive their reimbursement, which will come but only in installments: it is certain that as long as they have not been completely repaid, they will not openly contest our opinions; this is a small advantage, of which we must take advantage.
>
> I had instructed your predecessor to have only decorous relations with them. I recommend to you, as I did him, to be cautious of them, but I do not forbid you from making use of their credit, if you believe this to be of use to our affairs; in such a case you must make use of it without allocating it and make your claim for it directly. Recourse to their intervention is somewhat unworthy of the republic.[64]

Need, and discomfort in the face of this need, jostled with one another.

Nonetheless, the Directory began the process of making agreements to repay the money owed. Perhaps this was, as Plantet would have it, in the interest of keeping good relations with the regency. A sum of 150,000 livres was now to be paid in fortnightly installments.[65] However, before any payment could be made, war broke out, and Bacri and Busnach now received further requests, not for money but for wheat, to feed the expeditionary army. These requests came from Napoleon himself. On December 23, 1800, he wrote to Talleyrand, setting out in some detail what was required: two million bottles of wine, brandy, and liquors, as well as sheets, medicines, and oil; on their return, their ships were to carry rice, coffee, indigo, and sugar. "Several people," he noted, "are offering to take on this venture, but I prefer the House of Bacri, if it is available."[66] He may have been choosing to give the right impression to the dey rather than select the best business. A month later he ordered Talleyrand "to present this Jew to me in my apartment" and noted that this should be understood as a mark of his consideration for the dey.[67] "This Jew" was Jacob Bacri.[68] If Napoleon wished to impress the dey, it was because he understood how closely what he called the House of Bacri was linked with the Algerian ruler. Their business dealings, to a significant extent, were his. The debt that France owed to them was also, in part, owed to him. When Napoleon was sending instructions to Talleyrand, the House of Bacri was in debt to the regency for the sum of approximately three hundred thousand francs.

The events of 1798 brought Bacri and Busnach to the center of relations between France and the regency in a new way. When the conflict between France and the Ottoman Empire erupted, bringing about a rupture between France and the regency, all French citizens were arrested and sentenced to hard labor. The staff of the agence were imprisoned in Algiers, and their headquarters was pillaged and destroyed. Bacri and Busnach, drawing on their position in Algerian society, came to their rescue. When in late January 1800 the new consul, Charles-François Dubois-Thainville, wrote to Talleyrand, he included letters written to his predecessor from Astoin Sielve, France's agent of the agence in Algiers. "We owe our deliverance to the Jews," he told the consul, and they "still continue to behave well toward us."[69] Dubois-Thainville was happy to confirm, some weeks later, that the French had been freed and their possessions returned to them. He could report, too, that "the Bacri merchants appear to have behaved with much skill and devotion."[70] A few months later, Dubois-Thainville wrote, "As soon as I had returned home, Busnach, whom I was with in the palace, had the coral and silver from the concessions and the rings and watches belonging to officers transported to the consulate." A day later, he reported, the government's advisory body for the concessions was released from the navy through the appeals of Bacri and Busnach. They also managed to free other concession employees, subject to forced labor, "through appeals and sacrifices" and "in spite of the opposition of those people who are against us."[71]

Following the measures taken against French citizens in the regency, the Directory had ordered similar measures to be taken against Algerian subjects in France. This included the sequestration of all possessions, an embargo on all ships, the sale of all perishable goods, the placing of seals on residences, and arrest. Jacob Bacri found himself imprisoned in the Temple Prison, along with Simon Aboucaya. Dubois-Thainville was concerned for the fate of the Bacris and Busnachs beyond Algiers. He wrote to Talleyrand that "justice and recognition oblige the consul to declare that what these Jews did to prevent the declaration of war is public knowledge and that having been unsuccessful, they have not stopped using their credit to sweeten the fate of the French."[72] However, the procedures undertaken by the republic were not worthy of it. "There is no true retaliation where there is not parity of rank, dignity, or esteem between the people who are its targets, on both sides."[73] Dubois-Thainville wrote to Talleyrand that the imprisonment of Bacris and Busnachs in France "wounded the dignity of the republic." Thus he put them firmly, once again, in the place he wished them to occupy. "These Algerians are vile, despised Jews, to whom the dey attaches no importance at all and whom he would not buy back through the restitution of a single Frenchman. It is *of great importance* to ensure that Bacri, in Paris, and Busnach, in Marseilles, do not escape, but it is a good thing to bring much politeness and generosity to this surveillance."[74]

Dubois-Thainville's clear ambivalence was soon to temper his praise for the actions of Bacri and Busnach in Algiers. In his report, completed in late March 1799, he noted to Talleyrand that the true motive for "the tender interest that [Bacri and Busnach] showed" was the fear that the war might cause the cancellation of the debts owed to them by France. By June the consul was expressing frustration that Bacri and Busnach had not sent a ship to Bona to collect the belongings of the unfortunate employees, as they had promised. The consul found their "lack of willingness" to be "inconceivable." "It would appear," he mused, "that they are awaiting the outcome of events."[75] However, the treatment of Bacri and Busnach remained central to the restoration of relations between the two regimes. The king of Spain had recently received a letter from the dey, Dubois-Thainville told Talleyrand. In the letter, the dey asked the king to make a case for Bacri and Busnach to the Directory, to ask, in the king's name, that their sequestered goods be released and that they be treated as friends.[76]

Jacob was writing letters, too, and he drew on the notion of the agreement, established at the very beginning of relations between the House of Bacri and Busnach and the French regime. In a letter he sent to Talleyrand in August or September 1799, Jacob claimed to be writing on the dey's behalf, reminding Talleyrand that prior to the outbreak of war, the dey had requested payment for the cargo of two ships taken by French pirates. The matter was before the Tribunal of Cassation, the court that acted as a revisory power. "I am awaiting the outcome of this judgment," Jacob told Talleyrand, "in order to make known the loyalty of the French to the dey and to prevent the taking [of these two ships] from becoming an obstacle to the reestablishment of good harmony between the two powers."[77] In the same month, writing to request the return of his goods, he told Talleyrand that this was "absolutely necessary for me to be able to fulfill the engagements I have undertaken with several French trading houses, both here [in Paris] and in Marseilles." He asked that Talleyrand settle this matter with the police minister. A note in the letter's margin affirms that this should be done.[78] Talleyrand understood the centrality and significance of both the debt and the Bacris and Busnachs in diplomatic relations. In a much-cited letter, Talleyrand stated to the minister of finance that "the current state of our relationship with the regency demands that we manifest the best goodwill possible to the Jews. This affair must be considered not as specific to them, but as an affair of state."[79]

Bacris and Busnachs were involved in affairs of state in other, equally significant ways. In 1799, the French consul in Tunis, Devoize, had written to Talleyrand that "if the Executive Directory decides to suspend its resentment to fabricate a peace with Algiers, it needs only the secret involvement of Bacri."[80] As the war drew to a close, Talleyrand drew on Devoize's advice and made use of Joseph Cohen Bacri in the peace negotiations with the dey that took place over the course of 1800 and 1801.[81] The debt was at the heart of the peace. One of the stipulations of the peace treaty that Dubois-Thainville negotiated with the dey was Article Thirteen, which stated that "his excellency the dey promises to have all sums that might be owing to French citizens by his subjects reimbursed, just as citizen Dubois-Thainville makes the commitment, in the name of his government, to have all those [debts] that might be legally claimed by Algerian subjects settled."[82] The French understood that the phrase "Algerian subjects" referred specifically to the House of Bacri and Busnach,[83] and the regime's consul promised, in the name of his government, that as soon as political and commercial relations had been reestablished, the government's first priority would be to set dates for resurrection of those payments "interrupted by the rupture."[84]

Indeed, as soon as peace had been reestablished with Algiers in 1800, the Bacris began once again to request repayment. Their supply of the French armies meant that the debt had risen by five and a half million francs. Dubois-Thainville felt obliged to acknowledge to his minister that "the Jews have served the French government warmly at times; they have delivered supplies to us at difficult moments and have even made great sacrifices in order to do that; and Busnach, who enjoys unequaled credit in Algiers, has often brought the extravagant governing prince around to view France according to principles of equity."[85] Dubois-Thainville also believed that it would be wise, however, if France were to advance funds as repayment of the debt, "to maintain guarantees of [Bacri and Busnach's] sincerity. . . . It is impossible," he went on, "to charter a boat here without the Jews, who hold everything in their hands, finding out about it."[86] A month later he wrote, regarding the export of wheat from the regency, that this would simply have to be shared with the Jews, since their power was such that it would be unwise, if not impossible, "to fight them." In 1803, he was "begging" his minister to send some message to the dey that would assuage his anger regarding the debt, since he feared that this prince's "ignorance and the desperation of the Bacris" could well cause him "much trouble." Like his predecessor Saint-André, Dubois-Thainville sought to maintain what he considered to be his greater dignity. "[Bacri and Busnach] must understand," he wrote to Talleyrand, "that the republic's agent cannot be supervised by them like an instrument that they can direct according to their will."[87] The perception of Jewish power came up, once again, against the desire to deny it.

Talleyrand, notwithstanding the occasional outburst, was pragmatic about the debt and the place of the Bacris and Busnachs in France's relations with the regency. In early 1801, he reported to Napoleon that the dey was demanding that the treaty be enacted. It was important to attend to the dey's wishes, Talleyrand stated, since it was in his person that "Barbary Coast power effectively resided." "We should not doubt his sincerity," Talleyrand advised his master, "when he demonstrates so much solicitude for those merchants in their monetary affairs, in which he, personally, has considerable interest. *We cannot hope to succeed fully in our given goals, in our dealings with the Barbary States, unless we deal efficiently with the settlement and reimbursement of the debts.* It is, in a word, the only way to avoid and prevent problems and worries of all kinds, which will continue to arise, as long as we do not give our specific attention to satisfying them."[88] Napoleon must have trusted the judgment of his foreign minister. Sometime later, Talleyrand wrote to the director of settlement of the public debt, with the express authorization of the first consul, to set in train the payment of the monies owed to Bacri and Busnach. Payment was to take a specific form. "Payment in installments," as Talleyrand informed his colleague de Fermont, "has already been used, so as to satisfy them sufficiently for their influence over the Regency of Algiers to be favorable to us."[89]

Then, in 1801, peace negotiations stalled, and Dubois-Thainville was exiled yet again, this time to Spain. He had intended to remove himself to Barcelona for what he hoped would be a short-lived exile. However, Busnach and Bacri conspired, as he saw it, to send him where it suited them, to Alicante. Before his departure, Dubois-Thainville was visited in his home in Algiers by Busnach and Bacri. "They trembled for their heads," he told Talleyrand. He tried to instill courage in them, but, as he put it, "I was talking to Jews, and all I found was fainthearted souls." Dubois-Thainville, whose verbosity can be as trying for the researcher as I can only imagine it must have been for his minister, went on to describe at length how he had taken Busnach to task for his cowardliness.[90] Whatever power Busnach and Bacri might have possessed in the determination of Dubois-Thainville's fate, Dubois-Thainville remained, nonetheless, the greater man. This was the position that allowed him to explain away his constant reliance on "those Jews" as intermediaries in his work as the republic's representative. In this way, he was able to put all Busnachs and Bacris in their place. Yet this was an ongoing task, since Bacris and Busnachs continued to play a central role in the renewed attempts to end hostilities. Dubois-Thainville wrote to Talleyrand in mid-1801, still from Alicante, that he had complained to "the Jews" regarding the ease with which English boats were picking up supplies from African ports. While he was "far from believing in the Jews' assurances," it was nonetheless the case, he noted, that the English had recently been encountering great difficulties when they attempted to dock.[91] Dubois-Thainville may have been reliant on the Bacris and Busnachs. He may have been prepared to recognize and acknowledge their centrality in the processes he was seeking to put in train. Throughout his letters these facts stand in contrast to his desire to dislike those he most commonly referred to as "the Jews."[92] (This level of familiarity—or belittlement?—was not limited to Dubois-Thainville. Talleyrand did the same.)

One more installment of 1.2 million francs was paid to the House of Bacri. However, external affairs were again to stymie the progress of the repayments. By 1802, the relationship between France and Algeria was again breaking down. Algerian corsairs were making repeated attacks on vessels, including French ships, and this enraged Napoleon, who warned the dey that he could—and would—destroy the regency if he so desired. In 1802, an apparently furious Napoleon sent a list of instructions to Talleyrand. Napoleon wished Dey Baba Mustapha to understand that he would not accept that pirates were attacking French ships and that he was ready to punish the dey "as I punished the beys of Egypt." Talleyrand was to instruct the consul, Dubois-Thainville, to demand that all sequestered boats be reinstated, enslaved French citizens freed, and instigators punished. And apparently to ensure that the dey had properly understood the depth of Napoleon's rage, the first consul added a note to Talleyrand's report. A furious scrawl instructed Talleyrand to "send someone to find the Bacris and tell them that the first consul is very displeased; if the ship's captain who allowed himself to mistreat a Frenchman is not given capital punishment, the first consul will know how to get revenge. Inform them that a letter should come from them."[93] A second letter was to be sent by Talleyrand to the Ottoman ambassador, outlining Napoleon's outrage. Talleyrand was to ensure that the letter be forwarded to Constantinople as well as to Algiers, "or if [the ambassador] does not wish [to send the letter to Algiers], that he summon Bacri and give it to him so that Bacri can have it sent to Algiers by special courier."[94] Very clearly, Napoleon saw the Bacris as his political intermediaries.

The position of intermediary could bestow power, but it was also a position of vulnerability. In 1805, the ambivalent position of Jews in regency society was brought home forcefully. In June of that year, Naphtali Busnach was murdered by a Janissary. The following day was the Sabbath. As the Jews of Algiers were in prayer, they were attacked. In one synagogue, fourteen men were murdered and the Torah scroll was torn to shreds. A Jewish account of the violence set the number of dead at forty-two and many wounded.[95] However, the mob's first aim was pillage, and it also sacked Busnach's warehouses. The violence continued for three hours until the dey put a stop to it. The following day, the dey named Joseph Bacri as *mokadem* in Busnach's place. Most members of the Bacri and Busnach families had left Algiers for Livorno, and only Joseph and his son David remained to take care of family affairs in Algiers. The dey, claiming himself Busnach's creditor to the value of two million francs, then confiscated all his goods and seized and sold his ships. But on August 31, the dey went the way of his Jewish victim. He was replaced by Ahmed ben Ali, who was no friend of the Bacris and Busnachs. Less than two weeks after he came to power, he called on the Bacris to pay Busnach's debt to the Treasury, a sum of four million francs. Bacris and Busnachs in Algiers were saved from imprisonment and threats of death only by friends among the consular staff, who persuaded the dey to come to an arrangement whereby the sum owed would be paid in bimonthly installments.

Uncertainty continued in Algiers, as tensions between different beys, regional rulers, and the dey played out. Dubois-Thainville returned in 1811 to difficult diplomatic circumstances. Frequent changes of regime, as deys were murdered in quick succession, ensured instability. Napoleon had been ordering and then lifting the sequestration of goods belonging to Algerians in France and Italy, as well as the imprisonment of the same, as a diplomatic response to poor relations between France and the regency. Bacris and Busnachs were the constant victims of these sequestrations, and in this way, they remained at the center of the political relationship. For example, Napoleon's 1808 sequestration decree affected Jacob Bacri, who was arrested and imprisoned in his home. Shortly following his arrest, Jacob wrote to the police minister, as well as to the prefect of his own department, the Bouches-du-Rhône. He included a long list of the services that he had had "the happiness of offering France." If he hadn't formally applied to be naturalized as French, he was, nonetheless, "French, in my heart, my feelings, and my customs." For these reasons, he was hopeful that the police minister would order his freedom.[96] Jacob's hopes were not to be fulfilled, however. On the advice of Dubois-Thainville, it was decided that Jacob was simply too important to be released. In a sense, he was caught in a trap of his own making. In the correspondence that followed, between the foreign and police ministers, and the minister of the navy and colonies, it was decided that since Jacob's family in Algiers was "very much favored by the dey,"[97] Jacob's imprisonment would serve as "the surest guarantee of the safety of the French under arrest in Algiers."[98] In 1812, Foreign Minister Bassano reported to the police minister, the Duke de Rovigo, that "measures taken in Livorno against the Bacri Jews have produced an impression on the members of this family in Algiers whose effect has not been devoid of use in the reestablishment of our affairs in this land."[99] Jacob may have considered himself to be French "in the heart," but the authorities were not necessarily convinced.

The question of the belonging of the Bacris and Busnachs runs through the discourse surrounding them, up to and beyond the invasion. Once again, the questions and fantasies raised in Gautier's *Juive de Constantine* are replicated— or, more correctly, introduced—in this concrete setting. In 1806, Michel Busnach was the subject of some concern to French authorities. Dubois-Thainville had written to Talleyrand to warn him that Busnach's behavior in Marseilles was causing the dey to demand that Busnach "be delivered to him and that all his goods be sequestered," profiting the regency. Talleyrand was inclined to believe his consul's claim that Naphtali Busnach had spirited a great deal of the dey's money out of the regency, and that Michel Busnach was now misusing those same funds. "It is certain," he wrote to Marseilles, that Busnach, "who stayed Algerian for as long as it suited him to be so and who became French when it no longer suited him to be Algerian, fatigues the regency daily with his intrigues."[100] Debate over the belonging of the Bacris was still not settled at the time of the invasion of the regency. In a report on a ball hosted by the Bacris in Marseilles in January 1831, the *Sémaphore* responded indignantly to the claim of the *Gazette du Midi* that the Bacris were Algerian, that they were, in fact, "well and truly French and very good Frenchmen."[101]

Throughout this period, the idea of the debt as a political issue was maintained, too. In fact, it was only through politics that the debt survived. Then, in 1815, a change of regime brought a change of approach. Louis XVIII, the restored Bourbon king, appointed Pierre Deval as his consul to Algiers. Deval's first mission was to declare to the regency that the Restoration would satisfy all outstanding issues of contention. The great political survivor Talleyrand had returned, and he ordered Deval to promise the Bacris that their debts would be repaid in full. Talleyrand had been hard at work. In October 1815, he presented a report to King Louis XVIII, recommending that if the dey were to be promised repayment, then "the debts claimed by Messrs. Bacri to be owing by the French government [would] be examined and settled in France according to the law [and] that France alone had the right to judge the legitimacy of the said debts, and consequently, this affair could never be considered by the regency as public grievance; nor could it give rise to any retaliation but only to friendly reproach, which France would not fail to take into consideration."[102] The report effectively gave France the control it had always sought ever since it first became indebted to the House of Bacri and Busnach. Louis approved it because relations were "severely compromising the safety of sea trade."[103] It was finally time to consider repaying the debt in full. Deval wrote from Algiers, respectfully, that conditions there also demanded "a general resolution of the whole of Bacri's claims."[104] However, repayment of the debt no longer came under the aegis of the Ministry of Finance or related departments. It had entered "the domain of diplomacy."[105] Repayment, therefore, had to be demonstrated to be of diplomatic and political necessity. In 1812, the Duke de Bassano, now foreign minister, had written to Gaudin, his colleague in Finance, requesting that he seek evidence that the debt owed to Bacri and Busnach was "ill founded." Gaudin replied that given that this debt was now no longer valid in law, only "political considerations" could constitute an exception.[106] Two reports were now written that laid out the history of the debt and its part in the story of relations between the two regimes.[107] In their report, Deval and his fellow authors had little trouble establishing that the debt could legitimately be understood to be diplomatic. The author of a further report agreed. In their words, the contract between Bacri and Busnach and the French government "truly constitutes an engagement from government to government," since Bacri and Busnach only "contracted with the French government by order of the dey." However, even if the government were forced to rely on convenience alone as a reason for repayment, they would be rewarded, since conclusion of the debt would give the regency "a satisfaction that it cannot be denied, without inciting violent displeasure and perhaps a rupture."[108] A final report then considered the validity of each of the claims being made by Bacri and Busnach and set their value.[109] This report opened by repeating the acknowledgment that the House of Bacri and Busnach had been aggressively recruited by France to supply grain. (In fact, it was the then consul, Jean-Antoine Vallière, who, on the instructions of his regime, first approached the House of Bacri and Busnach in 1794.)[110] Since the house had begun to complain about slow repayments in 1796, the report noted that "they have, constantly and without success, demanded payment," but "they had received only small advances," and "they were constantly given the hope that they would soon be repaid" on the basis of which they continued to supply shipments.[111]

Following protracted negotiations, all parties in France agreed that the sum of seven million francs was to be paid in twelve equal installments of 582,333 francs each. On October 28, 1819, both parties signed an agreement that this figure would be paid to the Bacris, less any amount owed to French creditors. Major creditors were named on a separate list, on which the dey did not feature, even though he was owed seventy thousand piasters by the House of Bacri and Busnach.[112] Passage of the act then required the agreement of the dey that "in the name of the regency, that given the said transaction, he no longer had any demands to be made of the French government relative to the debts owed to Bacri and Busnach."[113] On December 23, 1819, Deval, together with Jacob Bacri, *mokadem* since 1816, met with Hussein to confirm his agreement to the act, which was then registered at the consulate and sent to Paris. When the dey declared himself satisfied, a bill proposing the opening of an account for seven million francs was presented to the Chamber of Deputies on June 20, 1820, by Baron Pasquier, then minister for foreign affairs. "The king," the minister stated in his accompanying speech,

> recognizes that the main cause of the interruption in our relationship with Algiers was the failure to carry through the article in the treaty of 1801 that guaranteed the payment of outstanding debts owed to Algerian subjects. The king promised what justice imperiously demanded. A declaration was given to the Regency of Algiers that its subjects' claims would be satisfied. The regency, believing in the sincerity of the French government's actions to this

end, immediately reestablished good relations between the two countries, and this felicitous change was followed soon after by the restitution to France of the concessions. It remained for France to fulfill its engagements.[114]

And thus, in the words of Gabriel Esquer, "it was solemnly confirmed, once again," that the settling of the Bacri-Busnach debts had taken on the characteristic of an affair of state and that meeting the debt had become the condition for the dey remaining well disposed toward France.[115]

The bill was presented to the Chamber of Peers for adoption and was ultimately ratified on July 24. The line of credit was then opened, and thus began a process of misunderstanding. While the Bourbon regime now set about paying those creditors of the House of Bacri and Busnach who came forward to claim payment, the dey, who promised to satisfy the same creditors, awaited payment of the full seven million francs. However, payment was not forthcoming, and this angered the dey, who wrote to Charles X to express his discontent. The dey, according to Henri-Delmas de Grammont, drawing on a trope of fanaticism, was fueled by "an ancient warrior spirit and hatred of the Christian."[116] Yet even Grammont, who in his version of the tale is apparently prepared to use stereotypes to understand and present Bacri and Busnach, noted that their claims on the French government were "well founded." In the Orient, foreignness was relative. For Grammont, it would appear that Jews could belong in a middle category; not quite them (Muslims) but not quite us either. In his version of events, two and a half million francs were withheld by the regime to be used to repay French debtors of Bacri and Busnach, as well as of the dey. The remaining four and a half million francs were given to "the two Jewish associates," who, "foreseeing the fate that awaited their four and half million, and perhaps their very heads, were very wary of returning to Algiers." No one, Grammont argued, could have made sense of all of this to the dey. Deval failed, but "all would have failed, in his place."[117] This, then, was the dey, misinformed, incapable of comprehending, and driven by ancient impulses, who took out his frustration on a consul whom he did not trust, bringing us back to the events with which we began this chapter.

Commentators, both at the time and from a distance, appear to be seduced by the idea of the Bacris and Busnachs as all powerful. Perhaps this still serves as the most accessible way of making sense of their role in this history—the lure of the power of a mix of fact and fantasy. Some cast our actors, particularly Joseph, Jacob, and Nathan Coen Bacri and Naphtali Busnach, variously, as honest—if slightly too clever—men of business. Others present them as willful, selfish double-dealers, entirely responsible for Algeria's downfall and everything in between.[118] A couple of works have been particularly influential in this regard in terms of the way they have dictated understanding. One of these is the 1936 work of Claude Martin, on Jews in Algeria, *Les Israélites algériens de 1830 à 1902*. In this work, Martin lays out what he sees as the reasons behind the families' rise to wealth and prominence. As bankers to the deys, in return for cash loans, they were given, little by little, the monopoly over the grain trade. They were then able to exploit this monopoly through their extraordinary networks. They had agents "disseminated throughout *beyliks* [territories under jurisdiction of the beys] and marketplaces in Europe," and their agents sent them information about ongoing political situations, as well as the state of crops and prices.[119] While the Bacris managed the business, Busnach, in Martin's words, "ran the state." "They reigned by corruption," he tells the reader, "buying viziers, like the Prince de Talleyrand, supplying both the English and the French in war, collecting all the takings and fooling the unfortunate dey, to whom they owed approximately three hundred thousand francs, which was never repaid."[120] Martin's work needs to be treated carefully. For example, he regularly cites one Claude-Antoine Rozet as a "witness."[121] Rozet, an army captain and engineer-geographer, produced two volumes of observations, mixed with gossip and information about his time in the regency. In his close descriptions of the Jewish community, he informed readers that the Jews of the Barbary States were "exactly the same variety" of Jew as those who lived in Europe.[122] "An air of humility and deceitfulness" was imprinted on the face of each and every Jewish man, "and their conduct did not contradict it."[123] His work, which would not be out of place with the travel accounts of Gautier and Didier from chapter 2, continues in the same vein, a tone that Claude Martin chooses to cite verbatim as fact. In this way he entombs prejudices and fantasy. Martin's work is generally cited as a standard text in the literature.[124] Yet his antipathy must, at the very least, be considered in the context of the date of publication, a period of political uncertainty, when the place of Jews in both France and Algeria was called into question.

Other commentators are no more generous. Gabriel Esquer, writing in the 1920s, hardly promises to be fair-minded when he states that it is no straightforward task to get to the bottom of whether "such characters" were sincere in their feelings and their attitudes.[125] If Esquer paints a picture of the Bacris and Busnachs as "despised but indispensable,"[126] Charles-André Julien, whose history of Algeria was published in 1964, builds up the Bacris and Busnachs to be "the government's best source of information, masters of foreign trade, and the regency's official diplomats to the European consulates."[127] "Masters of the market," the families ruined the Arabs among whom they lived, "their only concern the enormous profits they made on their exports, even in times of famine." The effect of their greed on the Algerian economy was nothing short of "disastrous." Julien refers to Bacri and Busnach in his work as "the Livornese."[128] Is this to imply that these men were not even true Algerians? Non-French commentators have found these stereotypes to be easily accessible, too. Peter Dunwoodie drew on the work of Charles-Robert Ageron to describe the affair of the dey striking Deval with the fan as "shady," "led by the all-powerful Jewish traders of Algiers, with the complicity of disreputable politicians in Paris."[129] In the words of Jules Roy, the Bacris and Busnachs were "sovereigns who possessed agents all across the Mediterranean . . . , ruining the competition, . . . masters of ports and the sea, of trade and of the prisons, making and unmaking peace through the intervention of the deys."[130] The work of the Algerian-born Roy was fictionalized history, part of his series of novels on the history of French Algeria. The image he creates of the House of Bacri and Busnach comes together, however, in striking resonance with the historiography. Said was perhaps right: Orientalism continues to inform and shape our understanding of a West opposed to an East. What these works suggest is that Jews can also be used to project ideas and prejudices about the Orient. Or, indeed, the Orient can be used to explain Jews.

If fact has been pushed aside to make space for fantasy in tales of the Bacris and Busnachs, this is particularly clear in depictions of Jacob Bacri. Thus, for example, the sole physical description we have of him comes from an 1844 history of Marseilles, written by one Lautard:

> Bacri, then in his prime, looked entirely a fool. He was of small, spindly stature, pallid in color, with a dazed look, and his speech was slow and labored. He spoke only a few words, in Barbary gibberish. It must be said that this aspect, barely pleasing, did not in any way suggest the favorite of the African despot. "Nonetheless, this favorite was an important man, for he was made of gold!" He had sumptuously furnished the Hotel Samatan, bought by mutual agreement, without taste and without moderation. He had accumulated so many priceless objects that the house looked like one of the large stores on the rue Vivienne. Shortly after he moved in, one day, at the house of Madame G. B. he lost approximately sixty thousand francs at [the card game] Trente et Quarante, with the stoic sangfroid of a Muslim on fire. He would probably have tripled his loss if the winners, worried about not being paid, had not held him back. They regretted their actions, for the descendant of Abraham honored his debts the very next day. . . . His affairs and his pleasures kept him [in Paris] a long time, and cheats and women made wide holes in his fortune. While he was away, in 1797, his hotel was completely and methodically pillaged and emptied over several nights by thieves.[131]

This is an interesting contrast to the few words we have from an American special agent in Algiers, who reported that he found Bacri to be "in every way polite and accommodating."[132] Yet Lautard's work has become, like that of Rozet and Martin, curiously authoritative, even though Lautard himself acknowledged in his preface that he had "stigmatized the wicked [and] glorified the good."[133] In December 1798, while Bacri was in Paris, his home in Marseilles was burgled. According to the police minister's report, a group of fifty "brigands" systematically emptied the Hotel Samatan of jewels, diamonds, gold, and money to the value of

four hundred thousand livres, the greater part of which, according to the minister, was the property of the dey.[134] Esquer's description of the burglary begins with
a commentary on Bacri's taste, quoting from Lautard, as fact, that Bacri "had ac-
cumulated expensive furniture, with neither taste nor moderation." Esquer goes
on to report that "the investigation raised doubts about the truth of the burglary,
and the police reports hint that the victim might have burgled himself."[135]

Jacob was not the only family member to be lifted into the realm of creative
fantasy. Nathan-Joseph Cohen Bacri, the son of Jacob's elder brother, Joseph, became the subject of an epic poem. While politicians were arguing in 1830 over the
value of war, the French public maintained stubborn apathy over the question of
Algeria. The lack of success of a satirical poem about Algeria from the otherwise
enormously popular authors Joseph Méry and Auguste-Marseille Barthélemy
can be read as an example of this disinterest. Méry and Barthélemy were both
born in Marseilles and moved to Paris in the 1820s, where they found one another
and began a fertile collaboration. They wrote political satire in the form of poetry
and enjoyed enormous popularity. *La Bacriade* is an exception in their oeuvre,
both in terms of its form and its lack of success. Nonetheless, the poem tells us
that writers, as well as politicians, were aware of the story of the Bacri-Busnach
debt, for the poem sets out to explain the reason why the two authors are unable
to travel to Algiers as they wish to.[136] The subject of the "heroicomic" poem is Nathan Bacri, "the Helen of the Algerian war."[137] Their *Bacriade*, much cited since,
offers a fascinating look into the way a Bacri entered the popular imagination in
France. Nathan Bacri was born in Algiers, but in 1823, he requested French citizenship. On his unsuccessful application he declared himself to be living in Paris
and to have spent several years in Marseilles; all in all, he claimed, he had been
living in France for fifteen years.[138] As is the case for Jacob, there is little or nothing that reveals Nathan to us. In one source, he is described as "puny looking,
with a dazed expression."[139] An undated police report describes Nathan as having "squandered a great deal and done bad business."[140] In the *Bacriade*, Barthélemy and Méry present Nathan as a complex figure. He is the opportunistic Jew
for whom "Christianity armed itself."[141] He is weak, giving in to the pleasures of
wealth. Yet he is also capable of honorable self-sacrifice.

The *Bacriade* opens with the dey, who is furious that Nathan has held on
to the seven million francs he has received in payment from France rather than
repaying what he owes the dey. The dey describes himself to his henchman Osmin as the victim of a plot. While Algiers came to the aid of France "in danger,"
"nourishing" the republic with African grain, a "son of Israel" called Nathan
Bacri, "known throughout the universe," served as intermediary.[142] Yet the name
of Bacri has meant nothing but setbacks for the dey. And France, "going through
twenty regimes," has consistently refused to settle the debt. Bacri assures the dey
that if he goes to France, he will have the debt repaid. The dey, trusting Nathan,

allows him to leave, and Nathan is indeed true to his word: the money owed is repaid. But "Israel never had a more false charlatan!"[143] For while the dey has waited, there has been no word from Bacri, who is still living in Paris, "accustoming his tongue to the Christian jargon," "shaving off his pointed beard," and spending the dey's seven million francs freely,[144] perhaps an allusion to newly emancipated Jews who were now making their way to the capital. The dey sends Osmin to find Nathan in Paris and bring him back to Algiers for judgment. Osmin goes to Alexandria to beg Mustapha Pasha's support and to request the use of fifty men. The image that Osmin paints of the damage Nathan could do if allowed to remain in Paris is a strikingly Christian one. In Nathan's skilled hands, Osmin tells his leader, the money will double, and Nathan, "the impure son of a proscribed people," will leave France as a "new Moses," leading three hundred thousand of his people in "a Jewish crusade" (and a fascinating conflation of Judaism and Christianity) to Jerusalem, to reawaken Zion.[145]

Nathan, meanwhile, is living the high life in Paris, consuming the dey's gold. His life is one of "indolent days," "gay meals," and "noble friends." At the stock exchange he is "another Rothschild."[146] However, while Nathan is out walking, he recognizes Osmin and realizes that Osmin has been sent to take him back to Algiers. Nathan formulates a plan to trick Osmin out of fulfilling his duty and, delighted with himself, announces this to the patrons of the Café Tortoni, where he is a regular. Soon after, Osmin and his fifty guards receive invitations to a special performance of the opera *Aladdin*. The men, enchanted by the performance, all take mistresses from the corps of dancers. Osmin quickly realizes that he has been duped into betraying his mission. He tries to persuade his soldiers to repent and reapply themselves to their mission, but they prefer to return to their beds, "still warm."[147] Osmin returns directly to Algiers to admit his failure and dies, dignified, having chosen impalement over suffocation. The dey is still determined to bring Nathan back to Algiers, however. He sends a giraffe to Paris, hoping that the price for this marvel will be Bacri. The king's ministers agree. Two agents come to take him from his hotel when rescue appears in the form—or motif—of none other than James de Rothschild. Rothschild, "the hope of nations and the support of kings," who has rushed from his Hotel d'Artois to save Nathan, threatens to withdraw all of his "cosmopolitan gold" and let all of Europe go bankrupt, if even one hair on Nathan's head comes to harm.[148] The dey realizes he is beaten, and smarting from this humiliation, he has an angry exchange with the French consul, who counsels him to petition the government for payment of the debt and refuses to hand Bacri over because he is a "faithful" French citizen, "adopted and protected by France."[149] The dey, furious, strikes Deval with his fan. Nathan, meanwhile, is horrified to see the effect he has caused. He decides to return to Algiers and sacrifice himself. The poem ends with Nathan, who has now become a figure of courage. His sacrifice is honored.

The figure of Bacri/Rothschild, still unknown and yet, in so many ways, known to those steeped in church teaching, might have provided a fertile starting point for fantasy. The fantasy of Barthélemy and Méry, however, did not come to fruition. There was no sacrifice made by a Bacri or a Busnach. In May 1830, a French fleet left Toulon for the shores of Algeria. Yet while the invasion was to set off an occupation of more than a century, the story of the House of Bacri and Busnach suggests that the history of France and Algeria did not necessarily begin—or indeed end—in 1830. Behind the invasion is a tale of continuity, of involvement, and of entanglement. It is the Bacris and Busnachs who take us across these temporal boundaries. Even as France prepared for war, Bacri and Busnach remained at the center of this story. The story of the Bacris, in particular, extends beyond the invasion that marked the end of Grammont's work. In the lead-up to the invasion, readers of the Marseilles newspaper, the *Sémaphore*, enjoyed coverage of preparations and the eventual embarkation of the troops in minute detail under the regular rubric "Expedition to Algiers." Preparations created "an extraordinary increase in movement" in the city's port.[150] The troops were embarking from Toulon; however, it was nonetheless in the port of Marseilles that 582 auxiliary boats were chartered and armed. Paul Masson wrote that a similar level of activity had not been seen in the old port "for a long time."[151]

We cannot know for certain whether Bacris, Busnachs, or their agents in Marseilles were keeping the Algiers branch up to date. Paul Raynal, who fought with the invading army but was in Marseilles during the preparations for war, reported in a letter to family that "one of the Bacris is here [in Marseilles], and this morning I was chatting with one of his friends, who passed on a message to me from him that three regiments and ten cannons would be sufficient to take Algiers."[152] Raynal's letter suggests that at the very least, Bacris were interested in the forthcoming invasion, and their opinion was seen as carrying some weight. Given also the presence in the city of family members or their representatives and the readiness with which they corresponded, it is not a stretch to imagine that Jacob Bacri, then living in Algiers and *mokadem* of that city's Jewish community since 1816 under four successive deys, was fully prepared to receive the new representatives of the nation at whose heart he had rested for so long.[153]

Just as they had been deeply implicated in the relationship between France and the regency, Bacri and Busnach now became central to the invading forces. Ian Coller has discussed the significance of the lack of Orientalists on the Egyptian expedition. "Because of this almost total absence of Orientalist expertise," he notes,

> the French were forced to draw heavily upon local collaborators, particularly among Christians, Jews, and the resident Europeans, or "Franks." These were not, then, European "Orientalists," but members of long-established local

communities with a knowledge of European languages and customs. . . . But even this formulation does not express accurately the nature of these intermediary populations, whose role has largely been neglected in the history of the relationship between Europe and the Muslim world. Without them, no French administration could hope to survive even for a year.[154]

Jews in 1830s Algeria were, as Joshua Schreier states, "a significant component of the social and economic fabric of Algeria's cities." They "were intimately interwoven into regional and trans-regional trading networks."[155] When the expeditionary force reached Algeria, they looked again for Coller's "intermediary population," those who were both deeply implicated in, yet on the edges of, Algerian society, who could act as go-betweens. Rozet wrote that since the army had been in Africa, "we haven't been able to do without the Jews."[156] Unsurprisingly, the French invaders found Jacob Bacri. Martin paints a picture of Joseph (it was in fact Jacob) Bacri, mounted on a "richly harnessed" mule, offering his services "in his zeal" to be useful to the victors and to the general in chief.[157] General de Bourmont took them on, against the advice of the dey, who was reputed, according to Martin, to have told de Bourmont that the pair was "cowardly and corrupt." If he employed them for their intelligence in financial matters, the dey's advice supposedly went, he should "never lose sight of them."[158]

Bacri nonetheless became one of the general's advisers. Rozet described Bacri as "the richest and most respected of the Jews in Algiers," noting also that French officers were regularly invited to the Bacri home to take part in his soirées.[159] Jacob Bacri's power and influence were, apparently, to continue to grow. Martin tells us that Jacob became "one of the general's most trusted advisers: Nothing could be done at that time, in the army, and in administrative matters, without him being consulted."[160] With hindsight, Martin judged de Bourmont's choice to be poor:

> Doubtless, in this unknown land, the opinion of an intelligent local was precious, but the name of Bacri had been pronounced often enough in the controversies that had preceded the expedition, and his doubtful morality had been sufficiently brought to light for the favorable treatment of the "king of the Jews" to be surprising.[161]

In November 1830, Jacob Bacri was named head of the Jewish community in Algiers and invested with the powers of policing and surveillance of that town's Jewish community. He was to carry out any judgments handed down by the tribunal, and he took responsibility for the collection of taxes. He reported to the general in chief.[162] In his memoir of his time in Algiers, General Paul Azan noted how "the Jew Bacri" was permitted "to give himself an air of importance that disconcerted a number of Muslims disposed to offer their services to the French and distanced them from the latter."[163] Julien describes this appointment as Jacob

Bacri's "triumph."[164] It shocked everyone, Julien tells us, all the way to the English consul, by its ostentation. Under Julien's pen, Bacri's influence grew. Not only was he de Bourmont's adviser; he also took part in meetings of the government commission, on his own initiative, and he assumed control of the provision of food to Algiers. It was an open fact, according to Julien's understanding, that Jacob Bacri "bartered his influence."[165] Bacri does seem to have gained the complete trust of the French administration, even if others were not so trusting. When General de Bourmont was fighting resisters outside Algiers, he took refuge in Bacri's country house. It was judged too far from battle to make a suitable headquarters, we are told, but de Bourmont stayed there long enough to take "badly needed refreshment."[166] Bacri was also supplying cattle to the army.[167] A Busnach, too, one of the sons of Naphtali, worked as an adviser and negotiator.[168] Indeed, such was the value of the Jewish elite as go-betweens that in his work Martin labeled them—perhaps borrowing from Grammont—"political intermediaries."[169] Yet the deep ambivalence present in the letters of Saint-André and Dubois-Thainville can still be discerned. The desire to put these Jews in their place still existed. Minister of War Simon Bernard wrote to General Damrémont, governor general of the French possessions in 1837, regarding payment of Mouchi (Moses) Busnach, who had acted as a go-between in peace negotiations with the bey of Constantine. Busnach, according to Minister Bernard, "as a good Israelite, did not offer his services free of charge," an entirely gratuitous comment, given that he saw it as perfectly reasonable that some reward be given for work that was concluded "advantageously and honorably."[170]

The Bacris and Busnachs invite us to complete the circle of narrative that has shaped this book. They provide yet another and perhaps even the best example of how reality and fantasy were blurred when it came to the Oriental or Orientalized Jew. In their story, the priorities of politics and the license of creation come together. The Bacris and Busnachs were not quite Algerian and not entirely European. They were professional go-betweens, and they were—and apparently still are—imagined with all the deep ambivalence that their position invited. The story of the House of Bacri and Busnach allows us to reconsider the colonial face of Orientalism, which is perhaps its most recognizable. The Bacris and Busnachs suggest to us that Orientalism was not a straightforward process whereby knowledge prepared the ground for appropriation. Rather, Orientalism, insofar as it is linked to colonialism, was a process of intense negotiation, and Jews could be negotiators par excellence. The Bacris and Busnachs were agents in the French experience of Algiers. They shaped it, and their activities determined French understanding and responses to a deeply significant extent. They tell us that we must reconsider Orientalism as a process of entanglement. They tell us, also, that if we must go to histories of Western imperialism, then we must also consider the pre-imperial world and the role of intermediaries—Jewish and otherwise—in shaping perceptions and experiences.

# Conclusion

In this book, I have sought to tease apart three aspects of the one story, brought to life by three sets of figures. In some ways, these stories are not as disparate as the organization of this book has suggested. There was no clear delineation in the ways Jews were Orientalized, whether read through the prism of religious belief, the impetus of artistic creation, or the requirements of imperial design. Both artists and bureaucrats drew on church teaching to better understand and describe the Jews they encountered and invented. Catholic pilgrims and artists alike were highly politicized and used their writings on Jews to make pronouncements on the state of their nation. Bureaucrats and pilgrims gave themselves creative license, telling stories as a way to explore and enlarge on the themes that were important to them.

Yet these same figures—pilgrims, artists, and bureaucrats—also allowed me to divide these stories into separate chapters, through their sense of the France that they belonged in, as well as the interplay between the meanings that they assigned to the Jews that they knew and encountered and their understanding of their place in their world. Without this, their own context, this story becomes unintelligible. Their experience of their context explains the particular Frenchness of this tale. The protagonists in this work lived through a time that gave them the liberty to imagine an ideal of France and, along with this, to express a sense of grievance in the face of realities in France, which, in their eyes, did not meet their ideal. When French Catholic pilgrims relived the Crusades in Jerusalem, they were articulating an ideal that made France once again the eldest daughter of the church. To discover that the Jews of Jerusalem were degraded was to write them into this schema. When writer-travelers discovered that Jews in the Orient were secretly and deceptively wealthy, they were giving full voice to their sense of outrage in the face of the individualistic materialism that was taking hold in France. And when diplomats and bureaucrats revealed the ways in which the House of Bacri and Busnach enjoyed extraordinary power, they were venting their frustration at their inability to impose the will of a nation that they wanted to see as powerful.

Indeed, the figure of the Orientalized Jew was powerful because it was created from a combination of this type of imagining and the reality of encounters. Jews, both in France and in the Orient, held enormous and unique significance. Jews, after all, were intrinsic to the story of Christianity, and they were familiar figures to anyone schooled in its ideology. Church teaching offered the tools to create imagined Jews, obstinate, blind, and malevolent. The combination of contact with very real Jews and the tradition of imagining Jews allowed for a creative space. This is not to imply that Jews in the Orient or, for that matter, in France were all that their observers claimed them to be. We know, for example, that the House of Bacri and Busnach did all in its power to have the money owed to it refunded. From this reality came tropes of manipulation, greed, and duplicity, which provided a welcome and convenient explanation for an unwanted indebtedness.

Just as these French writings on the Orientalized Jew tell a story of France, so Orientalism has been the prism through which other national stories have been told in other contexts. Eitan Bar-Yosef has written about "the various cross-exchanges" between the external British Protestant project of building presence and influence in Palestine and the British Protestant tradition of applying an imagined biblical Holy Land to England itself.[1] What he called "the long, intricate, intimate relationship" between England and Palestine was also, he argued, England's intricate, intimate relationship with itself.[2] In this story, the meeting of the real and the imagined, applied to a sense of national identity, is exemplified by William Blake's hymn "Jerusalem." John Efron has written about the process of German-Jewish self-fashioning in the eighteenth and nineteenth centuries that involved a valorization and appropriation of Sephardic—Oriental—Jewish culture in a German key. As German Jews sought avenues of entry into broader German societies, they reinvented themselves, idealizing Sephardic culture as a way of distancing themselves from their fellow Ashkenazic Jews farther East.[3] As these examples suggest, Orientalism was not a phenomenon outside history. If it has any value as a blanket term, it is in the sense that it invites us to explore its many, varying contexts.

In terms of nineteenth-century France, context tells us, also, that the meanings that pilgrims, artists, and bureaucrats assigned to Jews had limits. There were roles that the Jew could not fill. Or more precisely, there was one. The Orientalized Jew was never understood, simply, as being Jewish. Their Jewishness always carried some greater significance or meaning, and the real, living Jew marked the limit of that meaning. This is why, for example, Rachel's Jewishness was largely irrelevant to Gautier, except when she represented the ancient. Her idealized Jewishness explained antiquity but not modernity. That was the job of Catulle Mendès and the many other hateful figures that filled the pages of Gautier's work. This Orientalized Jew was made to be whatever would feed an awaited explanation. Pilgrims, artists, and bureaucrats posed questions, anticipating the answers they would find. Yet as the examples of Rachel and Catulle Mendès suggest, meaning stemmed also from the concrete.

While the Orientalized Jew was, at times, created in hateful terms, this is not a history of antisemitism. Western antisemitism was not Orientalism's "strange, secret sharer," as Said had it. Nor was Orientalism the "Islamic branch" of anti-semitism.[4] The history of the Orientalized Jew is a history of a middle space in relations between Jews and non-Jews, where contact, interchange, idealization, hatred, and even ambivalence could play out. This middle space largely char-acterizes the history of relations between Jews and non-Jews as the two came increasingly into contact with one another. This is not antisemitism; nor is it philosemitism. It is only partly Nirenberg's "anti-Judaism," a history of the ways Jews have been drawn negatively to make sense of the wider world.[5] All of these labels relegate Jews to a disciplinary silo in modern history, as a separate entity. They allow no space for us to make sense of the interaction between the con-crete and the imagined. For, as the figure of the Orientalized Jew demonstrates, the middle space was a space of contact, complexity, and fluidity. In this space, Gautier's reviews of and friendship with Rachel and his vulturelike Jews of the *Tableaux de siège* must be set side by side. If he created both, and sometimes within the same work, then should we seek to divide and categorize? Rather, we must ask why Gautier and his circle, French Catholic pilgrims, and consular staff could understand the Orientalized Jew in such apparently differing ways. Jews were indeed good to think, but this thinking could take different forms accord-ing to the needs of the thinker. In these writings, the Jew acts as a totemic fig-ure for the object of the author's desires or disgruntlements. The Jew serves as a means for expressing a particular view of the author's world. We gain the most meaningful access to works such as these when we seek to understand them not as an example of a particular category or idea overlaid onto history but, rather, as an expression of a particular understanding of time and place, or as revealing of their creator. The figure of the Orientalized Jew makes clear this middle space and, in doing so, opens up and complicates the idea of antisemitism.

If the figure of the Orientalized Jew cannot be explained and understood through antisemitism, then the framework of Orientalism breaks down, too. Just as the history of the Orientalized Jew is not a history of a monumental hatred, nor was Orientalism, and this becomes clear when we do not seek to employ Orien-talism to explain outcomes that occurred in the century to follow. Orientalism, rooted in context, was not necessarily, or not always, a meeting of two monolithic and unequal entities. Rather, in the history of the encounter between Europe and the Orient, we must make allowance for a vast diversity of populations in both locations. This includes both Muslims and Jews. This is not a story whereby the two simply swap places. Islam or anti-Islam does not take the place of antisemi-tism as the silent, secret sharer. Rather, in the history of French Orientalism in the nineteenth century, Islam and Judaism are both significant sharers. Jews and Muslims were used to define and explain one another: if one was industrious, the other was lazy; if one could be enlightened, the other was fanatical. A true history of Orientalism must make space for these processes.

We must also make allowance for mobility.[6] This entailed the literal trans-
port of peoples across the Mediterranean in both directions, but also, and most
important, we must allow for the movement of ideas and narratives back and
forth, between Europe and the Orient. In both senses, this is a history of criss-
crossing traffic. We cannot necessarily make a clear distinction between two distinct entities, be they West and East, Europe and Orient, or even just "here" and
"there." If the French did construct themselves against the backdrop of something they imagined as the Orient, this was a complex process, loaded with a
variety of possible meanings.

The discovery and depiction of Jews in the Orient by the French demonstrate
how Orientalism could be a process of drawing on, or making use of, the Orient,
whether imagined or real. This Orientalism might be a mechanism for domination, shackled to colonialism. But Orientalism was not simply a discourse of
colonialism. To understand it thus oversimplifies it and obscures its breadth. Orientalism has been hamstrung by its close association with colonialist discourse,
as a language of domination, applicable across different contexts. If Orientalism,
in the form of knowledge, did bring a sort of power, then this, surely, was the
power to choose what use was made of that knowledge. It is in this sense that
knowledge might be more than simply a tool for domination. In France, knowledge could also serve to express opposition to the phases through which French
society was passing in the nineteenth century or the subversion of these same
phases. Thus, Orientalism, as I frame it here, could also be projection or idealization. It could be an expression of hostility and power but also an expression of
disgruntlement and desire. Its own power lies, perhaps, in the combination of the
real and the imagined, in the fact that Orientalist fantasies generally arose from
something or someone concrete, however far the creator's imagination might
have traveled from that initial inspiration. This is precisely why Jews were so relevant to Orientalism. Those French who found Jews in the Orient brought their
inheritance to their understanding of what they discovered. In this sense, Jews
in the Orient were familiar. Jews were known; church teaching ensured this. Yet
Jews were also familiar in a much more concrete sense. In a place that was deeply
foreign in many ways, Jews were sufficiently familiar to be almost European. Foreignness could become relative, and the Jew, the inside Other, often performed
the role of vital intermediary. The Jew was the inside and outside Other, and, to
follow and build on Boyarin's schema, imposition and expansion without mir-
rored and interacted with imposition and expansion—in the nineteenth century,
of models of the nation—within. Bringing the figure of the Orientalized Jew to
light shows us this. The figure of the Jew in the history of Orientalism disrupts
categories and boundaries in productively messy ways: here and there, us and
them, powerful and disempowered, and even East and West.

# Notes

## Introduction

1. The emancipation of the Jews of France is best understood as a gradual and nonlinear process. See, for example, Paula Hyman, *The Jews of Modern France* (Berkeley: University of California Press, 1998).

2. See Christine Piette, *Les Juifs de Paris (1808–1840): La Marche vers l'assimilation* (Quebec: Presses de l'Université Laval, 1983); and Michael Graetz, *The Jews in Nineteenth-Century France: From the French Revolution to the Alliance Israélite Universelle*, trans. Jane Marie Todd (Stanford, CA: Stanford University Press, 1996). Many Jews, particularly in Alsace, maintained their prerevolutionary village life for some time after the Revolution. See Paula Hyman, *The Emancipation of the Jews of Alsace: Acculturation and Tradition in the Nineteenth Century* (New Haven, CT: Yale University Press, 1991).

3. For a recent review of the literature on Middle Eastern and Sephardi Jewry, see Sarah Stein, "Sephardi and Middle Eastern Jewries since 1492," in *The Oxford Handbook of Jewish Studies*, ed. Martin Cohen, Jeremy Goodman, and David Sorkin (Oxford: Oxford University Press, 2002), 327–362.

4. Théophile Gautier, *Loin de Paris* (Paris: Michel Lévy, 1865); Théophile Gautier, *Constantinople* (Paris: Michel Lévy, 1853).

5. Edward Said, *Orientalism* (1978; repr., New York: Vintage, 1994).

6. Gyan Prakash, "Orientalism Now," *History and Theory* 34, no. 3 (1995): 200.

7. Said, *Orientalism*, 28, 27. Said states in his introduction, "In addition, and by an almost inescapable logic, I have found myself writing the history of a strange, secret sharer of Western anti-Semitism. That anti-Semitism and, as I have discussed it in its Islamic branch, Orientalism resemble each other is a historical, cultural, and political truth that needs only to be mentioned to an Arab Palestinian for its irony to be perfectly understood" (27–28).

8. Ivan Davidson Kalmar and Derek Penslar, eds., *Orientalism and the Jews* (Lebanon, NH: Brandeis University Press, 2004), xv. See also Sander L. Gilman, "'We're Not Jews': Imagining Jewish History and Jewish Bodies in Contemporary Multicultural Literature," in Kalmar and Penslar, *Orientalism and the Jews*, 201.

9. James Pasto, "Islam's 'Strange Secret Sharer': Orientalism, Judaism, and the Jewish Question," *Comparative Studies of Society and History* 40, no. 3 (1998): 472.

10. Kalmar and Penslar, *Orientalism and the Jews*, xv.

11. Brian Cheyette, "White Skin, Black Masks: Jews and Jewishness in the Writings of George Eliot and Frantz Fanon," in *Cultural Readings of Imperialism: Edward Said and the Gravity of History*, ed. Keith Ansell-Pearson, Benita Parry, and Judith Squires (New York: St. Martin's Press, 1997), 124. See also Pasto, "Islam's 'Strange Secret Sharer.'"

12. Kalmar and Penslar, *Orientalism and the Jews*, xv.

13. Bryan Cheyette, *Constructions of "the Jew" in English Literature and Society* (New York: Cambridge University Press, 1993), 4.

14. Jonathan Hess, *Germans, Jews and the Claims of Modernity* (New Haven, CT: Yale University Press, 2002), 13, 88. See also Susannah Heschel, *Abraham Geiger and the Jewish Jesus* (Chicago: University of Chicago Press, 1998), 19–22.

15. Hess, *Germans, Jews and the Claims of Modernity*, 57.

16. Heschel, *Abraham Geiger and the Jewish Jesus*, 21.

17. Jonathan Boyarin, *The Unconverted Self: Jews, Indians, and the Identity of Christian Europe* (Chicago: University of Chicago Press, 2009), 1.

18. Jonathan Boyarin, "Jews, Indians, and the Identity of Christian Europe," *AJS Perspectives*, Fall 2005, p. 13.

19. Boyarin, *The Unconverted Self*, 119n1 (intro) (emphasis in original). "Such an occlusion," he adds, "should not be allowed to stand for long" (119n1 [intro]). See also Cheyette, "White Skin, Black Masks," 124.

20. Said, *Orientalism*, 19.

21. See James McMillan, "Priest Hits Girl: The Front Line of the War of the Two Frances," in *Culture Wars: Secular-Catholic Conflict in Nineteenth-Century Europe*, ed. Christopher Clark and Wolfram Kaiser (New York: Cambridge University Press, 2003), 81. Carol Harrison has recently questioned the notion that Catholics were opposed to modernity in *Romantic Catholics: France's Postrevolutionary Generation in Search of a Modern Faith* (Ithaca, NY: Cornell University Press, 2014).

22. Daniel Schroeter, *The Sultan's Jew: Morocco and the Sephardi World* (Stanford, CA: Stanford University Press, 2002), 121.

23. On the role of Jews as go-betweens in the Ottoman Empire, see ibid.; Thomas Philipp, "The Farhi Family and the Changing Position of the Jews in Syria, 1750–1860," *Middle Eastern Studies* 20, no. 4 (1984): 37–52; Colette Zytnicki, *Les Juifs du Maghreb: Naissance d'une historiographie coloniale* (Paris: Presses de l'Université Paris-Sorbonne, 2011), 21–24; and H. Z. (J. W.) Hirschberg, "Jews and Jewish Affairs in the Relations between Great Britain and Morocco in the 18th Century," in *Essays Presented to Chief Rabbi Israel Brodie on the Occasion of His Seventieth Birthday*, ed. H. J. Zimmels, J. Rabbinowitz, and I. Finestein (London: Soncino Press, 1967), 153–182.

24. Ronald Schechter, *Obstinate Hebrews: Representations of Jews in France, 1715–1815* (Berkeley: University of California Press, 2003), 7–8; Julie Kalman, *Rethinking Antisemitism in Nineteenth-Century France* (New York: Cambridge University Press, 2010), 1–22.

25. French Jewish interest in what they called "Eastern" or "Oriental" Jews dates essentially from around 1840, the Damascus Affair, and the colonization of Algeria. See Lisa Moses Leff, *Sacred Bonds of Solidarity: The Rise of Jewish Internationalism in Nineteenth-Century France* (Stanford, CA: Stanford University Press, 2006), 117–119.

26. See, for example, Maurice Samuels's work on Eugénie Foa in *Inventing the Israelite: Jewish Fiction in Nineteenth-Century France* (Stanford, CA: Stanford University Press, 2010), 37–73; and Leff, *Sacred Bonds of Solidarity*, 102–116.

27. This includes work by David Nirenberg, *Anti-Judaism: The Western Tradition* (New York: Norton, 2013); Schechter, *Obstinate Hebrews*; Cheyette, *Constructions of "the Jew"*; Nadia Valman, *The Jewess in Nineteenth-Century British Literary Culture* (Cambridge: Cambridge University Press, 2007); and Maurice Samuels, "Zola's Philosemitism: From *L'Argent* to *vérité*," in "Zola," special issue, *Romanic Review* 102, no. 3–4 (2011): 503–519.

28. Nirenberg, *Anti-Judaism*, 2.

29. Ibid., 3. See also the work of Ronald Schechter, which predates Nirenberg's work. Schechter suggested that we might understand discourses about Jews in France as a history of the Jew being "good to think" about bigger issues, such as nation and citizenship. Schechter, *Obstinate Hebrews*, 7.

30. Jonathan Karp and Adam Sutcliffe, eds., *Philosemitism in History* (New York: Cambridge University Press, 2011).

31. Gautier, *Loin de Paris*, 28, 30.

32. Ian Coller, *Arab France: Islam and the Making of Modern Europe, 1798–1831* (Berkeley: University of California Press, 2011), 2.

## 1. Pilgrimage to the Holy Land Within

1. René-François de Chateaubriand, *Itinéraire de Paris à Jérusalem*, ed. Jean-Claude Berchet (Paris: Gallimard, 2005), 75–76. Unless otherwise stated, all translations are mine.

2. Paul Bénichou, *Romantismes français*, vol. 1, *Le Sacre de l'écrivain: Le Temps des prophètes* (Paris: Gallimard, 2004), 142.

3. In his *Histoire du romantisme*, literary critic Théophile Gautier called Chateaubriand "the grandfather, or if you prefer, the Sachem of Romanticism in France." Quoted in Fernande Bassan, *Chateaubriand et la terre sainte* (Paris: Douniol, 1959), 217.

4. Charles Baudelaire, "Qu'est-ce que le romantisme?," in *Salon de 1846* (Paris: Lévy, 1846), 6.

5. Joseph Joubert, quoted in Bénichou, *Le Sacre*, 143.

6. Chateaubriand, *Itinéraire*, 448–450. On Catholic criticism of *philosophie* and its association with the Enlightenment, see Darrin McMahon, *Enemies of the Enlightenment: The French Counter-Enlightenment and the Making of Modernity* (New York: Oxford University Press, 2001).

7. In an interesting echo of Jonathan Boyarin's thesis, Chateaubriand's two works could be linked as a project of fantasizing about the spread of Christianity into the New World and returning to the Old.

8. See Eitan Bar-Yosef, *The Holy Land in English Culture, 1799–1914: Palestine and the Question of Orientalism* (Oxford: Oxford University Press, 2005), 6–7.

9. See Ivan Davidson Kalmar and Derek Penslar, "Orientalism and the Jews: An Introduction," in *Orientalism and the Jews*, ed. Ivan Davidson Kalmar and Derek Penslar (Lebanon, NH: Brandeis University Press, 2005), xiv, xxi.

10. Thomas Kselman, *Miracles and Prophecies in Nineteenth-Century France* (New Brunswick, NJ: Rutgers University Press, 1983), 199. See also Raymond Jonas, *France and the Cult of the Sacred Heart: An Epic Tale for Modern Times* (Berkeley: University of California Press, 2000); Ralph Gibson, *A Social History of French Catholicism, 1789–1914* (London: Routledge, 1989); Gérard Cholvy and Yves-Marie Hilaire, *Histoire religieuse de la France contemporaine*, vol. 1, *1800–1880* (Toulouse: Privat, 1990); Ruth Harris, *Lourdes: Body and Spirit in the Secular Age* (London: Allen Lane, 1999).

11. The question of how we might understand the pilgrim is one that anthropologists have been considering for some time. See Victor Turner and Edith Turner, *Image and Pilgrimage in Christian Culture: Anthropological Perspectives* (New York: Columbia University Press, 1978); and a recent summary of theoretical critiques of this work in Ellen Badone and Sharon R. Roseman, eds., *Intersecting Journeys: The Anthropology of Pilgrimage and Tourism* (Champaign: University of Illinois Press, 2004), 3–5. John Eade and Michael Sallnow have argued that the study of pilgrimage is terrain for the formation of competing discourses. The pilgrimage shrine, they argue, is powerful precisely because it functions as a "religious void, a ritual space capable of accommodating diverse meanings and practices." John Eade and Michael J. Sallnow, eds., *Contesting the Sacred: The Anthropology of Christian Pilgrimage* (Urbana: University of Illinois Press, 2000), 15. In this way, each pilgrim group can then impose its own understanding of the shrine's significance or meaning. Eade and Sallnow's understanding of the

pilgrimage space comes together, for Jerusalem, with Halbwachs's notion that Christian memory changes the way that it recollects in each generation, adapting past events to fit current needs. Maurice Halbwachs, "The Legendary Topography of the Gospels in the Holy Land," in *On Collective Memory*, ed. and trans. Lewis A. Coser (Chicago: University of Chicago Press, 1992), 234. These are useful frameworks for thinking about the site of disputed holiness that was—and still is—Jerusalem. (On Jerusalem as a contested holy site, see Simon Goldhill, *Jerusalem: City of Longing* [Cambridge, MA: Belknap Press of Harvard University Press, 2008].)

12. Joseph d'Estourmel, *Journal d'un voyage en Orient* (Paris: Crapelet, 1844), 1:n.p. (preface).

13. On the transition from ultraroyalism to Legitimism, see André Jardin and André-Jean Tudesq, *Restoration and Reaction, 1815–1848*, trans. Elborg Forster (Cambridge: Cambridge University Press, 1983), 189, 236; and René Rémond, *The Right Wing in France from 1815 to De Gaulle*, 2nd ed., trans. James Laux (Philadelphia: University of Pennsylvania Press, 1969), chaps. 1 and 2.

14. François Furet, *Revolutionary France, 1770–1880*, trans. Antonia Nevill (Oxford: Blackwell, 1992), 420.

15. Ibid., 431.

16. Jean Chelini and Henry Branthomme, *Les Chemins de Dieu: Histoire des pèlerinages chrétiens des origines à nos jours* (Paris: Hachette, 1982), 303.

17. James F. McMillan, "Rediscovering Louis Veuillot: The Politics of Religious Identity in Nineteenth-Century France," in *Visions/Revisions: Essays on Nineteenth-Century French Culture*, ed. Nigel Harkness, Paul Rowe, Tim Unwin, and Jennifer Yee (Bern: Peter Lang, 2003), 308. See also Ralph Gibson, *A Social History of French Catholicism, 1789–1914* (London: Routledge, 1989).

18. Louis Bunel, *Jérusalem, la côte de Syrie et Constantinople, en 1853* (Paris: Sagnier et Bray, 1854), v.

19. Kselman, *Miracles and Prophecies*, 196.

20. Constantin-François Volney, *Voyage en Syrie et en Egypte* (Paris: Volland, 1787).

21. Bassan, *Chateaubriand*, 35.

22. Sixty-six pilgrimage accounts are known to have been produced in nineteenth-century France following the publication of Chateaubriand's work. Bassan, *Chateaubriand*, 226. The first guidebook to the Orient, *Guide du voyageur en Orient: Itinéraire artistique et pittoresque*, was produced in 1844 by Quétin.

23. Alexander William Kinglake, *The Invasion of the Crimea: Its Origin, and an Account of Its Progress, down to the Death of Lord Raglan*, vol. 1 (New York: Harper and Brothers, 1863), 49.

24. D'Estourmel, *Journal*, 2:iii. Pilgrims interacted beyond reading one another's work, too. For example, Estourmel received advice from Marcellus and Beugnot, and he traveled for some time with Géramb.

25. Charles-Marie Rosset de Létourville, *Jérusalem: Notes de voyage* (Paris: Amyot, 1856), n.p. (preface).

26. Michel Butor, "Travel and Writing," cited in Robin Jarvis, "Self-Discovery from Byron to Raban: The Long Afterlife of Romantic Travel," *Studies in Travel Writing* 9, no. 2 (2005): 187. Said was the first, of course, to trace the textual tradition in Orientalism.

27. Bassan, *Chateaubriand*, 5.

28. Chateaubriand, quoted in ibid., 221.

29. Bénichou, *Le Sacre*, 259.

30. E.-H. Langlois, *Essai historique et descriptif sur l'Abbaye de Fontenelle*, quoted in James Smith Allen, *Popular French Romanticism: Authors, Readers and Books in the Nineteenth Century* (Syracuse, NY: Syracuse University Press, 1981), 54.

31. Martyn Lyons, *Le Triomphe du livre: Une Histoire sociologique de la lecture dans la France du XIXe siècle* (Paris: Promodis, 1987).

32. Torquato Tasso, *Jerusalem Delivered*, ed. and trans. Anthony Esolen (Baltimore: Johns Hopkins University Press, 2000), 391.

33. Ibid., 400.

34. Ibid., 56.

35. Ibid., 413.

36. James Smith Allen undertook a sampling of the more than one hundred thousand new titles that appeared between 1820 and 1840 and found a strong interest in the medieval period. Allen, *Popular French Romanticism*, 54.

37. R. J. Zwi Werblowsky, "The Meaning of Jerusalem to Jews, Christians, and Muslims," in *Jerusalem in the Mind of the Western World, 1800–1948*, ed. Yehoshua Ben Arieh and Moshe Davis (Westport, CT: Praeger, 1997), 7.

38. Norman Roth, ed., *Medieval Jewish Civilization: An Encyclopedia* (New York: Routledge, 2003), 491.

39. Tudor Parfitt, *The Jews in Palestine, 1800–1882* (Woodbridge, UK: Boydell Press, 1987), 1–10.

40. Naomi Shepherd, *The Zealous Intruders: The Western Rediscovery of Palestine* (London: Collins, 1987), 73.

41. Among these societies were the Société asiatique, established in 1821, which produced the *Journal asiatique*; the Société de géographie, which printed a *Bulletin* from 1822 to 1899; the Société orientale, of which Chateaubriand was a member and which produced the *Revue de l'Orient* from 1843 to 1868.

42. In his work on historical fiction in France, Maurice Samuels has described in detail how reading audiences developed a strong taste for descriptive histories, such as those produced by Walter Scott. See Maurice Samuels, *The Spectacular Past: Popular History and the Novel in Nineteenth-Century France* (Ithaca, NY: Cornell University Press, 2004), 151–194.

43. Untitled article, *Bulletin de l'oeuvre des pèlerinages*, July 1856–October 1858, p. 9.

44. Ibid., 58. It is interesting to note in this context that Abbé Delorme, perhaps hoping for a similar effect, addressed his work to an imagined cohort of "young readers." Abbé Delorme, *Un Pèlerinage en Terre Sainte, par l'abbé Delorme* (Limoges: Barbou frères, 1860), n.p. His work had the stamp of the *Bibliothèque chrétienne et morale* (the Christian moral library, a publishing series similar to, and in competition with, the *Bibliothèque morale de la jeunesse*) and approval from the bishop of Limoges.

45. Chelini and Branthomme, *Chemins de Dieu*, 317.

46. Louis Enault, *La Terre sainte: Voyage de quarante pèlerins de 1853* (Paris: Maison, 1854); Abbé Azaïs, *Pèlerinage en Terre-Sainte* (Paris: E. Giraud, 1855); R. P. Amédée de Damas, *Voyages en Orient: Jérusalem* (Paris: Delhomme et Briguet, [1866]); Marie-Joseph Daspres, *Pèlerinage en Terre-Sainte: Journal de la caravane partie de Marseille le 28 août et dissoute à Beyrouth, le 20 octobre 1869* (Paris: J. Lefort, 1875).

47. The dispute centered on who had the right to be keeper of the key to the Church of the Nativity in Bethlehem. The Orthodox Church had held the key, but the Ottomans had bestowed this right on the French, as the representative of Catholicism in the Holy Land. On the Crimean War in the Holy Land, see Goldhill, *Jerusalem*, 237–238; Bernard Wasserstein, *Divided Jerusalem: The Struggle for the Holy City*, 3rd ed. (New Haven, CT: Yale University Press, 2008), 42–44; and Candan Badem, *The Ottoman Crimean War (1853–1856)* (Leiden, Netherlands: Brill, 2010), 343–346.

48. Delorme, *Pèlerinage*, 73.

49. Edouard Blondel, *Deux ans en Syrie, 1838–9* (Paris: Dufart, 1840), 212.

50. Félicien de Saulcy, *Les Derniers jours de Jérusalem* (Paris: L. Hachette, 1866), 2. Simon Goldhill has described Saulcy as a "nineteenth-century French travel writer, social climber and archaeologist." Goldhill, *Jerusalem*, 216.

51. See Léon E. S. J. Laborde, *Voyage de la Syrie, par MM. Alexandre de Laborde, Becker, Hall et Léon de Laborde, rédigé et publié par Léon de Laborde [et A. de Laborde]* (Paris: Firmin-Didot frères, 1837); and Léon E. S. J. Laborde, *L'Orient et le moyen âge, par M. Léon de la Borde* (Paris: 20, rue des Grands-Augustins, 1833). In 1842 Laborde was elected a member of the Académie des inscriptions et belles lettres. In 1847 he was appointed curator of the Department of Antiquities at the Louvre, and a year later he became the curator of the collections of the Middle Ages and the Renaissance.

52. Laborde, *Voyage de la Syrie*, 73.

53. Bar-Yosef, *Holy Land*, 8.

54. Halbwachs, "Legendary Topography," 200.

55. Ibid., 205.

56. Enault, *La Terre sainte*, 110.

57. Ibid., 97.

58. Laborde, *Voyage de la Syrie*, 3.

59. Xavier Marmier, *Du Rhin au Nil: Souvenirs de voyages*, vol. 2 (Paris: Bertrand, 1847), quoted in Bassan, *Chateaubriand*, 225.

60. Laborde, *Voyage de la Syrie*, 2.

61. Laborde, *L'Orient*, 47.

62. Chateaubriand, *Itinéraire*, 425.

63. Ibid., 427, 430.

64. Ibid., 440.

65. Vidal de Langon, *Jérusalem et la Terre Sainte* (Bordeaux: J. Dupuy, 1846), 110.

66. Henri Cornille, *Souvenirs d'Orient*, 2nd ed. (Paris: Bertrand, 1836), 333.

67. Damas, *Voyages en Orient*, 5.

68. Jean-Hippolyte Michon, *Voyage religieux en Orient* (Paris: Vve Comon, 1853), 2:390.

69. J.-V. de la Roière, *Voyage en Orient* (Paris: Debécourt, 1836), 131.

70. Damas, *Voyages en Orient*, 508.

71. Vidal, *Jérusalem*, 9, 7, 145.

72. Marmier, *Impression et souvenirs*, 192–193.

73. Chateaubriand, *Itinéraire*, 317. According to Laborde, "You must understand the Orient and its traditions, as you listen to a traveler and his memories. In Syria, everything breathes biblical antiquity; the sites are commentaries on the sacred texts. There, every stone, every stream, everything, even the worm-eaten tree trunks, offers itself as guide to the pilgrim traveler, showing him the way he must follow to discover each event." Laborde, *Voyage de la Syrie*, 2.

74. Bryan Cheyette calls it "encompassing the unruly Jew." Bryan Cheyette, *Constructions of "the Jew" in English Literature and Society* (New York: Cambridge University Press, 1993), 269.

75. Vidal, *Jérusalem*, 130–131.

76. On this point, see Ivan Kalmar, "Jesus Did Not Wear a Turban: Orientalism, the Jews, and Christian Art," in *Orientalism and the Jews*, ed. Ivan Davidson Kalmar and Derek Penslar (Lebanon, NH: Brandeis University Press, 2004), 19.

77. Delorme, *Pèlerinage*, 78.

78. Vidal, *Jérusalem*, 9.

79. Blondel, *Deux ans en Syrie*, 212.

80. Cornille, *Souvenirs d'Orient*, 336.

81. Auguste de Forbin, *Voyage dans le Levant, en 1817 et 1818* (Paris: L'Imprimerie royale, 1819), 444; R. P. Marie-Joseph de Géramb, *Pèlerinage à Jérusalem et au mont Sinaï, en 1831, 1832, et 1833*, 2nd ed., 2 vols. (Paris: Leclère, 1836), 89; Marmier, *Impressions et souvenirs*, 220, 279.

82. Vidal, *Jérusalem*, 118.

83. Forbin, *Voyage dans le Levant*, 86.

84. P.-Gérardy Saintine [Xavier Boniface], *Trois ans en Judée* (Paris: Hachette, 1860), 190, 185.

85. Enault, *Terre Sainte*, 170–171.

86. Vidal, *Jérusalem*, 118.

87. Forbin, *Voyage dans le Levant*, 86. See also Vidal, *Jérusalem*, 119.

88. Forbin, *Voyage dans le Levant*, 86.

89. D'Estourmel, *Journal*, 355.

90. Marie-Louis-Jean-André-Charles Marcellus, *Souvenirs de l'Orient* (Paris: Debucourt, 1839), 2:74.

91. Géramb, *Pèlerinage*, 102.

92. Marmier, *Impressions et souvenirs*, 279.

93. Ibid., 250.

94. Forbin, *Voyage dans le Levant*, 86.

95. Marmier, *Impressions et souvenirs*, 254.

96. Géramb, *Pèlerinage*, 104. The rhetoric of these pilgrims forms a contrast with Evangelical Protestant visitors from Britain and America, for whom the Jews of Jerusalem served a very different purpose. Jews in Palestine were a disappointment to them, but they disappointed the Protestant clergyman who visited the Holy Land in two ways, both very different from the ways they were drawn by French Catholic pilgrims. These two ways speak to the priorities and desires of Evangelical Protestants. First, the Sephardic Jews in Jerusalem were no longer warlike or agrarian and could not be seen or described as descendants of the original Israelites. They had to be eliminated from efforts to authenticate them as "contemporary 'illustrations'" of the Bible. Shepherd, *The Zealous Intruders*, 93. Second, they showed no signs of wishing to convert and bring about the return of the Jews, the necessary precursor to the Second Coming of Christ. See Bar-Yosef, *Holy Land*, 182–202.

97. Damas, *Voyages*, 108, 109.

98. Charles-Louis de Secondat, Baron de Montesquieu, *Lettres persanes*, letter 60, quoted in Marcellus, *Souvenirs*, 2:75.

99. Montesquieu, *Lettres persanes*, letter 60, 127–128. On Jews in Montesquieu's letters, see Ronald Schechter, *Obstinate Hebrews: Representations of Jews in France, 1715–1815* (Berkeley: University of California Press, 2003), 38–39.

100. Marcellus, *Souvenirs*, 2:75.

101. Vidal, *Jérusalem*, 191–192.

102. Cornille, *Souvenirs d'Orient*, 338.

103. Ibid., 337–338.

104. Marmier, *Impression et souvenirs*, 276.

105. Géramb, *Pèlerinage*, 95.

106. Marmier, *Impressions et souvenirs*, 277.

107. Ibid., 276.

108. Daspres, *Pèlerinage en Terre-Sainte*, 130.

109. Marcellus, *Souvenirs*, 2:75; see also Delorme, *Pèlerinage*, 128.

110. Daspres, *Pèlerinage en Terre-Sainte*, 130.

111. Géramb, *Pèlerinage*, 95.

112. Damas, *Voyages*, 110.

113. Saintine, *Trois ans en Judée*, 187–188.

114. Marmier, *Impressions et souvenirs*, 279.

115. Géramb, *Pèlerinage*, 94. One rare voice of dissent in this tide was that of the Viscount de Vogüé, who understood there to be a clear distinction between the Jews of the East and those of the West:

> We must add that these paintings and reflections, that the singularity of the Jews of Palestine inspire in all travelers, have nothing at all to do with the many Israelites who, through their industry, intelligence, and patriotism, have created an honorable place in our European societies for themselves. The majority of them would be the first to be saddened by the moral and material degeneration in which their coreligionists in Syria seem to revel and to pity a cast that has voluntarily separated itself from the rest of humanity.

Eugène Melchior de Vogüé, *Syrie, Palestine, Mount Athos: Voyage au pays du passé* (Paris: Plon, 1876), 110.

116. Joseph d'Estourmel stayed in the home of a Polish Jew named Weissman in Tiberius. D'Estourmel, *Journal*, vol. 1, especially p. 354. Laborde had a rabbi as his host in Nablus. Maxime du Camp, traveling through Palestine, was offered a meal by a Jewish family from Jerusalem. Maxime du Camp, *Voyage en Orient, 1849–1851*, ed. Giovanni Bonaccorso (Messina: Peloritana Editrice, 1972), 205–207.

117. Gillot de Kerhardène, *Voyage en Orient: Course de Tibériade à Capharnaüm* (Roanne, France: Ferlay 1860), 3.

118. Saintine, *Trois ans en Judée*, 191.

119. Damas, *Voyages*, 106.

120. Géramb, *Pèlerinage*, 96–98.

121. Clara Filleul de Petigny, *La Palestine, ou Une visite aux Lieux-Saints* (Rouen: Mégard, 1867), 131. The *Bibliothèque morale de la jeunesse* was a series of moral works for young readers, produced by the Mégard publishing house of Rouen. Over the nineteenth and into the twentieth centuries, it produced twenty-seven hundred titles and ten million copies. Each title was reviewed by a committee of bishops before publication.

122. A. Berthon, *Bérénice, ou Le Pèlerinage à Jérusalem* (Tours: Pornin, 1843).

123. Georges Darboy, *Jérusalem et la Terre-Sainte: Notes de voyage* (Paris: Belin-Leprieur et Morizot, [1852]), vi.

124. Vidal, *Jérusalem*, 191.

125. Forbin, *Voyage dans le Levant*, n.p. (preface).

126. Pierre-Antoine Lebrun, "Voyages: Voyage dans le Levant en 1817 et 1818 par M. le Comte de Forbin," *La Renommée* 30 (1819): 120.

127. Marcellus, *Souvenirs*, 86. Charles Ferdinand d'Artois, the Duke de Berry, was assassinated at the Paris Opera in 1820 by Louis Pierre Louvel, an antiroyal Bonapartist.

128. D'Estourmel, *Journal*, 2:509–510.

129. Chateaubriand, *Itinéraire*, 301, 446, 351.

130. Cornille, *Souvenirs*, 353.

131. Delorme, *Pèlerinage*, 55–56.

132. Saulcy, *Jérusalem*, 1–2.

133. Enault, *Terre Sainte*, 169.

134. Alphonse de Lamartine, *Voyage en Orient: 1832–1833* (Paris: C. Gosselin, 1841), 1:324.

135. Concern regarding the Orthodox Church was a theme in other works, too. Abbé Jean-Hippolyte Michon visited the Jewish quarter early in the 1850s. He had read Chateaubriand and made reference to him. But for Michon, the Satan to Catholicism's Jesus was not the Jews but the Greek Orthodox Church. Michon, *Voyage religieux en Orient*; see also Jacques Mislin, *Les Saints lieux*, 2 vols. (Paris: Guyot frères, 1851). Victor Guérin wrote a report on pilgrimage to the Holy Land in 1873, and he was driven by a sense that the need to ensure the presence of French Catholicism there, in opposition to the forces of Greek Orthodoxy, was overwhelming. For him, the phenomenon of pilgrimage was vital work that rendered "true service" to France, a country

"certainly more Catholic at heart than its government." Victor Guérin, *Rapport sur les pèleri-nages en Terre Sainte, par M. Guérin* (Paris: Imprimerie de G. Chamerot, [1873]), 10. For these men, the Orthodox Church was unwanted and frankly illegal competition in the Holy Land.

136. Xavier Marmier, *En pays lointains* (Paris: Hachette, 1876), 99.

137. Gustave Flaubert, *Voyage en Palestine* (Paris: Magellan, 2008), 31.

138. Du Camp, *Voyage en Orient*, 213–214.

139. Frédéric August Antoine Goupil, *Voyage en Orient fait avec Horace Vernet en 1839 et 1840* (Paris: Challamel, [1843]), 174.

140. Jean-Baptiste Morot, *Journal de voyage: Paris à Jérusalem, 1839 et 1840* (Paris: Claye, 1869), 205, 213.

141. Flaubert, *Voyage*, 32. He did note that the Armenian quarter was "well swept."

142. Du Camp, *Voyage en Orient*, 208 (emphasis mine).

143. Morot, *Journal de voyage*, 2.

144. Halvor Moxnes, "Renan's *Vie de Jésus* as Representation of the Orient," in *Jews, Antiquity, and the Nineteenth-Century Imagination*, ed. Hayim Lapin and Dale B. Martin (Bethesda, MD: University Press of Maryland, 2003), 92, 103–107.

145. On Renan and Jews, see, for example, Maurice Hayoun, *Renan, la bible et les juifs* (Paris: Gallimard, 2008).

146. Ernest Renan, *Vie de Jésus*, 13th ed. (Paris: Julliard, 1962), 311.

147. Ernest Renan, *Mission de Phénicie* (Paris: Lévy, 1864), 791.

148. Ibid., 786.

149. Ibid., 789.

150. Ibid., 786.

151. In his conclusion, Renan states that he sought "less to shine than to be a servant in the progression of science." Ibid., 815.

152. See Jonathan Boyarin, *The Uncoverted Self: Jews, Indians, and the Identity of Christian Europe* (Chicago: University of Chicago Press, 2009), 2.

153. On the culture wars, see McMillan, "Rediscovering Louis Veuillot"; Robert Gildea, *The Past in French History* (New Haven, CT: Yale University Press, 1994), chap. 1; and Pierre Nora, dir., *Realms of Memory: Rethinking the French Past*, ed. Lawrence D. Kritzman, trans. Arthur Goldhammer (New York: Columbia University Press, 1996), 1:22–23.

154. See Julie Kalman, "Going Home to the Holy Land: The Jews of Jerusalem in Nineteenth-Century French Catholic Pilgrimage," *Journal of Modern History* 84, no. 2 (2012): 336–340.

155. Félicien de Saulcy, *Voyage autour de la Mer Morte et dans les terres bibliques, executé de décembre 1850 à avril 1851* (Paris: Gide et J. Baudry, 1853), 2:514.

156. Ibid.

## 2. Travel and Intimacy

1. Françoise Court-Perez, *Gautier, un romantique ironique* (Paris: Champion, 1998), 11–12.

2. Letter from Wilhelm Ténint to Théophile Gautier, January 15, 1844, in Claudine Lacoste-Veysseyre [Théophile Gautier], ed., *Correspondance générale* (Geneva: Droz, 1985), 2:117.

3. "The highly benevolent remarks that you wrote, in your edition of the first of October, in terms that were so flattering to me, convince me that you are indulgent, and good. . . . Permit me, Sir, to express, here, all my gratitude, as well as that of my family, who you have made very happy." Letter from Bouffé to Théophile Gautier, October 8, 1844, in Lacoste-Veysseyre, *Correspondance*, 2:184.

4. Gautier has his own devoted society and bulletin (see http://www.theophilegautier .fr/presentation-societe).

5. Mary Louise Pratt, *Imperial Eyes: Travel Writing and Transculturation*, 2nd ed. (New York: Routledge, 2008), 4.

6. Ibid., 53.

7. Nigel Leask, *British Romantic Writers and the East: Anxieties of Empire* (Cambridge: Cambridge University Press, 1992), 2.

8. Edward Said, *Culture and Imperialism* (New York: Knopf, 1993), xxi.

9. Ibid., 99.

10. Pratt, *Imperial Eyes*; see also David Spurr, *The Rhetoric of Empire* (Durham, NC: Duke University Press, 1993); Timothy Fulford and Peter J. Kitson, eds., *Romanticism and Colonialism: Writing and Empire, 1780–1830* (Cambridge: Cambridge University Press, 1998); Amanda Gilroy, ed., *Romantic Geographies: Discourses of Travel 1775–1844* (Manchester, UK: Manchester University Press, 2000); Jocelyn Hackforth-Jones and Mary Roberts, eds., *Edges of Empire: Orientalism and Visual Culture* (Oxford: Blackwell, 2005).

11. Anthony Pagden, *European Encounters with the New World: From Renaissance to Romanticism* (New Haven, CT: Yale University Press, 1993), 184.

12. Théophile Gautier, *Portrait de Balzac, précédé de Portrait de Théophile Gautier, par lui-même* (1859; repr., Montpellier: L'Anabase, 1994), 15–16.

13. Emile Bergerat, *Théophile Gautier: Entretiens, souvenirs et correspondance; Avec une préface de Edmond de Goncourt, et une eau-forte de Félix Bracquemond* (Paris: Charpentier, 1879), 48.

14. Théophile Gautier, *Histoire du romantisme* (Paris: Charpentier, 1882), 4.

15. Paul Bénichou, *Romantismes français*, vol. 2, *Les Mages romantiques: L'Ecole du désenchantement* (Paris: Quarto/Gallimard, 1992).

16. Charles Sainte-Beuve, "Du Mouvement littéraire et poétique après la Révolution de 1830," *Le Globe*, October 11, 1830.

17. Bénichou, *Romantismes français*, 2:1478–1479.

18. Bergerat, *Théophile Gautier*, xiv.

19. Gautier, *Histoire du romantisme*, 3.

20. Bénichou, *Romantismes français*, 2:1997.

21. For example, Françoise Court-Perez titled her work *Gautier, un romantique ironique*.

22. Théophile Gautier, "Liminaire," *La Revue de Paris*, 1851, p. 11, quoted in Bénichou, *Romantismes français*, 2:1993.

23. Marcel Voisin, "Théophile Gautier et la politique," *Bulletin de la Société Théophile Gautier* 15 (2003): 327. On Romanticism in opposition to modernity, see also Michael Löwy and Robert Sayre, *Romanticism against the Tide of Modernity*, trans. Catherine Porter (Durham, NC: Duke University Press, 2001), 1.

24. Löwy and Sayre, *Romanticism*, 19, 29–30. See also Voisin, "Théophile Gautier et la politique," 329.

25. On Romanticism and nostalgia for the Middle Ages, see Maurice Cranston, "Romanticism and Revolution," *History of European Ideas* 17, no. 1 (1993): 24–25.

26. Charles Baudelaire, "Théophile Gautier," *L'Artiste*, March 13, 1859, p. 166.

27. Théophile Gautier, preface to *Jeunes-France*, 28, quoted in Bénichou, *Romantismes français*, 2:1964.

28. Théophile Gautier, "Sommités contemporaines: M. Th. Gautier," *L'Illustration*, March 9, 1867, quoted in Bénichou, *Romantismes français*, 2:1965.

29. Voisin, "Théophile Gautier et la politique," 327.

30. Théophile Gautier, *Les Vendeurs du temple*, in *La Comédie de la mort* (Paris: Desessart, 1838); Théophile Gautier, *Constantinople* (Paris: Michel Lévy, 1853); Théophile Gautier, *Le Roman de la momie* (Paris: Charpentier, 1955); Théophile Gautier, *Voyage en Russie* (Paris: Garnier-Flammarion, 1867); and Théophile Gautier, *Tableaux de siège: Paris 1870–1871* (Paris: Charpentier, 1871).

31. Martine Lavaud, *Théophile Gautier: Militant du romantisme* (Paris: Champion, 2001), 476.

32. Ibid., 492.

33. *Les Français à Constantine* was one such example. See Louis Péricaud, *Le Théâtre des Funambules, ses mimes, ses acteurs, et ses pantomimes, depuis sa fondation, jusqu'à sa démolition* (Paris: Sapin, 1897), cited in Claude Book-Senninger, *Théophile Gautier: Auteur dramatique* (Paris: Nizet, 1972), 234.

34. On the background to the writing of the play, see Claudine Lacoste, "La Juive de Constantine," *Bulletin de la Société Théophile Gautier* 26 (2004): 305; and Book-Senninger, *Théophile Gautier*, 233. These two short pieces were for a long time the only studies of this play—both in French. Both assess the play on its merits as a melodrama but do not seek to take it beyond these limits. Maurice Samuels's recent article is a significant addition to the scholarship on the play. See Maurice Samuels, "Philosemitism and the *Mission Civilisatrice* in Gautier's *La Juive de Constantine*," *French Forum* 38, no. 1–2 (2013): 19–33.

35. Book-Senninger, *Théophile Gautier*, 230.

36. Théophile Gautier, untitled article, *La Presse*, November 16, 1846.

37. Samuels, "Philosemitism," 29.

38. Jennifer Sessions has described how the army was understood as representing "the standard of patriotic and masculine virtue against which men of the July Monarchy were to be measured." Jennifer Sessions, *By Sword and Plow: France and the Conquest of Algeria* (Ithaca, NY: Cornell University Press, 2011), 141.

39. See, for example, Luce Klein, *Portrait de la juive dans la littérature française* (Paris: Nizet, 1970).

40. See Book-Senninger, *Théophile Gautier*, 236.

41. Lacoste, "La Juive de Constantine," 306.

42. Théophile Gautier, *La Juive de Constantine* (Paris: Marchant, 1846), 2.

43. Ibid., 3. It is possible that Nathan's invocation of blood both references and inverts Shylock's famous speech from act 3, scene 1 of *The Merchant of Venice*. I am grateful to David Feldman for this suggestion.

44. This is known in Judaism as *kapparot*.

45. Gautier, *La Juive de Constantine*, 27.

46. Book-Senninger, *Théophile Gautier*, 240–241.

47. Gautier's inclusion of patriotic statements could also be understood, as Sessions has argued, as a form of criticism of the July Monarchy and its "cautious diplomacy." Sessions, *Sword and Plow*, 141. To express patriotism as the will to invade Algeria, in this context, was to express a patriotism that harkened back to Napoleon: it was hard and virile. Samuels argues that the play should be read in the context of discussions over whether to extend rights to Jews and Muslims in Algeria. Samuels, "Philosemitism," 23.

48. Gautier, *La Juive de Constantine*, 2.

49. Ibid., 17.

50. Ibid., 15.

51. Ibid., 4.

52. Ibid., 8.

53. Ibid., 22. Maurice uses the familiar *tu*.

54. The one rabbi who has a speaking part is referred to in the script as "First Rabbi."

55. Gautier, *La Juive de Constantine*, 23.

56. Ibid., 12.

57. According to Samuels's reading of the play, the Jews can be redeemed because they are prepared, in contrast to the Arabs, to renounce the authority of their own religious law. Samuels, "Philosemitism," 30.

58. Ibid., 24. Samuels reads Kadidja's veiling as significant in that it signifies her backwardness and, by extension, that of Islam more generally. He argues also that this makes Kadidjah invisible and thus unknowable, in contrast to Léa, whose beauty can be seen and celebrated. This is another possible reading of the ways that Jews and Arabs work to define one another in the play. Ibid., 28.

59. Ibid., 18.

60. Ibid., 21.

61. Paul Lamy, untitled review, *La Patrie*, November 15, 1846.

62. Auguste Vacquerie, untitled review, *L'Epoque*, November 16, 1846.

63. T. Sauvage, untitled review, *Le Moniteur universel*, November 16, 1846, p. 4.

64. Paul Lamy, untitled review, *La Patrie*, November 22, 1846.

65. The play is named for the Mazagran fortress in Algiers, ceded to France in 1837.

66. Théophile Gautier, untitled review, *La Presse*, April 27, 1840.

67. Gautier, untitled article, *La Presse*, November 16, 1846.

68. Ibid.

69. Ibid. In this context, it is interesting to note that when he was consulted in 1849 during the preparation of a law on the theater, Gautier was to plead for the wisdom of the audience: "Use no censors other than the public: they are rigorous and enlightened critics who cannot be gainsaid. . . . Have faith in their wisdom and intelligence." Charles Spoelberch de Lovenjoul, *Histoire des oeuvres de Théophile Gautier* (Geneva: Slatkine, 1968), 2: 579, quoted in Voisin, "Théophile Gautier et la politique," 328.

70. Lamy, untitled review, *La Patrie*, November 15, 1846.

71. F.D., untitled review, *Le Furet de Paris*, November 16, 1846, p. 3.

72. Colette Zytnicki, *Les Juifs du Maghreb: Naissance d'une historiographie coloniale* (Paris: Presses de l'Université Paris-Sorbonne, 2011), 24.

73. Ronald Schechter, *Obstinate Hebrews: Representations of Jews in France, 1715–1815* (Berkeley: University of California Press, 2003), 5–10.

74. Jean-Claude Berchet, ed., *Le Voyage en Orient: Anthologie des voyageurs français dans le Levant au XIXe siècle* (Paris: Robert Laffont, 1985), 5.

75. Jean Richer, *Etudes et recherches sur Théophile Gautier, prosateur* (Paris: Nizet, 1981), 76–77. See also Lavaud, *Théophile Gautier*, 334–335.

76. John Sellards, *Dans le sillage du romantisme: Charles Didier (1805–1864)* (Paris: Champion, 1933).

77. Gérard de Nerval, *Le Voyage en Orient*, 3rd ed., 2 vols. (Paris: Charpentier, 1851).

78. Daniel Roche, "Les Livres de voyage à l'époque moderne XVIe–XVIIIe siècles," *Dossier: Voyages, Revue de la Bibliothèque nationale de France* 22 (2006): 5–13; Yasmine Marcil, "'Voyage écrit, voyage vécu?' La Crédibilité du voyageur, du Journal encyclopédique au Magasin encyclopédique," in "Le Siècle du voyage," special issue, *Sociétés et représentations* 21 (2006): 25–43, cited in Elisabeth Fraser, "Books, Prints, and Travel: Reading in the Gaps of the Orientalist Archive," *Art History* 31, no. 3 (2008): 343. For a discussion of the popularity of travel books in England, see Nigel Leask, *Curiosity and the Aesthetics of Travel Writing, 1770–1840*:

*"From an Antique Land"* (Oxford: Oxford University Press, 2002), 11–12. Leask writes of travel writing permeating "all levels of eighteenth- and nineteenth-century literary culture" (12). Elisabeth Fraser has shown that, up to 1850, the travel account could be an extravagant affair: "Lavish engravings, and then lithography from the early nineteenth century, became the norm. Of high artistic quality and often folio-sized, these prints were produced at great expense and disseminated in instalments to subscribers." Fraser, "Books, Prints, and Travel," 343. The *Voyage de la Syrie*, a travel account written by Count Léon de Laborde, is one example of such productions. Léon Laborde, *Voyage de la Syrie, par MM. Alexandre de Laborde, Becker, Hall et Léon de Laborde, rédigé et publié par Léon de Laborde [et A. de Laborde]* (Paris: Firmin-Didot frères, 1837). My consultation of this work in the Bibliothèque nationale required the organizational involvement of several members of staff and barely used equipment.

79. Richer, *Etudes et recherches*, 76. See also Alphonse de Lamartine, *Souvenirs, impressions, pensées et paysages pendant un voyage en Orient (1832–1833) ou Notes d'un voyageur*, 4 vols. (Paris: Gosselin, 1835); Alphonse de Lamartine, *Voyage en Orient: 1832–1833*, 2 vols. (Paris: Gosselin, 1841); Alexandre Dumas and Adrien Dauzats, *Quinze jours au Sinaï* (Paris: Editions d'aujourd'hui, 1839), which was published in multiple editions; Alexandre Dumas, *Le Véloce, ou De Cadix à Tunis* (1848, repr., Paris: Bourin, 1990); Maxime du Camp, *Souvenirs et paysages d'Orient* (Paris: Bertrand, 1848); Gustave Flaubert, *Voyage en Egypte*, ed. Pierre-Marc de Biasi (Paris: Grasset, 1991). Flaubert traveled in 1849–1850. Gautier and Nerval were close friends with Joseph Lingay, secretary to the chairman of the Council of Ministers from 1816 to 1848. He used his position to obtain grants for his friends to travel. C. W. Thompson, *French Romantic Travel Writing: Chateaubriand to Nerval* (Oxford: Oxford University Press, 2012), 84.

80. Guy Dumur believes that the choice of Delacroix for the role was no coincidence: not only was he known for his *Liberty Guiding the People*; he was also, according to Dumur, a "child of the Empire." Guy Dumur, *Delacroix et le Maroc* (Paris: Herscher, 1988), 9. Delacroix's father was a minister under the Directory and later an ambassador and prefect. His two brothers were officers in the Napoleonic army; the youngest lost his life at the Battle of Austerlitz. Maurice Regard explains that Delacroix was present on the expedition because he had been chosen as a traveling companion by the Count de Mornay "to make an unbearable journey bearable." Maurice Regard, "Eugène Delacroix et le comte de Mornay au Maroc," *Etudes d'Art* 7 (1952): 32.

81. Charles de Pardieu, *Excursion en Orient: L'Egypte, le Mont-Sinaï, l'Arabie, la Palestine, la Syrie, le Liban* (Paris: Garnier, 1851), 1.

82. Emile Barrault and E. De Cadalvène, *Deux années de l'histoire d'Orient, 1839–1840: Faisant suite à l'histoire de la guerre de Méhemed-Ali en Syrie et en Asie mineure (1832–1833)* (Paris: Delloye, 1840), 1:vii.

83. Court-Perez, *Gautier, un romantique ironique*, 11–12.

84. Théophile Gautier, *Portrait de Balzac*, 19.

85. Letter from Théophile Gautier to Gérard de Nerval, July 25, 1843, in Lacoste-Veysseyre, *Correspondance*, 2:41. The letter was also published in *La Presse*, July 25, 1843.

86. [Julie Bernat], *La Vie d'une grande comédienne: Mémoires de Madame Judith, de la comédie française, et souvenirs sur ses contemporains* (Paris: Tallandier, 1911), 236–377.

87. Bergerat, *Théophile Gautier*, 67.

88. "In this way, we came to a strange quarter." Gautier, *Constantinople*, 231. Gautier employed the same tool for his description of the Venice ghetto and used almost identical language. See Théophile Gautier, *Italia*, 2nd ed. (Paris: Hachette, 1855), 384–390; Julie Kalman, "The Jew in the Scenery: Historicising Nineteenth-Century French Travel Literature," *French History* 27, no. 4 (2013): 519–521.

89. Gautier, *Constantinople*, 231.

90. Ibid., 232.

91. Ibid.

92. Ibid.

93. Gautier described himself as the "painter" of his group: "I laid out all the colors of the sunrise on the palette of my style." Bergerat, *Théophile Gautier*, 117, quoted in Malcolm Easton, *Artists and Writers in Paris: The Bohemian Idea, 1803–1867* (London: Edward Arnold, 1964), 70.

94. Gautier, *Constantinople*, 233.

95. Lavaud, *Théophile Gautier*, 479. Of his travels in Egypt in 1854, Charles Didier wrote in his preface, "The author has invented nothing; as always, he has only recounted what he saw." Charles Didier, *Cinquante Jours au désert*, quoted in John Sellards, *Dans le sillage du romantisme*, 179.

96. Gautier, *Constantinople*, 231.

97. Steve Clark, ed., *Travel Writing and Empire: Postcolonial Theory in Transit* (London: Zed Books, 1999), 1.

98. Victoria Thompson, "'I Went Pale with Pleasure': The Body, Sexuality, and National Identity among French Travelers to Algiers in the Nineteenth Century," in *Algeria and France, 1800–2000: Identity, Memory, Nostalgia*, ed. Patricia Lorcin (Syracuse, NY: Syracuse University Press, 2006), 23.

99. Robin Jarvis, "Self-Discovery from Byron to Raban: The Long Afterlife of Romantic Travel," *Studies in Travel Writing* 9, no. 2 (2005): 185.

100. See David Wrobel, "Exceptionalism and Globalism: Travel Writers and the Nineteenth-Century American West," *The Historian* 68, no. 3 (2006): 431.

101. Andrew Aisenberg, *Contagion: Disease, Government and the Social Question in Nineteenth-Century France* (Stanford, CA: Stanford University Press, 1999), 28. See also Catherine Kudlick, *Cholera in Post-revolutionary Paris: A Cultural History* (Berkeley: University of California Press, 1996), especially 31–64.

102. Gautier, *Constantinople*, 231.

103. Ibid., 233.

104. Ibid.

105. Lavaud, *Théophile Gautier*, 493.

106. Gautier, *Loin de Paris* (Paris: Michel Lévy, 1865), 28.

107. Ibid., 30.

108. The imagery is borrowed from Klein, *Portrait de la juive*, 174.

109. Théophile Gautier, *Voyage pittoresque en Algérie*, ed. Madeleine Cottin (Geneva: Droz, 1973), 187.

110. Baron Marie-Théodore Renoüard de Bussièrre, *Lettres sur l'Orient, écrites pendant les années 1827 et 1828* (Paris: Levrault, 1829), 2:49.

111. Louis Enault, *Constantinople et la Turquie: Tableau historique, pittoresque, statistique et moral de l'empire ottoman* (Paris: Hachette, 1855), 371.

112. Abbé Azaïs, *Journal d'un voyage en Orient* (Avignon: Seguin, 1858), 274.

113. Bussièrre, *Lettres sur l'Orient*, 2:49.

114. Enault, *Constantinople et la Turquie*, 371.

115. Samuel Romanelli, a Jew from Italy, traveled in Morocco at the end of the eighteenth century and described his coreligionists there in strikingly similar terms: they were ignorant and superstitious. Daniel Schroeter has discussed the way that Romanelli's attitudes inscribed him in "the European image of Barbary," underscoring, perhaps, Romanelli's place in Europe. Daniel J. Schroeter, "Orientalism and the Jews of the Mediterranean," *Journal of Mediterranean Studies* 4, no. 2 (1994): 184.

116. Charles Didier, *Promenade au Maroc* (Paris: Labitte, 1844), 171.

117. Ibid., 162.

118. Ibid., 153.

119. Joseph-François Michaud and Jean-Joseph-François Poujoulat, *Correspondance d'Orient, 1830–1831* (Paris: Ducollet, 1833), 2:227.

120. Didier, *Promenade au Maroc*, 147.

121. Raoul de Malherbe, *L'Orient: 1718 à 1845—histoire, politique, religions et mœurs* (Paris: Gide, 1846), 1:388–389.

122. For more on the Damascus Blood Libel, see Jonathan Frankel, *The Damascus Affair: "Ritual Murder," Politics, and the Jews in 1840* (Cambridge: Cambridge University Press, 1997).

123. Florimond Jacques Basterot, *Le Liban, la Galilée et Rome: Journal d'un voyage en Orient et en Italie, septembre 1867–mai 1868* (Paris: Douniol, 1869), 120.

124. See, for example, Julie Kalman, *Rethinking Antisemitism in Nineteenth-Century France* (New York: Cambridge University Press, 2010), chap. 4.

125. Joseph d'Estourmel, *Journal d'un voyage en Orient* (Paris: Crapelet, 1844), 1:302.

126. Michaud and Poujoulat, *Correspondance d'Orient*, 2:226.

127. Pierre-Nicolas Hamont, *L'Egypte sous Méhémet-Ali* (Paris: Léautey et Lecointe, 1848), 2:114.

128. Charles Marcotte de Quivières, *Deux ans en Afrique* (Paris: Librarie nouvelle, 1855), 84.

129. Dumas, *Le Véloce*, 44.

130. Baptistin Poujoulat, *Voyage à Constantinople, dans l'Asie mineure, en Mésopotamie, à Palmyre, et Syrie, en Palestine et en Egypte* (Paris: Ducollet, 1840), 1:17.

131. Michaud and Poujoulat, *Correspondance d'Orient*, 2:225.

132. Didier, *Promenade au Maroc*, 128.

133. Hamont, *L'Egypte*, 114.

134. Basterot, *Le Liban*, 36.

135. Malherbe, *L'Orient*, 1:389.

136. In fact, under Islam, Jews were subject to sartorial restrictions designed to prevent them from wearing bright colors, in particular green, the color of Islam. On the exoticization of the Jewish woman, see Julie Kalman, "Sensuality, Depravity and Ritual Murder: The Damascus Blood Libel and Jews in France," *Jewish Social Studies: History, Culture, Society* 13, no. 3 (2007): 35–58.

137. Didier, *Promenade au Maroc*, 155–160.

138. Marcotte de Quivières, *Deux ans en Afrique*, 81.

139. Eugène Delacroix, *Souvenirs d'un voyage dans le Maroc*, ed. Laure Beaumont-Maillet, Barthélémy Jobert, and Sophie Join-Lambert (Paris: Gallimard, 1999), 21.

140. Dumas, *Le Véloce*, 48.

141. Nerval, *Voyage en Orient*, 2:185.

142. Didier, *Promenade au Maroc*, 282.

143. Michaud and Poujoulat, *Correspondance d'Orient*, 2:226.

144. Maxime du Camp, *Voyage en Orient, 1849–1851*, ed. Giovanni Bonaccorso (Messina: Peloritana Editrice, 1972), 283.

145. Azaïs, *Journal*, 274–275.

146. Hamont, *L'Egypte*, 2:365–356.

147. Didier, *Promenade au Maroc*, 123.

148. Ibid., 163.

149. Du Camp, *Souvenirs et paysages*, 281. Du Camp was writing about Damascus.

150. Didier, *Promenade au Maroc*, 183.

151. Ibid., 152–153.

152. Charles Didier, *Nationalité française* (Paris: Pagnerre, 1841), 10, 5.
153. Quoted in Sellards, *Dans le sillage du romantisme*, 106.
154. See Kalman, *Rethinking Antisemitism*, 128–154.
155. See, for example, Sand's play *Les Mississipiens* (1840) or her novel *Valvèdre* (1861).
156. Kalman, *Rethinking Antisemitism*, 148–152.
157. Dumas, *Le Véloce*, 41–42.
158. Ibid., 42.
159. Didier, *Promenade au Maroc*, 304.
160. The phrase, which was to become widespread, was first introduced in a speech given by Louis-Philippe in 1831. See Guy Antonetti, *Louis-Philippe* (Paris: Fayard, 1994), 713.
161. Bénichou, *Romantismes français*, 2:1991–1992.
162. Court-Perez, *Gautier, un romantique ironique*, 11–12.
163. Michaud and Poujoulat, *Correspondance d'Orient*, 2:227.
164. The name of Delacroix's host is variously written ben Chimol or Benchimol.
165. Jean Guiffrey, *Le Voyage d'Eugène Delacroix au Maroc* (Paris: André Marty, 1909), 2:11.
166. Delacroix, *Souvenirs*, 111.
167. Maurice Arama, ed., *Eugène Delacroix, le voyage au Maroc*, (Paris: Editions du Sagittaire, 1992), 71.
168. Delacroix, *Souvenirs*, 113–114.
169. Dumas, *Le Véloce*.
170. Renoüard de Bussièrre, *Lettres sur l'Orient*, 2:50.
171. Ibid., 2:142.
172. Ibid., 1:145.
173. Count de Mornay, *Ma Mission au Maroc, par le Comte Charles de Mornay*, in Arama, *Eugène Delacroix*, 16.
174. On the place of Jews in Moroccan society, see Daniel Schroeter, *The Sultan's Jew: Morocco and the Sephardi World* (Stanford, CA: Stanford University Press, 2002).
175. Ibid., 121.
176. Delacroix, *Souvenirs*, 85.
177. Dumas, *Le Véloce*, 44, 39, 40.
178. Ibid., 63.
179. Ibid., 395.
180. Ibid., 47, 48.
181. Ibid., 63.
182. Ibid., 52.
183. Ibid., 70, 45.
184. Ibid., 71.
185. On the Farhi family, see Thomas Philipp, "The Farhi Family and the Changing Position of the Jews in Syria, 1750–1860," *Middle Eastern Studies* 20, no. 4 (1984): 37–52.
186. Marie-Louis-Jean-André-Charles Marcellus, *Souvenirs de l'Orient* (Paris: Deboucourt, 1839), 1:420. Marcellus, like his fellow Legitimist Bussièrre, had been secretary to the French ambassador in Constantinople.
187. Ibid.; and Auguste de Forbin, *Voyage dans le Levant, en 1817 et 1818* (Paris: L'Imprimerie royale, 1819), 71.
188. Charles Lewis Meryon, *Travels of Lady Hester Stanhope* (London: Henry Colburn, 1846), 2:9–11, quoted in Philipp, "The Farhi Family," 42.
189. Marcellus, *Souvenirs de l'Orient*, 1:420.
190. Forbin, *Voyage dans le Levant*, 71.

191. Ibid., 71.

192. Marcellus, *Souvenirs de l'Orient*, 1:421.

193. Ibid., 1:420.

194. Ibid.

195. Forbin, *Voyage dans le Levant*, 71. The ambivalence of Farhi's position is well illustrated by his own fate. In 1794 Farhi was imprisoned on the orders of Ahmad Pasha, who had appointed him chief *sarraf*, or treasurer. He was blinded in one eye, and one of his ears and part of his nose were cut off. All visitors referred to this disfigurement. In 1820 Farhi was murdered on the orders of his own ward, Abdallah, whom he had recently brought to power.

196. Poujoulat, *Voyage à Constantinople*, 1:17–19.

197. Didier, *Promenade au Maroc*, 127.

198. Ibid., 127–128.

199. Michaud and Poujoulat, *Correspondance d'Orient*, 2:226.

200. Renoüard de Bussièrre, *Lettres sur l'Orient*, 2:142.

201. Basterot, *Le Liban*, 36.

202. Hamont, *L'Egypte*, 1:364.

203. Nerval, *Voyage en Orient*, 2:185.

204. Malherbe, *L'Orient*, 1:389n.

205. Ibid., 1:387.

206. Dumas, *Le Véloce*, 40–41.

207. Basterot, *Le Liban*, 120–121.

208. Dumas, *Le Véloce*, 43.

209. Victor Fontanier, *Voyages en Orient, entrepris par ordre du gouvernement français, de 1830 à 1833: Deuxième Voyage en Anatolie* (Paris: Librairie de Dumont, 1834), iv.

210. Ibid., 153.

211. Isidore Justin Séverin Taylor and Louis Reybaud, *La Syrie, l'Egypte, la Palestine, et la Judée, considérées sous leur aspect historique, archéologique, descriptif et pittoresque* (Paris: Chez l'éditeur, 1839).

212. See, for example, Lamartine, *Voyage en Orient*, 2:208, 243.

213. Frédéric August Antoine Goupil, *Voyage en Orient fait avec Horace Vernet en 1839 et 1840* (Paris: Challamel, [1843]), 47.

214. Ibid., 215.

215. Théophile Gautier, *Les Beaux-Arts en Europe* (Paris: Michel Lévy, 1856), 1:180–181.

216. Théophile Gautier, *Voyage pittoresque en Algérie*, ed. Madeleine Cottin (Geneva: Droz, 1973), 186.

217. Michael Graetz, *The Jews in Nineteenth-Century France: From the French Revolution to the Alliance Israélite Universelle*, trans. Jane Marie Todd (Stanford, CA: Stanford University Press, 1996), 43, 44.

218. Deborah Hertz, *How Jews Became Germans: The History of Conversion and Assimilation in Berlin* (New Haven, CT: Yale University Press, 2007), 103.

219. Marie Lathers has discussed how the ideal of beauty changed—and with it the ethnicity of the ideal model—through the nineteenth century. Marie Lathers, *Bodies of Art: French Literary Realism and the Artist's Model* (Lincoln: University of Nebraska Press, 2001).

220. Very little is known of Marix's life. The most thorough retelling is in Jean Ziegler, *Gautier, Baudelaire: Un Carré de dames* (Paris: Nizet, 1978). Marie Lathers also discusses Joséphine Marix in her *Bodies of Art*, chap. 4.

221. L. G. de Marsay [Albert-André Patin de la Fizelière], *La Danse, ses temples et ses desservants en 1850* (Paris: Pilloy, 1850).

222. Alexandre Privat d'Anglemont, *La Closerie des Lilas: Quadrille en prose* (Paris: Frey, 1848), 55–56.

223. Claude-Marie Senninger, ed., *Baudelaire par Théophile Gautier* (Paris: Klincksieck, 1986), 118.

224. Ziegler, *Gautier, Baudelaire*, 37–74. See also letter from Théophile Gautier to Ernesta Grisi, September 25, 1858, in Lacoste-Veysseyre, *Correspondance*, 7:80.

225. Ibid.

226. Letter from Théophile Gautier to Ernesta Grisi, February 18, 1859, in Lacoste-Veysseyre, *Correspondance*, 7:107–108.

227. Letter from Théophile Gautier to Ernesta Grisi, September 10, 1859, in Lacoste-Veysseyre, *Correspondance*, 7:170.

228. Letter from Théophile Gautier to Jules Hetzel, June (?) 25, 1857, in Lacoste-Veysseyre, *Correspondance*, 6:317.

229. Letter from Théophile Gautier to Arsène Houssaye, February (?) 1850, in Lacoste-Veysseyre, *Correspondance*, 4:121. Houssaye was the director of the Comédie-Française. See also letter from Théophile Gautier to Arsène Houssaye, March 20 (?), 1850, in Lacoste-Veysseyre, *Correspondance*, 4:126; and letter from Théophile Gautier to Siona Lévy, n.d., in Lacoste-Veysseyre, *Correspondance*, 4:381. An 1862 edition of Gautier's *Poésies complètes* was dedicated as "a book that I would have liked to give to Miss Siona Lévy." Spoelberch de Lovenjoul, *Histoire des oeuvres de Théophile Gautier*, 1:301. The 1877 edition of the second volume of his *Poésies complètes* included a quatrain titled "A Mademoiselle Siona Lévy":

> Child, twice acclaimed
> You sing, and you recite poetry;
> And your tragic mask
> Is crowned with green laurels.

Quoted in Spoelberch de Lovenjoul, *Histoire des oeuvres de Théophile Gautier*, 1:455.

230. [Julie Bernat], *La Vie d'une grande comédienne*.

231. Gautier, untitled reviews, *La Presse*, December 14, 1846; January 11, March 1, April 26, June 21, October 25, November 1 and 29, and December 27, 1847; March 27 and September 4, 1848.

232. Théophile Gautier, untitled review, *La Presse*, December 14, 1846, p. 2.

233. Théophile Gautier, untitled review, *La Presse*, January 11, 1847, p. 2.

234. Gautier, untitled review, *La Presse*, December 14, 1846, p. 2.

235. Letter from Gautier to Houssaye, February (?) 1850.

236. See Giovanna Bellati, *Théophile Gautier, journaliste à la presse: Point de vue sur une esthétique théâtrale* (Turin: Harmattan Italia, 2008), 45–46.

237. Théophile Gautier, "Revue dramatique: Melle Rachel," *Le Moniteur universel*, January 11, 1858, p. 423.

238. Théophile Gautier, untitled review, *La Presse*, March 3, 1851.

239. Théophile Gautier, untitled review, *La Presse*, February 14, 1853.

240. Théophile Gautier, untitled review, *La Presse*, December 28, 1840.

241. Théophile Gautier, untitled review, *La Presse*, May 22, 1842.

242. Théophile Gautier, untitled review, *La Presse*, May 27, 1850.

243. Théophile Gautier, untitled review, *La Presse*, April 7, 1845.

244. Théophile Gautier, "Sommités contemporaines: M. Th. Gautier," *L'Illustration*, March 9, 1867, quoted in Bénichou, *Romantismes français*, 2:1965.

245. Gautier, "Revue dramatique," 424.

246. Gautier, untitled review, *La Presse*, April 7, 1845.

247. Théophile Gautier, untitled review, *La Presse*, December 8, 1845.

248. Théophile Gautier, untitled review, *La Presse*, March 9, 1846.

249. Gautier, untitled review, *La Presse*, May 8, 1848.

250. Gautier, untitled review, *La Presse*, May 27, 1850. See also his review in *La Presse*, December 3, 1849:

> Everything has been said about Mademoiselle Rachel; her talent has been analyzed in its most subtle nuances, but in our opinion, not enough attention has been paid to the sculptural side of her art: it is not possible to make or break a stance in a more harmonious and more sculptural manner; each one of her roles is a series of antique statues of the greatest style. . . . The way that she places and moves her feet, or bends her arm, with primitive gestures that recall the beautiful era of Greek statuary, or that she bends and lifts her head, is truly astonishing.

251. Letter from Rachel Félix to Théophile Gautier, January 23, 1843, in Lacoste-Veysseyre, *Correspondance*, 2:5.

252. Letter from Théophile Gautier to Adèle Gautier, June 26, 1846, in Lacoste-Veysseyre, *Correspondance*, 3:61.

253. Letter from Théophile Gautier to Rachel Félix, before July 20, 1846, in Lacoste-Veysseyre, *Correspondance*, 3:64.

254. Letter from Rachel Félix to Théophile Gautier, late November 1846(?), in Lacoste-Veysseyre, *Correspondance*, 3:116.

255. Letter from Rachel Félix to Théophile Gautier, 1854(?), in Lacoste-Veysseyre, *Correspondance*, 4:111.

256. In the long obituary Gautier wrote for Rachel, there is not one mention of her religious adherence.

257. Gautier, untitled review, *La Presse*, March 9, 1846.

258. Gautier, untitled review, *La Presse*, January 11, 1847, p. 2.

259. Théophile Gautier, review of *Suzanne au bain*, by Théodore Chassériau, *La Presse*, April 13, 1839, p. 5.

260. Théophile Gautier, review of *Sabbat des Juifs de Constantine*, by Théodore Chassériau, *La Presse*, April 27, 1848, p. 2. This painting has been destroyed.

261. Edmond de Goncourt and Jules de Goncourt, *Journal: Mémoires de la vie littéraire* (Monaco: Flammarion, 1956), 2:43–44.

262. Lacoste-Veysseyre, *Correspondance*, 1:2.

263. Théodore Faullain de Banville, funeral oration for Gautier, quoted in P. E. Tennant, *Théophile Gautier* (London: Athlone Press, 1975), 102.

264. Court-Perez, *Gautier, un romantique ironique*, 11–12.

265. Letter from Théophile Gautier to Isaac Péreire, between December 1853 and March 1857, in Lacoste-Veysseyre, *Correspondance*, 6:295. On the Péreires, see Helen Davies, *Emile and Isaac Péreire: Bankers, Socialists and Sephardic Jews in Nineteenth-Century France* (Manchester, UK: Manchester University Press, 2015).

266. Joanna Richardson, *Théophile Gautier: His Life and Times* (London: Max Reinhardt, 1958), 93.

267. Théophile Gautier, untitled article, *La Presse*, January 29, 1850.

268. Senninger, *Baudelaire par Théophile Gautier*, 118.

269. Gautier, review of *Sabbat des Juifs*, 2.

270. Ibid. See also Théophile Gautier, *Salon de 1847* (Paris: Hetzel, 1847), 21.

271. Théophile Gautier, untitled review, *Le Moniteur universel*, March 10, 1862.

272. Gautier, untitled article, *La Presse*, January 29, 1850.

273. See letter from Alphonse Toussenel to Théophile Gautier, March 24, 1848, in Lacoste-Veysseyre, *Correspondance*, 3:329, in which Toussenel addresses Gautier as his "Dear and illustrious master."

274. See Kalman, *Rethinking Antisemitism*, 128–154.

275. Bellati, *Théophile Gautier*, 53.

276. Jules Canonge, *Pradier et Ary Scheffer: Notes, souvenirs et documents d'art contemporain* (Paris: Paulin, 1858), 31.

277. Gautier, *Le Roman de la momie*, 277.

278. Ernest Feydeau, *Théophile Gautier: Souvenirs intimes* (Paris: Plon, 1874), 91–92.

279. Ibid., 92.

280. Ibid., 93.

281. Gautier, *Le Roman de la momie*, 274.

**282.** On the Damascus Blood Libel, see Frankel, *The Damascus Affair*.

283. Gautier, *Le Roman de la momie*, 269.

284. Ibid., 275.

285. Ibid., 275–276.

286 See Geneviève Van Den Bogaert, preface to Gautier, *Le Roman de la momie*, 11–13.

287. Ibid., 20.

288. Ibid., 21.

289. Ibid., 18.

290. For example, Gautier's editor at the *Moniteur*, Julien Turgan, noted, "As a friend and one who appreciates literature, I find that, to this point, your characters, with the exception of Tahoser, are too much like dead Egyptians, and that by dint of having seen engravings and paintings, in spite of yourself you are making frescos instead of a tableau vivant." Letter from Julien Turgan to Théophile Gautier, March 20, 1857, in Lacoste-Veysseyre, *Correspondance*, 6:290.

291. Gautier, *Le Roman de la momie*, 289, 299.

292. Ibid., 290, 316, 304, 290.

293. Ibid., 304, 316.

294. *Crapule m'embête* translates loosely as the "scoundrel annoys me."

295. Quoted in Joanna Richardson, *Judith Gautier: A Biography* (London: Quartet, 1986), 29.

296. Letter from Théophile Gautier to Julien Turgan, February 1866, quoted in ibid., 42.

297. Letter from Théophile Gautier to Ernesta Grisi, between February 28 and March 15, 1866, in Lacoste-Veysseyre, *Correspondance*, 9:185.

298. Letter from Théophile Gautier to Carlotta Grisi, late March 1866, in Lacoste-Veysseyre, *Correspondance*, 9:193.

299. Letter from Théophile Gautier to Ernesta Grisi, between February 28 and March 15, 1866, in Lacoste-Veysseyre, *Correspondance*, 9:184.

300. Diary of Eugénie Fort, quoted in Richardson, *Judith Gautier*, 45.

301. Goncourt and Goncourt, *Journal*, 10:82, quoted in Richardson, *Judith Gautier*, 95. Journalist Maxime Rude described him as a "presumptuous half-caste" in *Confidences d'un journaliste* (Paris: Sagnier, 1876), 160. Another account of the time refers to his "inferior origins." Maurice Talmeyr, *Souvenirs d'avant le deluge, 1870–1914* (Paris: Perrin, 1927), 113.

302. Richardson, *Théophile Gautier*, 31; Claude-Marie Senninger, *Théophile Gautier, une vie, une œuvre* (Paris: Sedes, 1994), 434. Lavaud argues that Gautier's hostility to Mendès "was not exactly due to his Jewish background." Lavaud, *Théophile Gautier*, 498.

303. Letter from Théophile Gautier to Carlotta Grisi, April 5, 1866, in Lacoste-Veysseyre, *Correspondance*, 9:206.

304. Letter from Théophile Gautier to Carlotta Grisi, April 21 (?), 1866, in Lacoste-Veysseyre, *Correspondance*, 9:212.

305. Letter from Théophile Gautier to Julien Turgan, early March 1866, in Lacoste-Veysseyre, *Correspondance*, 9:181.

306. Lacoste-Veysseyre, *Correspondance*, 9:82n1.

307. Letter from Théophile Gautier to Carlotta Grisi, mid-February 1865, in Lacoste-Veysseyre, *Correspondance*, 9:24. Carlotta replied that Manheim would appear to be "too Jewish." Letter from Carlotta Grisi to Théophile Gautier, February 20, 1865, in Lacoste-Veysseyre, *Correspondance*, 9:29.

308. Letter from Théophile Gautier to Carlotta Grisi, June 30, 1865, in Lacoste-Veysseyre, *Correspondance*, 9:81.

309. Honoré de Balzac, quoted in Charles Lehrmann, *The Jewish Element in French Literature*, trans. George Klin (Rutherford, NJ: Fairleigh Dickinson University Press, 1971), 166. On Jewish figures in Balzac, see Kalman, *Rethinking Antisemitism*, 118–122.

310. On *La Juive*, see Diana Hallman, *Opera, Liberalism and Antisemitism in Nineteenth-Century France: The Politics of Halévy's* La Juive (Cambridge: Cambridge University Press, 2002). On *Ivanhoe*, see Martyn Lyons, "The Audience for Romanticism: Walter Scott in France, 1815–1851," *European History Quarterly* 14, no. 1 (1984): 27–28.

311. Nadia Valman conceptualizes this as "uncertainty" in *The Jewess in Nineteenth-Century British Literary Culture* (Cambridge: Cambridge University Press, 2007), 2.

312. Hallman, *Opera, Liberalism*, 102.

313. Maurice Samuels, *Inventing the Israelite: Jewish Fiction in Nineteenth-Century France* (Stanford, CA: Stanford University Press, 2010), 62.

314. Lisa Moses Leff, *Sacred Bonds of Solidarity: The Rise of Jewish Internationalism in Nineteenth-Century France* (Stanford, CA: Stanford University Press, 2006), 99.

315. Gautier, *Tableaux de siège*.

316. Ibid., 226, 225.

317. Ibid., 228.

318. Ibid., 229.

319. Ibid., 230.

320. Ibid., 231.

321. Letter from Théophile Gautier to Giacomo Meyerbeer, March or April 1839, in Lacoste-Veysseyre, *Correspondence*, 1:146.

322. Kerry Murphy has detailed the role of Meyerbeer's Jewishness in criticism of his music. Kerry Murphy, "Berlioz, Meyerbeer, and the Place of Jewishness in Criticism," in *Berlioz: Past, Present, Future: Bicentenary Essays*, ed. Peter Bloom (Rochester, NY: University of Rochester Press, 2003), 90–104.

323. Review of *Les Huguenots*, by Giacomo Meyerbeer, *La France*, March 2, 1836.

324. Untitled review, *Gazette de France*, March 10, 1836, p. 1.

325. Louis Desnoyers, untitled review, *Le National*, March 16, 1836.

326. Gustave Planche, untitled review, *Chronique de Paris*, March 1836, p. 1.

327. Ibid. See also Castil-Blaze, untitled reviews, *La France musicale*, May 22 and 27, 1838.

328. Théophile Gautier, *Souvenirs de théâtre, d'art et de critique* (Paris: Charpentier, 1883), 94–95.

329. Théophile Gautier, review of *Le Prophète*, by Giacomo Meyerbeer, *La Presse*, October 29, 1849.

330. See letter from Théophile Gautier to Henry Rouy, before April 1855, in Lacoste-Veysseyre, *Correspondence*, 6:136, in which Gautier tells Rouy that yesterday, he accompanied "our friend

Meyerbeer" to the gare du Nord. Gautier also maintained a friendly correspondence with the writer Henri [Heinrich] Heine, who converted from Judaism.

331. Toward the end of his life, Gautier appears to have reconciled himself to the idea of Mendès, and even, perhaps, to his person. In 1868, Mendès wrote to thank Gautier for a positive review of his poetry. See letter from Catulle Mendès to Théophile Gautier, April 16, 1868, in Lacoste-Veysseyre, *Correspondance*, 10:519. In June 1872 Gautier gave Mendès permission to turn his book, *Le Capitaine Fracasse*, into an opéra-comique. Richardson suggests that at this point, in ill health and aware that he would not live much longer, Gautier sought to "reconcile and forgive." He is reputed to have said of Mendès, "I had an enemy, once, but now I have lost him!" Richardson, *Théophile Gautier*, 275.

332. Schechter, *Obstinate Hebrews*, 7.

333. Ziegler, *Gautier, Baudelaire*, 95.

334. Goncourt and Goncourt, *Journal*, 1:164.

335. Ibid., 1:164–165.

## 3. The Kings of Algiers

1. Henri-Delmas de Grammont, *Histoire d'Alger sous la domination turque (1515–1830)* (Paris: Leroux, 1887), 235. Grammont belonged to one of France's oldest military families. His father, part of the military guard to Charles X, had accompanied the king on the way to exile to Cherbourg in 1830, after which he broke his sword in two. Gilbert Jacqueton, *H. D. de Grammont* (Algiers: Jourdan, n.d.), 3.

2. Joshua Schreier, *Arabs of the Jewish Faith: The Civilizing Mission in Colonial Algeria* (New Brunswick, NJ: Rutgers University Press, 2010); Lisa Moses Leff, *Sacred Bonds of Solidarity: The Rise of Jewish Internationalism in Nineteenth-Century France* (Stanford, CA: Stanford University Press, 2006), 127–137; Colette Zytnicki, *Les Juifs du Maghreb: Naissance d'une historiographie coloniale* (Paris: Presses de l'Université Paris-Sorbonne, 2011), 56–57.

3. Quoted in Gabriel Esquer, *Les Commencements d'un empire: La Prise d'Alger (1830)*, 2nd ed. (Paris: Larose, 1929), 63n1.

4. La Bretonnière, quoted in ibid., 63.

5. Quoted in ibid., 27; and Eugène Plantet, ed., *Correspondance des deys d'Alger avec la cour de France, 1579–1833* (Paris: Alcan, 1889), 2:491.

6. The sources reveal a variety of contemporary spellings of the two names. Given that these have since become fixed in the forms used here, for the sake of consistency I use these spellings throughout this chapter.

7. Francesca Trivellato, *The Familiarity of Strangers: The Sephardic Diaspora, Livorno, and Cross-cultural Trade in the Early Modern Period* (New Haven, CT: Yale University Press, 2009), 58. This was in contrast, Trivellato tells us, to "the most prosperous group of Livorno Sephardim," who "worked to develop connections between the Levant and Northern Europe." Ibid.

8. Claude Martin, *Les Israélites algériens de 1830 à 1902* (Paris: Herakles, 1936), 30. According to Trivellato, "'Franks' was the generic term for Europeans in the Muslim world." Trivellato, *Familiarity*, 66.

9. Trivellato, *Familiarity*, 67.

10. Maurice Eisenbeth, "Les Juifs en Algérie et en Tunisie à l'époque turque (1516–1830)," *Revue africaine* 46 (1952): 373.

11. According to Haddey, Naphtali's father, also named Naphtali, had established the family in Algiers in 1723. M. J. M. Haddey, *Le Livre d'or des israélites algériens: Recueil de*

*renseignements inédits et authentiques sur les principaux négociants juifs d'Alger pendant la période turque* (1871; repr., Paris: Cercle de généalogie juive, 2005), 41. Plantet says that Louis XV's consul, Taitbout de Marigny, dealt with the "intrigues" of a Nephtali Busnach, the grandfather of the Naphtali who features here, in 1739. Plantet, *Correspondance*, 2:189. Isaac Bloch notes that Busnach is, in fact, an Arabic name, Bou Djenah (the winged man). Isaac Bloch, *Inscriptions tumulaires des anciens cimetières israélites d'Alger* (Paris: Durlacher, 1888), 72.

12. Eisenbeth, "Les Juifs en Algérie," 373.

13. Schreier, *Arabs of the Jewish Faith*, 13.

14. See Paul Masson, *Marseille et la colonisation française: Essai d'histoire coloniale* (Marseilles: Barlatier, 1906), 534; Esquer, *Les Commencements d'un empire*, 19–20; Martin, *Les Israélites algériens*, 20.

15. Report on the Bacri family by Foreign Minister Bassano, August 8, 1812, dossier 1633/2, F/7/6537, Archives nationales (AN), Paris.

16. Trivellato discusses the lucrative nature of the coral trade in *Familiarity*, 225–226.

17. Paul Masson, "A la veille d'une conquête: Concessions et compagnies d'Afrique (1800–1830)," *Bulletin de géographie historique et descriptive* 24 (1909): 49.

18. Masson, who admittedly sees the concessions as being at the center of the story of the invasion of Algeria, argues that this unique exception to the principle of free trade is worthy of note. It demonstrates, as he puts it, "the importance that the government placed on the concessions." Paul Masson, "Concessions et compagnies," 56.

19. Quoted in Esquer, *Les Commencements d'un empire*, 20.

20. Quoted in Masson, "Concessions et compagnies," 58; and Masson, *Marseille et la colonisation française*, 538.

21. Masson, "Concessions et compagnies," 61.

22. Ibid., 58.

23. Charles-André Julien, *Histoire de l'Algérie contemporaine: La Conquête et les débuts de la colonisation (1827–1871)* (Paris: Presses universitaires de France, 1964), 18.

24. For example, in 1800, Jacob wrote to his correspondent in Cadiz that if he had been without news from Algiers for some time, it was because wheat was now being sent to Lisbon to take advantage of the high prices there. In 1801, Bacri wrote to his brothers in Algiers, requesting that wheat be sent to Lisbon, following the failure of crops there. Françoise Hildesheimer, "Grandeur et décadence de la maison Bacri de Marseille," *Revue des études juives* 86, no. 3–4 (1977): 400.

25. Morton Rosenstock, "The House of Bacri and Busnach: A Chapter from Algeria's Commercial History," *Jewish Social Studies* 14, no. 4 (1952): 345. Some scholars have used what facts are available to dispute the widely held and repeated perceptions. For example, Morton Rosenstock argued that the extent of Jewish control over trade was "frequently exaggerated." He made use of a different source, which stated that Jews paid a 10 percent tax on imports, whereas non-Jews paid 5 percent. Morton Rosenstock, "Economic and Social Conditions among the Jews of Algeria: 1790–1848," *Historia Judaica* 18 (1956): 4. See also his source, Venture de Paradis, "Alger au XVIII siècle," *Revue africaine* 39 (1895): 292–293. Another scholar of Bacri and Busnach, Françoise Hildesheimer, has taken issue with Masson's interpretation of events. She notes that the activities of both importers—the House of Bacri and Busnach and the Agence d'Afrique—follow a parallel evolution at the mercy of markets and events. Thus, she argues, any bankruptcy would surely have had more to do with the vagaries of trade between France and Algeria than with Bacri and Busnach. Hildesheimer, "Grandeur et décadence," 395. Benjamin Braude has argued more generally that "the common European belief that Jews dominated the Ottoman economy" most probably had more to do with the exaggerated claims of Jewish intermediaries and the European desire to claim proximity to power than with having

roots in fact. Benjamin Braude, "The Myth of the Sephardi Economic Superman," in *Trading Cultures: The Worlds of Western Merchants*, ed. Jeremy Adelman and Stephen Aron (Turnhout, Belgium: Brepols, 2001), 186. Francesca Trivellato argues for the inclusion of complaints by European consuls in Braude's list. Trivellato, *Familiarity*, 128.

26. Pierre Deval, *Mémoire analytique de la correspondance du département des affaires étrangères depuis 1794 jusqu'en 1818, concernant les réclamations des Sieurs Bacri et Busnach, sujets algériens, sur le gouvernement français*, October 1818, Correspondance Consulaire et Commerciale (8CCC), folder 44, Archives diplomatiques (AD), Paris.

27. Hildesheimer found his name in the columns of Marseilles' trade tribunal in June 1795. Hildesheimer, "Grandeur et décadence," 391–392.

28. Letter from Sidi Hassan to the members of the Committee for Public Safety, July 12, 1795, in Plantet, *Correspondance*, 2:451–452. Charles-François Delacroix replied, "It was with pleasure that we saw the sincere expression of your friendship and your gratitude for the welcome that this merchant has received since he arrived in France [in your letter]. Be assured that he will have nothing but satisfaction, too, with the way in which we will continue to conduct ourselves with him, as with all those whom you recommend to us, and we will not miss any opportunity to further strengthen the bonds of this ancient friendship." Letter from Delacroix (minister for foreign affairs) to Sidi Hassan, June 1796, in Plantet, *Correspondance*, 2:455–456.

29. Letter from Hassan to Committee for Public Safety, July 12, 1795.

30. As does the spelling of Bacri and Busnach, the orthography of Simon Aboucaya's last name varies wildly in the literature.

31. Letter from Jacob Cohen Bacri to the members of the Committee for Public Safety, 6 Thermidor an 3 (July 24, 1795), 8CCC, folder 32, AD.

32. The first chief rabbi for the city took office in 1804, "with great pomp." Pierre Guiral and Paul Amargier, *Histoire de Marseille* (Paris: Mazarine, 1983), 210.

33. Julien, *Histoire de l'Algérie contemporaine*, 18. Contrary to Julien, Françoise Hildesheimer concluded, from her examination of the departmental archive, that Jacob Bacri appeared to have been the only Algerian to set himself up in business in Marseilles in 1795. Hildesheimer, "Grandeur et décadence," 398. We can be more certain about the presence of Jews in the city a decade later, when the mayor of Marseilles, Antoine-Ignace Anthoine, wrote to the prefect of the Département des Bouches-du-Rhone, Antoine Thibaudeau, on the occasion of the arrival of seventy-four Egyptians in the city. Anthoine complained that Marseilles was "already full of refugee Jews from Algiers." Ian Coller, *Arab France: Islam and the Making of Modern Europe, 1798–1831* (Berkeley: University of California Press, 2011), 62. In the eyes of this mayor, the presence of Jews, who would have been fleeing the 1805 massacres in Algiers, was less of a problem than the presence of what he called "Egyptian negresses."

34. Hildesheimer, "Grandeur et décadence," 398.

35. Guiral and Amargier, *Histoire de Marseille*, 191.

36. Masson, *Marseille*, 533.

37. Pierre Guiral, "Les Juifs de Marseille en 1808," in *Actes du 85e Congrès national des Sociétés savantes: Section d'histoire moderne et contemporaine* (Paris: Imprimerie nationale, 1961), 281.

38. Rosenstock, "The House of Bacri and Busnach," 347. See also Haddey, *Livre d'or*, 75.

39. Rosenstock, "The House of Bacri and Busnach," 346.

40. Consular report, *Bulletin des nouvelles d'Alger*, 3–7 Germinal an 2 (March 23–27, 1794), 8CCC, folder 32, AD.

41. Esquer, *Les Commencements d'un empire*, 20.

42. Letter from Jean Bon Saint-André to minister of external relations, 24 Pluviôse an 5 (February 12, 1797), 8CCC, folder 32, AD.

43. Letter from Jean Bon Saint-André to minister of external relations, 19 Germinal an 5 (April 8, 1797), 8CCC, folder 32, AD.

44. Letter from Jean Bon Saint-André to minister of external relations, 1 Nivôse an 5 (December 21, 1796), 8CCC, folder 33, AD.

45. Letter from Jean Bon Saint-André to minister of external relations, 25 Pluviôse an 5 (February 14, 1797), 8CCC, folder 33, AD.

46. Letter from Jean Bon Saint-André to minister of external relations, December 21, 1796.

47. Ibid.

48. Letter from Jean Bon Saint-André to minister of external relations, 3 Nivôse an 5 (December 23, 1796), 8CCC, folder 33, AD.

49. Letters from Jean Bon Saint-André to minister of external relations, 12 Nivôse (January 1) and 29 Ventôse an 5 (March 17, 1797), 8CCC, folder 33, AD.

50. Letter from Sidi Hassan to the directory, May 18, 1797, in Plantet, *Correspondance*, 2:462–463.

51. Letter from Jean Bon Saint-André to minister of external relations, 19 Floréal an 5 (May 8, 1797), 8CCC, folder 33, AD.

52. Letter from Jean Bon Saint-André to minister of external relations, 9 Vendémiaire an 5 (September 30, 1797), 8CCC, folder 33, AD. This understanding of the state of affairs in Algiers was supported by another observer. Captain Barré wrote to Talleyrand, following his return from a long stay in Algiers, that "the Jews Busnach and Bacry" had complete power over the dey. Letter from Captain Barré to Talleyrand, 9 Germinal an 6 (March 29, 1798), 8CCC, folder 34, AD.

53. Letter from Jean Bon Saint-André to minister of external relations, 25 Pluviôse an 6 (February 13, 1798), 8CCC, folder 34, AD.

54. Letter from Jean Bon Saint-André to minister of external relations, 10 Nivôse an 5 (December 30, 1796), 8CCC, folder 33, AD.

55. Letter from Jean Bon Saint-André to minister of external relations, 4 Germinal an 5 (March 24, 1797), 8CCC, folder 33, AD.

56. Letter from Jean Bon Saint-André to minister of external relations, 30 Germinal an 5 (April 19, 1797), 8CCC, folder 33, AD.

57. Letter from Jean Bon Saint-André to minister of external relations, 9 Vendémiaire an 5 (September 30, 1797), 8CCC, folder 33, AD.

58. Letter from Mustapha to the Directory, June 1798, in Plantet, *Correspondance*, 2:477–478.

59. Letter from Mustapha to the Directory, September 17, 1798, in Plantet, *Correspondance*, 2:480.

60. Mustapha continued to write. In his next letter, he wrote that his claims with regard to the *Good Hoffnung* "had not been heard, and the rules necessary for peace and understanding between us have not been observed." Letter from Mustapha to the Directory, October 13, 1798, in Plantet, *Correspondance*, 2:485.

61. Deval, *Mémoire analytique*.

62. Letter from Lacroix to Ramel, April 24, 1798, in Plantet, *Correspondance*, 2:462–463.

63. Letter from Talleyrand to Dubois-Thainville, 9 Vendémiaire an 7 (September 30, 1798), 8CCC, folder 33, AD.

64. Ibid.

65. Plantet, *Correspondance*, 2:484.

66. Letter from Napoleon to Talleyrand, December 23, 1800, in *Correspondance de Napoléon Ier, publiée par ordre de l'empereur Napoléon III*, vol. 6, *1799–1801* (Paris: Imprimerie impériale, 1865), 544. Documents from the sequestration of Jacob Bacri's boats in Marseilles

at the time of the outbreak of war demonstrate that the Bacris did, indeed, meet Napoleon's request. Seven boats were bound for Malta. Their cargo included wine, salted meat, brandy, vinegar, haricot beans, wood for burning, and paper. Hildesheimer, "Grandeur et décadence," 398. It is ironic that these deliveries would have been held up by order of Napoleon himself.

67. Letter from Napoleon to Talleyrand, January 26, 1801, in *Correspondance de Napoléon Ier*, 6:589.

68. See Deval, *Mémoire analytique*. The same story is told in Deval, *Rapport concernant les réclamations des Sr Bacri, négociants algériens, envers le gouvernement français, extrait de la correspondance du consulat général et de celle des divers ministères du gouvernement*, undated, 8CCC, folder 44, AD, although *juif* is changed to *négociant* (merchant).

69. Letter from Dubois-Thainville to Talleyrand, 9 Pluviôse an 7 (January 28, 1799), 8CCC, folder 34, AD. Dubois-Thainville's letter included extracts of letters from Citizen Sielve in Algiers to Citizen Vallière in Marseilles, 19 and 27 Pluviôse an 7 (February 7 and 15, 1799) and 2 Ventôse an 7 (February 20, 1799). Before he took up his post, Dubois-Thainville had written to ask his minister what "attitude he should display in Algiers vis-à-vis the Bacri Jews." Until that advice was received, he had chosen to "enclose himself within the boundaries of an extreme reserve," without rejecting them. Dubois-Thainville was well aware of the influence that "the Bacri Jews" held with the dey and the importance, on this basis, of maintaining caution in his dealings with them. Letter from Dubois-Thainville to Talleyrand, 11 Vendémiaire an 7 (October 2, 1798), 8CCC, folder 33, AD.

70. Letter from Dubois-Thainville to Talleyrand, 5 Germinal an 7 (March 15, 1799), 8CCC, folder 34, AD.

71. Letter from Dubois-Thainville to Talleyrand, 7 Floréal an 7 (April 26, 1799), quoted in Laurent-Charles Féraud, *Histoire des villes de la province de Constantine: La Calle et documents pour servir à l'histoire des anciennes concessions françaises d'Afrique* (Algiers: Aillaud, 1877), 551.

72. Letter from Dubois-Thainville to Talleyrand, 9 Pluviôse an 7 (January 28, 1799), 8CCC, folder 34, AD.

73. Report to the Directory, 7 Germinal an 7 (March 27, 1799), 8CCC, folder 34, AD.

74. Letter from Vallière to Talleyrand, 14 Ventôse an 7 (March 4, 1799), 8CCC, folder 34, AD (emphasis in original).

75. Letter from Dubois-Thainville to Talleyrand, 1 Messidor an 7 (June 19, 1799), quoted in Féraud, *Constantine*, 553.

76. Report to the Directory.

77. Letter from Jacob Cohen Bacri to Talleyrand, (?) Fructidor an 7 (August or September 1799), 8CCC, folder 34, AD.

78. Letter from Jacob Cohen Bacri to Talleyrand, 15(?) Fructidor an 7 (September 1[?], 1799), 8CCC, folder 34, AD. In March, Talleyrand had written to Dubois-Thainville, making it clear that he was aware of the help given the French by Joseph Bacri and Naphtali Busnach in Algiers. Letter from Talleyrand to Dubois-Thainville, 5 Germinal an 7 (March 25, 1799), 8CCC, folder 34, AD.

79. Letter from Talleyrand to the minister of finance, August 24, 1800, quoted in Esquer, *Les Commencements d'un empire*, 27; and Plantet, *Correspondance*, 2:491.

80. Esquer, *Les Commencements d'un empire*, 21.

81. Eisenbeth, "Les Juifs en Algérie," 374.

82. *Traité de paix entre la Régence d'Alger et la France, le 17 décembre 1801*, reproduced in Alexandre de Laborde, *Au roi et aux chambres, sur les véritables causes de la rupture avec Alger et sur l'expédition qui se prépare* (Paris: Truchy, 1830), v.

83. See Deval, *Mémoire analytique*, and [Deval], *Rapport concernant les réclamations des Sr Bacri*. (See note 107 for more information about these two reports.)

84. Deval, *Mémoire analytique*.

85. Letter from Dubois-Thainville to Talleyrand, undated, 8CCC, folder 35, AD.

86. Letter from Dubois-Thainville to Talleyrand, 11 Vendémiaire an 9 (October 3, 1800), 8CCC, folder 35, AD.

87. Letter from Dubois-Thainville to Talleyrand, 8 Ventôse an 11 (February 27, 1803), quoted in Deval, *Rapport*.

88. Letter from Talleyrand to Napoléon Bonaparte, 27 Nivôse an 9 (January 17, 1801), quoted in Deval, *Mémoire analytique* (emphasis in original).

89. Letter from Talleyrand to de Fermon, 12 Brumaire an 11 (November 3, 1802), quoted in Deval, *Mémoire analytique*.

90. Letter from Dubois-Thainville to Talleyrand, 17 Pluviôse an 9 (February 6, 1801), 8CCC, folder 35, AD. In an accompanying note to a report written by Dubois-Thainville and forwarded to the first consul, an anonymous author, presumably from the Department of Foreign Affairs, perhaps even Talleyrand himself, noted that Dubois-Thainville had produced a "rather voluminous" report covering all details of the peace negotiations. Anonymous note, 6 Pluviôse an 10 (January 26, 1802), 8CCC, folder 36, AD.

91. Letter from Dubois-Thainville to Talleyrand, 17 Messidor an 9 (July 6, 1801), 8CCC, folder 35, AD.

92. In 1801, when the French were able to return to Algiers, the Bacris and Busnachs redoubled their requests for repayment. In the copy of one letter, being forwarded to Talleyrand, Dubois-Thainville provided outraged commentary in the margin: "I have known them to be very deceitful and greedy men for some time, but I would never have thought them capable of raising such absurd claims." Letter from Dubois-Thainville to Talleyrand, 26 Brumaire an 10 (November 17, 1801), 8CCC, folder 35, AD.

93. Letter from Dubois-Thainville to Talleyrand, 12 Messidor an 10 (July 1, 1802), 8CCC, folder 36, AD. The letter was forwarded, with a report, to Napoleon.

94. Letter from Napoléon Bonaparte to Talleyrand, 10 Thermidor an 10 (July 29, 1802), quoted in Féraud, *Constantine*, 575.

95. "Elégie sur le sac d'Alger," cited in Bloch, *Inscriptions tumulaires*, 133–140.

96. Letter from Jacob Bacri to the police minister and prefect of Bouches-du-Rhône, March 26, 1808, F/7/824, AN.

97. Département des Bouches-du-Rhône, "Etat nominatif des algériens arrêtés à Marseille en exécution du décret du 17 février 1808," F/7/8524, AN.

98. Copy of letter from the foreign minister of Champagny to the minister of the navy and colonies, June 18, 1809, dossier 1633/2, F/7/6537, AN.

99. Letter from Bassano to Duke de Rovigo, August 8, 1812, dossier 1633/2, F/7/6537, AN.

100. Guiral, "Les Juifs de Marseille en 1808," 285.

101. Untitled article, *Le Sémaphore de Marseille*, January 29, 1831.

102. Deval, *Mémoire analytique*.

103. "Copie du projet de rapport annoncé dans le mémoire analytique adressé à la commission," August 1818, 8CCC, folder 44, AD.

104. Deval, *Mémoire analytique*.

105. Letter from Corvette to minister for foreign affairs, August 2, 1816, quoted in Deval, *Mémoire analytique*.

106. Letter from Bassano to Gaudin, March 28, 1812, cited in Deval, *Mémoire analytique*; letter from Gaudin to Bassano, April 1812, cited in Deval, *Mémoire analytique*. Bassano was

requesting information that he could feed to Dubois-Thainville, once again besieged by the dey's demands. Deval, *Mémoire analytique*.

107. A first report that summed up the background to the debt and the bureaucratic correspondence surrounding it was Deval, *Mémoire analytique*. Deval's *Mémoire* reads like a drafted document: the handwriting is poor, and there is a good deal of crossing out. A second report, the unsigned and undated *Rapport*, reads like the final version of the *Mémoire*.

108. "Copie du projet de rapport annoncé dans le mémoire analytique."

109. *Rapport à son excellence le ministre des affaires étrangères, sur les créances dont les Sr Bacri et Busnach, sujets algériens demandent le paiement au gouvernement français*, February 21, 1819, 8CCC, folder 44, AD.

110. Deval, *Mémoire analytique*.

111. *Rapport à son excellence le ministre*.

112. Plantet, *Correspondance*, 2:558.

113. Esquer, *Les Commencements d'un empire*, 45.

114. Quoted in Laborde, *Au roi et aux chambres*, xviii.

115. Esquer, *Les Commencements d'un empire*, 46.

116. Delmas de Grammont, *Histoire d'Alger*, 387.

117. Ibid., 387–388. In response to the claim made in the opposition press and picked up since that Deval colluded with Bacri and Busnach for financial reward, Grammont's own impulse is to protect the consul's reputation, stronger even than his desire to indict Bacri and Busnach. The fact that Deval died penniless a few years after these events is proof for Grammont that the consul's actions were pure.

118. See, for example, Julien, *Histoire de l'Algérie contemporaine*, chap. 2; Martin, *Israélites algériens*, 20–22.

119. Martin, *Israélites algériens*, 20. Martin gives no source for this information, and it may well be that much of it is exaggeration or fabrication.

120. Ibid.

121. Claude-Antoine Rozet, *Voyage dans la régence d'Alger, ou Description du pays occupé par l'armée française en Afrique; contenant des observations sur la géographie physique, la géologie, la météorologie, l'histoire naturelle, etc. suivies de détails sur le commerce, l'agriculture, les sciences et les arts, les mœurs, les coutumes et les usages des habitans de la régence, de l'histoire de son gouvernement, de la description complète du territoire, d'un plan de colonisation, etc.*, 3 vols. (Paris: Bertrand, 1833).

122. Ibid., 2:210.

123. Ibid., 2:215.

124. One recent article calls the work "the best history of Algerian Jews in the nineteenth century." Michael Shurkin, "French Liberal Governance and the Emancipation of Algeria's Jews," *French Historical Studies* 33, no. 2 (2010): 259n1.

125. Esquer, *Les Commencements d'un empire*, 42.

126. Ibid., 20.

127. Julien, *Histoire de l'Algérie contemporaine*, 12. Julien often does not cite sources; however, here he is relying on the outrage of the French consul, Jean Bon Saint-André.

128. Ibid., 19.

129. Peter Dunwoodie, *Writing French Algeria* (Oxford: Oxford University Press, 1998), 7; Charles-Robert Ageron, *Histoire de l'Algérie contemporaine, 1830–1964* (Paris: Presses universitaires de France, 1964).

130. Jules Roy, *Les Chevaux du soleil* (Paris: Grasset, 1967), 79.

131. L. Lautard, *Esquisses historiques: Marseille depuis 1789 jusqu'en 1815 par un vieux Marseillais* (Marseille: Olive, 1844), 1:410, 2:95. Lautard's passage is reproduced in full in Masson, *Marseille et la colonisation française*, 536–537. Lautard offers no source for his quote.

132. The special agent, named Keene, reported in 1814. Mordecai M. Noah, *Correspondence and Documents Relative to the Attempt to Negotiate for the Release of the American Captives at Algiers* (Washington, DC, 1816), 18, quoted in Rosenstock, "The House of Bacri and Busnach," 349.

133. Lautard, *Esquisses historiques*, v.

134. Hildesheimer, "Grandeur et décadence," 396.

135. Esquer, *Les Commencements d'un empire*, 32.

136. Auguste-Marseille Barthélemy and Joseph Méry, *La Bacriade, ou La Guerre d'Alger: Poème héroï-comique en cinq chants* (Paris: A. Dupont, 1827), 6.

137. Ibid., 5. Théophile Gautier wrote an obituary for Méry, in which he waxed lyrical about the poet's ability. Méry, wrote Gautier, "set off dazzling fireworks at all moments, in broad daylight." "In this century of richness of rhyme," in Gautier's assessment, "Méry was a millionaire." Théophile Gautier, obituary for Joseph Méry, *Le Moniteur*, June 19, 1866.

138. Hildesheimer, "Grandeur et décadence," 413.

139. *Le Caducée: Souvenirs marseillais, provençaux et autres* (Marseille: M. Olive, 1879), 2:207.

140. Police report, undated, series 2, dossier 1633, F/7/6537, AN.

141. Barthélemy and Méry, *La Bacriade*, 12.

142. Ibid., 16.

143. Ibid., 17. A footnote from the authors makes the disclaimer that "by putting these verses in the mouth of the dey, we have no intention of attacking either the highly estimable class of Israelites en masse or even Mr. Bacry's integrity. For even supposing that Mr. Bacry is in possession of the dey's funds, we do not believe that he is dishonored for appropriating the gold of a pirate who unjustly had several members of [Bacri's] family decapitated." Ibid. In this way, the lines between reality and fantasy are blurred, once again.

144. Ibid., 18.

145. Ibid., 30–32.

146. Ibid., 34, 36.

147. Ibid., 52.

148. Ibid., 61–62.

149. Ibid., 67.

150. "Expedition to Algiers," *Le Sémaphore de Marseille*, May 4, 1830.

151. Masson, *Marseille et la colonisation française*, 335.

152. Paul Raynal, *L'Expédition d'Alger (1830): Lettres d'un témoin* (Paris: Société d'éditions géographiques, maritimes et coloniales, 1930), 30.

153. Charles-André Julien, "Marseille et la question d'Alger à la veille de la conquête," *Revue africaine* 60 (1919): 16–61.

154. Coller, *Arab France*, 30. See also Zytnicki, *Les Juifs du Maghreb*, 43–48.

155. Schreier, *Arabs of the Jewish Faith*, 24.

156. Rozet, *Voyage*, 2:231.

157. Martin, *Israélites algériens*, 41.

158. Esquer, *Les Commencements d'un empire*, 335, 412–414, quoted in Martin, *Israélites algériens*, 42.

159. Rozet, *Voyage*, 2:258.

160. Martin, *Israélites algériens*, 43.

161. Ibid., 43. See also Edmond Pellissier de Reynaud, *Annales algériennes: Nouvelle édition revue, corrigée et continuée jusqu'à la chute d'Abd-el-Kader* (Paris: Dumaine, 1854), 1:78–79.

162. Martin, *Israélites algériens*, 44–45.

163. Paul Azan, *Général Paul Azan: L'Expédition d'Alger, 1830* (Paris: Plon, 1930), 142.

164. Julien, *Histoire de l'Algérie contemporaine*, 72.

165. Ibid.
166. Marquis de Bartillat, *Relation de la campagne d'Afrique en 1830*, 2nd ed. (Paris: Dento, 1832), 82.
167. Ibid., 208.
168. See Martin, *Israélites algériens*, 54; Pellissier, *Annales algériennes*, 1:367; Charles-Marie Denys Damrémont [Gabriel Esquer], *Correspondance du général Damrémont, gouverneur général des possessions françaises dans le nord de l'Afrique (1837)* (Paris: Honoré Champion, 1928), 237, 239, 240; Jean-Baptiste Drouet d'Erlon [Gabriel Esquer], *Correspondance du général Drouet d'Erlon, gouverneur général des possessions françaises dans le nord de l'Afrique (1834–1835)* (Paris: Honoré Champion, 1926), 185.
169. Martin, *Israélites algériens*, 52.
170. Letter from the minister of war to General Damrémont, August 9, 1837, quoted in Damrémont, *Correspondance*, 632.

## Conclusion

1. Eitan Bar-Yosef, *The Holy Land in English Culture, 1799–1917: Palestine and the Question of Orientalism* (Oxford: Oxford University Press, 2005), 4.
2. Ibid., 301.
3. John Efron, *German Jewry and the Allure of the Sephardic* (Princeton, NJ: Princeton University Press, 2015).
4. Edward Said, *Orientalism* (1978; repr., New York: Vintage, 1994), 27–28.
5. David Nirenberg, *Anti-Judaism: The Western Tradition* (New York: Norton, 2013).
6. Ian Coller, *Arab France: Islam and the Making of Modern Europe, 1798–1831* (Berkeley: University of California Press, 2010).

# Bibliography

Archival Collections

Archives diplomatiques, Paris
Archives nationales, Paris

French Periodicals

*L'Artiste*
*Les Beaux-arts en Europe*
*Bulletin de l'oeuvre des pèlerinages en Terre sainte*
*Chronique de Paris*
*L'Epoque*
*Le Furet de Paris*
*La France*
*La France industrielle, encyclopédie des arts, du commerce, de l'agriculture, et de l'industrie française*
*La France musicale*
*Gazette de France*
*Le Globe*
*L'Illustration*
*Le Magasin pittoresque*
*Le Moniteur universel*
*Le National*
*La Patrie*
*La Presse*
*La Renommée*
*La Revue des deux mondes*
*La Revue de Paris*
*Le Sémaphore de Marseille*

Other Sources

Adelman, Jeremy, and Stephen Aron, eds. *Trading Cultures: The Worlds of Western Merchants.* Turnhout, Belgium: Brepols, 2001.
Ageron, Charles-Robert. *Histoire de l'Algérie contemporaine, 1830–1964.* Paris: Presses universitaires de France, 1964.
Aisenberg, Andrew. *Contagion: Disease, Government and the Social Question in Nineteenth-Century France.* Stanford, CA: Stanford University Press, 1999.

Allen, James Smith. *Popular French Romanticism: Authors, Readers and Books in the Nineteenth Century*. Syracuse, NY: Syracuse University Press, 1981.

Antonetti, Guy. *Louis-Philippe*. Paris: Fayard, 1994.

Arama, Maurice, ed. *Eugène Delacroix, le voyage au Maroc*. Paris: Editions du Sagittaire, 1992.

Azaïs, Abbé. *Journal d'un voyage en Orient*. Avignon: Seguin, 1858.

———. *Pèlerinage en Terre-Sainte*. Paris: E. Giraud, 1855.

Azaïs, Abbé, and C. Domergue. *Journal d'un voyage en Orient*. Avignon, France: F. Seguin aîné, 1858.

Azan, Paul. *Général Paul Azan: L'Expédition d'Alger, 1830*. Paris: Plon, 1930.

Badem, Candan. *The Ottoman Crimean War (1853–1856)*. Leiden, Netherlands: Brill, 2010.

Badone, Ellen, and Sharon R. Roseman, eds. *Intersecting Journeys: The Anthropology of Pilgrimage and Tourism*. Champaign: University of Illinois Press, 2004.

Barrault, Emile, and E. de Cadalvène. *Deux années de l'histoire d'Orient, 1839–1840: Faisant suite à l'histoire de la guerre de Méhemed-Ali en Syrie et en Asie mineure (1832–1833)*. 2 vols. Paris: Delloye, 1840.

Barthélemy, Auguste-Marseille, and Joseph Méry. *La Bacriade, ou La Guerre d'Alger: Poème héroï-comique en cinq chants*. Paris: A. Dupont, 1827.

Bartillat, Marquis de. *Relation de la campagne d'Afrique en 1830*. 2nd ed. Paris: Dentu, 1832.

Bar-Yosef, Eitan. *The Holy Land in English Culture, 1799–1914: Palestine and the Question of Orientalism*. Oxford: Oxford University Press, 2005.

Bassan, Fernande. *Chateaubriand et la terre sainte*. Paris: Presses universitaires de France, 1959.

Basterot, Florimond Jacques. *Le Liban, la Galilée et Rome: Journal d'un voyage en Orient et en Italie, septembre 1867–mai 1868*. Paris: Douniol, 1869.

Baudelaire, Charles. "Qu'est-ce que le romantisme?" In *Salon de 1846*, 5–8. Paris: Lévy, 1846.

Beall, Chandler Baker. *Chateaubriand et le Tasse*. Baltimore: Johns Hopkins University Press, 1934.

———. *La Fortune du Tasse en France*. Eugene: University of Oregon and Modern Language Association of America, 1942.

Bellati, Giovanna. *Théophile Gautier, journaliste à la presse: Point de vue sur une esthétique théâtrale*. Torino: Harmattan Italia, 2008.

Ben Arieh, Yehoshua. *The Rediscovery of the Holy Land in the 19th Century*. Jerusalem: Magnes Press, Hebrew University, 1979.

Ben Arieh, Yehoshua, and Moshe Davis, eds. *Jerusalem in the Mind of the Western World, 1800–1948*. Westport, CT: Praeger, 1997.

Benbassa, Ester, and Aron Rodrigue. *Sephardi Jewry: A History of the Judeo-Spanish Community, 14th–20th Centuries*. Berkeley: University of California Press, 2000.

Bénichou, Paul. *Romantismes français*. Vol. 1, *Le Sacre de l'écrivain: Le Temps des prophètes*. Paris: Gallimard, 2004.

———. *Romantismes français*. Vol. 2, *Les Mages romantiques: L'Ecole du désenchantement*. Paris: Quarto/Gallimard, 1992.

Berben, Jacqueline. "The Romantic Traveler as Questing Hero: Théophile Gautier's *Voyage en Espagne*." *Texas Studies in Literature and Language* 25, no. 3 (1983): 367–389.

Berchet, Jean-Claude, ed. *Le Voyage en Orient: Anthologie des voyageurs français dans le Levant au XIXe siècle.* Paris: Robert Laffont, 1985.

Bergerat, Emile. *Théophile Gautier: Entretiens, souvenirs et correspondance; Avec une préface de Edmond de Goncourt, et une eau-forte de Félix Bracquemond.* Paris: Charpentier, 1879.

[Bernat, Julie]. *La Vie d'une grande comédienne: Mémoires de Madame Judith, de la comédie française, et souvenirs sur ses contemporains.* Paris: Tallandier, 1911.

Berthon, A. *Bérénice, ou Le Pèlerinage à Jérusalem.* Tours: Pornin, 1843.

Bloch, Isaac. *Inscriptions tumulaires des anciens cimetières israélites d'Alger.* Paris: Durlacher, 1888.

Blondel, Edouard. *Deux ans en Syrie, 1838–9.* Paris: Dufart, 1840.

Book-Senninger, Claude. *Théophile Gautier: Auteur dramatique.* Paris: Nizet, 1972.

Bornes-Varol, Marie-Christine. "Balat, vieille communauté judéo-espagnole d'Istanbul." *Revue des études juives* 140, no. 7 (1988): 495–504.

Boyarin, Jonathan. "Jews, Indians, and the Identity of Christian Europe." *AJS Perspectives,* Fall 2005, pp. 12–13.

———. *The Unconverted Self: Jews, Indians, and the Identity of Christian Europe.* Chicago: University of Chicago Press, 2009.

Braude, Benjamin. "The Myth of the Sephardi Economic Superman." In *Trading Cultures: The Worlds of Western Merchants,* edited by Jeremy Adelman and Stephen Aron, 163–191. Turnhout, Belgium: Brepols, 2001.

Bunel, Louis. *Jérusalem, la côte de Syrie et Constantinople en 1853.* Paris: Sagnier et Bray, 1854.

*Le Caducée: Souvenirs marseillais, provençaux et autres.* 10 vols. Marseilles: M. Olive, 1879.

Canonge, Jules. *Pradier et Ary Scheffer: Notes, souvenirs et documents d'art contemporain.* Paris: Paulin, 1858.

Carré, Jean Marie. *Voyageurs et écrivains français en Egypte.* Vol. 1, *Des pèlerins du Moyen Age à Méhémet Ali.* 2nd ed. Cairo: Imprimerie de l'institut français d'archéologie orientale, 1956.

Charles-Roux, François. "Les Travaux d'Herculais, ou une extraordinaire mission en Barbarie." *Revue de l'histoire des colonies françaises* 20 (1927): 321–368.

Chateaubriand, François-René. *Itinéraire de Paris à Jérusalem.* Edited by Jean-Claude Berchet. Paris: Gallimard, 2005.

Chelini, Jean, and Henry Branthomme. *Les Chemins de Dieu: Histoire des pèlerinages chrétiens des origines à nos jours.* Paris: Hachette, 1982.

Cheyette, Bryan. *Constructions of "the Jew" in English Literature and Society.* New York: Cambridge University Press, 1993.

———. "White Skin, Black Masks: Jews and Jewishness in the Writings of George Eliot and Frantz Fanon." In *Cultural Readings of Imperialism: Edward Said and the Gravity of History,* edited by Keith Ansell-Pearson, Benita Parry, and Judith Squires, 106–126. New York: St. Martin's Press, 1997.

Cholvy, Gérard, and Yves-Marie Hilaire. *Histoire religieuse de la France contemporaine.* Vol. 1, *1800–1880.* Toulouse: Privat, 2000.

Clark, Steve, ed. *Travel Writing and Empire: Postcolonial Theory in Transit.* London: Zed Books, 1999.

Coller, Ian. *Arab France: Islam and the Making of Modern Europe, 1798–1831.* Berkeley: University of California Press, 2010.

Cornille, Henri. *Souvenirs d'Orient.* 2nd ed. Paris: Bertrand, 1836.

*Correspondance de Napoléon Ier, publiée par ordre de l'empereur Napoléon III.* 32 vols. Paris: Imprimerie impériale, 1858–1869.

Court-Perez, Françoise. *Gautier, un romantique ironique.* Paris: Champion, 1998.

Cranston, Maurice. "Romanticism and Revolution." *History of European Ideas* 17, no. 1 (1993): 19–30.

Damas, R. P. Amédée de. *Voyages en Orient: Jerusalem.* Paris: Putois-Cretté, [1866].

Damrémont, Charles-Marie Denys [Gabriel Esquer]. *Correspondance du général Damrémont, gouverneur général des possessions françaises dans le nord de l'Afrique (1837).* Paris: Honoré Champion, 1928.

Darboy, Georges. *Jérusalem et la Terre-Sainte: Notes de voyage.* Paris: Belin-Leprieur et Morizot, [1852].

Daspres, Marie-Joseph. *Pèlerinage en Terre-Sainte: Journal de la caravane partie de Marseille de 28 août et dissoute à Beyrouth, le 20 octobre 1869.* Paris: J. Lefort, 1875.

Davies, Helen. *Emile and Isaac Péreire: Bankers, Socialists and Sephardic Jews in Nineteenth-Century France.* Manchester, UK: Manchester University Press, 2015.

[Delacroix, Eugène]. *Delacroix, le voyage au Maroc.* Translated by Tamara Blondel. Paris: Institut du monde arabe, 1994.

———. *Souvenirs d'un voyage dans le Maroc.* Edited by Laure Beaumont-Maillet, Barthélémy Jobert, and Sophie Join-Lambert. Paris: Gallimard, 1999.

Delmas de Grammont, Henri. *Histoire d'Alger sous la domination turque (1515–1830).* Paris: Leroux, 1887.

Delorme, Abbé. *Un Pèlerinage en Terre Sainte, par l'abbé Delorme.* Limoges: Barbou frères, 1860.

De Marsay, L. G. [Albert-André Patin de la Fizelière]. *La Danse, ses temples et ses desservants en 1850.* Paris: Pilloy, 1850.

Didier, Charles. *Nationalité française.* Paris: Pagnerre, 1841.

———. *Promenade au Maroc.* Paris: Labitte, 1844.

Drouet d'Erlon, Jean-Baptiste [Gabriel Esquer]. *Correspondance du général Drouet d'Erlon, gouverneur général des possessions françaises dans le nord de l'Afrique (1834–1835).* Paris: Honoré Champion, 1926.

Du Camp, Maxime. *Souvenirs et paysages d'Orient.* Paris: Bertrand, 1848.

———. *Voyage en Orient, 1849–1851.* Edited by Giovanni Bonaccorso. Messina: Peloritana Editrice, 1972.

Dumas, Alexandre. *Quinze jours au Sinaï.* 1839. Reprint, Plan de la Tour: Editions d'aujourd'hui, 1979.

———. *Le Véloce, ou De Cadix à Tunis.* 1848. Reprint, Paris: Bourin, 1990.

Dumur, Guy. *Delacroix et le Maroc.* Paris: Herscher, 1988.

Dunwoodie, Peter. *Writing French Algeria.* Oxford: Oxford University Press, 1998.

Eade, John, and Michael J. Sallnow, eds. *Contesting the Sacred: The Anthropology of Christian Pilgrimage.* Urbana: University of Illinois Press, 2000.

Easton, Malcolm. *Artists and Writers in Paris: The Bohemian Idea, 1803–1867.* London: Edward Arnold, 1964.

Efron, John. *German Jewry and the Allure of the Sephardic.* Princeton, NJ: Princeton University Press, 2015.

Eisenbeth, Maurice. "Les Juifs en Algérie et en Tunisie à l'époque turque (1516–1830)." *Revue africaine* 46 (1952): 114–187, 343–384.

Enault, Louis. *Constantinople et la Turquie: Tableau historique, pittoresque, statistique et moral de l'empire ottoman*. Paris: Hachette, 1855.

———. *La Terre sainte: Voyage de quarante pèlerins de 1853*. Paris: Maison, 1854.

Esquer, Gabriel. *Les Commencements d'un empire: La Prise d'Alger (1830)*. Paris: Larose, 1929.

———. "Les Poètes et l'expédition d'Alger." *Revue africaine* 60 (1919): 112–145.

d'Estourmel, Joseph. *Journal d'un voyage en Orient*. 2 vols. Paris: Crapelet, 1844.

Féraud, Laurent-Charles. *Histoire des villes de la province de Constantine: La Calle et documents pour servir à l'histoire des anciennes concessions françaises d'Afrique*. Algiers: Aillaud, 1877.

Feydeau, Ernest. *Théophile Gautier: Souvenirs intimes*. Paris: Plon, 1874.

Filippini Jean-Pierre. "A Jewish Family in Livorno between the Trading Ambitions and Vicissitudes of the Mediterranean World: The Coen Bacris" [in Italian]. *Richerche Storiche* 2 (1982): 287–333.

———. "Juifs émigrés et immigrés dans le port de Livourne pendant la période napoléonienne." *East and Maghreb* 4 (1983): 31–91.

———. "Les Séfarades en méditerranée occidentale." *Histoire, économie et société* 12, no. 3 (1993): 345–349.

Filleul de Petigny, Clara. *La Palestine, ou Une visite aux Lieux-Saints*. Rouen: Mégard, 1867. Originally published as *Les Jeunes voyageurs en Palestine*, 1843.

Flaubert, Gustave. *Voyage en Egypte*. Edited by Pierre-Marc de Biasi. Paris: Grasset, 1991.

———. *Voyage en Palestine*. N.p.: Magellan, 2008.

Fontanier, Victor. *Voyages en Orient, entrepris par ordre du gouvernement français, de 1830 à 1833: Deuxième voyage en Anatolie*. Paris: Librairie de Dumont, 1834.

Forbin, Auguste de. *Voyage dans le Levant, en 1817 et 1818*. Paris: L'Imprimerie royale, 1819.

Frankel, Jonathan. *The Damascus Affair: "Ritual Murder," Politics, and the Jews in 1840*. Cambridge: Cambridge University Press, 1997.

Fraser, Elisabeth. "Books, Prints, and Travel: Reading in the Gaps of the Orientalist Archive." *Art History* 31, no. 3 (2008): 342–367.

Fulford, Tim, and Peter J. Kitson, eds. *Romanticism and Colonialism: Writing and Empire, 1780–1830*. Cambridge: Cambridge University Press, 1998.

Furet, François. *Revolutionary France, 1770–1880*. Translated by Antonia Nevill. Oxford: Blackwell, 1992.

Gautier, Théophile. *Les Beaux-Arts en Europe*. 2 vols. Paris: Michel Lévy, 1856.

———. *La Comédie de la mort*. Paris: Desessart, 1838.

———. *Constantinople*. Paris: Michel Lévy, 1853.

———. *Histoire du romantisme*. Paris: Charpentier, 1882.

———. *Italia*. 2nd ed. Paris: Hachette, 1855.

———. *La Juive de Constantine*. Paris: Marchant, 1846.

———. *Loin de Paris*. Paris: Michel Lévy, 1865.

———. *L'Orient*. 2 vols. Paris: Charpentier, 1882.

———. *Portrait de Balzac, précédé de portrait de Théophile Gautier, par lui-même.* 1859. Reprint, Montpellier: L'Anabase, 1994.

———. *Portraits contemporains: Littérateurs, peintres, sculpteurs, artistes dramatiques; Avec un portrait de Théophile Gautier d'après une gravure a l'eau forte par lui-même vers 1832*. Paris: Charpentier, 1898.

———. *Le Roman de la momie*. Paris: Garnier-Flammarion, 1966.

———. *Salon de 1847*. Paris: Hetzel, 1847.

———. *Souvenirs de théâtre, d'art et de critique*. Paris: Charpentier, 1883.

———. *Tableaux de siège, Paris 1870–1871*. Paris: Charpentier, 1871.

———. *Les Vendeurs du temple*. In *La Comédie de la mort*. Paris: Desessart, 1838.

———. *Voyage en Russie*. Paris: Charpentier, 1867.

———. *Voyage pittoresque en Algérie*. Edited by Madeleine Cottin. Geneva: Droz, 1973.

Gaviglio-Faivre d'Arcier, Catherine. *Lovenjoul (1836–1907): Une vie, une collection*. Paris: Kimé, 2007.

Géramb, R. P. Marie-Joseph de. *Pèlerinage à Jérusalem et au mont Sinaï, en 1831, 1832, et 1833*. 2nd ed. 2 vols. Paris: Leclère, 1836.

Gibson, Ralph. *A Social History of French Catholicism, 1789–1914*. London: Routledge, 1989.

Gildea, Robert. *The Past in French History*. New Haven, CT: Yale University Press, 1994.

Gilman, Sander L. "'We're Not Jews': Imagining Jewish History and Jewish Bodies in Contemporary Multicultural Literature." In *Orientalism and the Jews*, edited by Ivan Davidson Kalmar and Derek Penslar, 201–221. Lebanon, NH: Brandeis University Press, 2004.

Gilroy, Amanda, ed. *Romantic Geographies: Discourses of Travel, 1775–1844*. Manchester, UK: Manchester University Press, 2000.

Goldhill, Simon. *Jerusalem: City of Longing*. Cambridge, MA: Belknap Press of Harvard University Press, 2008.

Goncourt, Edmond, and Jules de Goncourt. *Journal: Mémoires de la vie littéraire*. 11 vols. Monaco: Flammarion, 1956.

Goupil, Frédéric August Antoine. *Voyage en Orient fait avec d'Horace Vernet en 1839 et 1840*. Paris: Challamel, [1843].

Graetz, Michael. *The Jews in Nineteenth-Century France: From the French Revolution to the Alliance Israélite Universelle*. Translated by Jane Marie Todd. Stanford, CA: Stanford University Press, 1996.

Guérin, Victor. *Rapport sur les pèlerinages en Terre Sainte, par M. Guérin*. Paris: Imprimerie de G. Chamerot, [1873].

Guiffrey, Jean. *Le Voyage d'Eugène Delacroix au Maroc*. 2 vols. Paris: André Marty, 1909.

Guiral, Pierre. "Les Juifs de Marseille en 1808." In *Actes du 85e Congrès national des Sociétés savantes: Section d'histoire moderne et contemporaine*, 279–289. Paris: Imprimerie nationale, 1961.

———. *Marseille et l'Algérie: 1830–1841*. Gap, France: Ophrys, 1956.

Guiral, Pierre, and Paul Amargier. *Histoire de Marseille*. Paris: Mazarine, 1983.

Hackforth-Jones, Jocelyn, and Mary Roberts, eds. *Edges of Empire: Orientalism and Visual Culture*. Oxford: Blackwell, 2005.

Haddey, M. J. M. *Le Livre d'or des Israélites algériens: Recueil de renseignements inédits et authentiques sur les principaux négociants juifs d'Alger pendant la période turque*. 1871. Reprint, Paris: Cercle de généalogie juive, 2005.

Halbwachs, Maurice. "The Legendary Topography of the Gospels in the Holy Land." In *On Collective Memory*, edited and translated by Lewis A. Coser, 193–235. Chicago: University of Chicago Press, 1992.

———. *On Collective Memory*. Edited and translated by Lewis A. Coser. Chicago: University of Chicago Press, 1992.

Hallman, Diana. *Opera, Liberalism and Antisemitism in Nineteenth-Century France: The Politics of Halévy's* La Juive. Cambridge: Cambridge University Press, 2002.

Hamont, Pierre-Nicolas. *L'Egypte sous Méhémet-Ali.* 2 vols. Paris: Léautey et Lecointe, 1843.

Harris, Ruth. *Lourdes: Body and Spirit in the Secular Age.* London: Allen Lane, 1999.

Harrison, Carol E. *Romantic Catholics: France's Postrevolutionary Generation in Search of a Modern Faith.* Ithaca, NY: Cornell University Press, 2014.

Hayoun, Maurice. *Renan, la bible et les juifs.* Paris: Gallimard, 2008.

Hertz, Deborah. *How Jews Became Germans: The History of Conversion and Assimilation in Berlin.* New Haven, CT: Yale University Press, 2007.

Heschel, Susannah. *Abraham Geiger and the Jewish Jesus.* Chicago: University of Chicago Press, 1998.

Hess, Jonathan. *Germans, Jews and the Claims of Modernity.* New Haven, CT: Yale University Press, 2002.

Hildesheimer, Françoise. "Grandeur et décadence de la maison Bacri de Marseille." *Revue des études juives* 86, no. 3–4 (1977): 389–414.

Hirschberg, H. Z. (J. W.). *A History of the Jews in North Africa.* Vol. 2, *From the Ottoman Conquests to the Present Time.* Edited by Eliezer Bashan and Robert Attal. Leiden, Netherlands: Brill, 1981.

———. "Jews and Jewish Affairs in the Relations between Great Britain and Morocco in the 18th Century." In *Essays Presented to Chief Rabbi Israel Brodie on the Occasion of His Seventieth Birthday.* Edited by H. J. Zimmels, J. Rabbinowitz, and I. Finestein, 153–182. London: Soncino Press, 1967.

Hyman, Paula. *The Emancipation of the Jews of Alsace: Acculturation and Tradition in the Nineteenth Century.* New Haven, CT: Yale University Press, 1991.

———. *The Jews of Modern France.* Berkeley: University of California Press, 1998.

Jacqueton, Gilbert. *H. D. de Grammont.* Algiers: Jourdan, n.d.

Janin, Jules. *Rachel et la tragédie.* Paris: Amyot, 1858.

Jardin, André, and André-Jean Tudesq. *Restoration and Reaction, 1815–1848.* Translated by Elborg Forster. Cambridge: Cambridge University Press, 1983.

Jarvis, Robin. "Self-Discovery from Byron to Raban: The Long Afterlife of Romantic Travel." *Studies in Travel Writing* 9, no. 2 (2005): 185–204.

Jonas, Raymond. *France and the Cult of the Sacred Heart: An Epic Tale for Modern Times.* Berkeley: University of California Press, 2000.

Julien, Charles-André. *Histoire de l'Algérie contemporaine: La Conquête et les débuts de la colonisation (1827–1871).* Paris: Presses universitaires de France, 1964.

———. "Marseille et la question d'Alger à la veille de la conquête." *Revue africaine* 60 (1919): 16–61.

Kalman, Julie. "Going Home to the Holy Land: The Jews of Jerusalem in Nineteenth-Century French Catholic Pilgrimage." *Journal of Modern History* 84, no. 2 (2012): 335–368.

———. "The Jew in the Scenery: Historicising Nineteenth-Century French Travel Literature." *French History* 27, no. 4 (2013): 515–534.

———. *Rethinking Antisemitism in Nineteenth-Century France.* New York: Cambridge University Press, 2010.

———. "Sensuality, Depravity, and Ritual Murder: The Damascus Blood Libel and Jews in France." *Jewish Social Studies: History, Culture, Society* 13, no. 3 (2007): 35–58.

Kalmar, Ivan. "Jesus Did Not Wear a Turban: Orientalism, the Jews, and Christian Art." In *Orientalism and the Jews*, edited by Ivan Davidson Kalmar and Derek Penslar, 3–31. Lebanon, NH: Brandeis University Press, 2004.

Kalmar, Ivan Davidson, and Derek Penslar, eds. *Orientalism and the Jews*. Lebanon, NH: Brandeis University Press, 2004.

———. "Orientalism and the Jews: An Introduction." In *Orientalism and the Jews*, edited by Ivan Davidson Kalmar and Derek Penslar, xiii–xl. Lebanon, NH: Brandeis University Press, 2005.

Karp, Jonathan, and Adam Sutcliffe, eds. *Philosemitism in History*. New York: Cambridge University Press, 2011.

Kearns, James. *Théophile Gautier, Orator to the Artists*. London: Legenda, 2007.

Keller, Barbara G. *The Middle Ages Reconsidered: Attitudes in France from the Eighteenth Century through the Romantic Movement*. New York: Peter Lang, 1994.

Kerhardène, Gillot de. *Voyage en Orient: Course de Tibériade à Capharnaüm*. Roanne, France: Ferlay, 1860.

Kinglake, Alexander William. *The Invasion of the Crimea: Its Origin, and an Account of Its Progress, Down to the Death of Lord Raglan*. Vol. 1. New York: Harper and Brothers, 1863.

Klein, Luce. *Portrait de la juive dans la littérature française*. Paris: Nizet, 1970.

Kselman, Thomas. *Miracles and Prophecies in Nineteenth-Century France*. New Brunswick, NJ: Rutgers University Press, 1983.

Kudlick, Catherine. *Cholera in Post-revolutionary Paris: A Cultural History*. Berkeley: University of California Press, 1996.

Laborde, Alexandre de. *Au Roi et aux chambres, sur les véritables causes de la rupture avec Alger et sur l'expédition qui se prépare*. Paris: Truchy, 1830.

Laborde, Léon E. S. J. *L'Orient et le Moyen Age, par M. Léon de La Borde*. Paris: 20, rue des Grands-Augustins, 1833.

———. *Voyage de la Syrie, par MM. Alexandre de Laborde, Becker, Hall et Léon de Laborde, rédigé et publié par Léon de Laborde [et A. de Laborde]*. Paris: Firmin-Didot frères, 1837.

Lacoste, Claudine. *La Critique d'art de Théophile Gautier*. Montpellier: La Grande-Motte, 1985.

———. "La femme orientale vue et rêvée par le poète." *Bulletin de la Société Théophile Gautier* 12 (1990): 11–21.

———. "La Juive de Constantine." *Bulletin de la Société Théophile Gautier* 26 (2004): 303–308.

Lacoste-Veysseyre, Claudine [Gautier, Théophile], ed. *Correspondance générale*. 11 vols. Geneva: Droz, 1985.

Lamartine, Alphonse de. *Souvenirs, impressions, pensées et paysages pendant un voyage en Orient (1832–1833) ou Notes d'un voyageur*. 4 vols. Paris: Gosselin, 1835.

———. *Voyage en Orient: 1832–1833*. 2 vols. Paris: Gosselin, 1841.

Lapin, Hayim, and Dale B. Martin, eds. *Jews, Antiquity, and the Nineteenth-Century Imagination*. Bethesda: University Press of Maryland, 2003.

La Roière, J.-V. de. *Voyage en Orient*. Paris: Debécourt, 1836.

Lathers, Marie. *Bodies of Art: French Literary Realism and the Artist's Model*. Lincoln: University of Nebraska Press, 2001.

Lautard, Laurent. *Esquisses historiques: Marseille depuis 1789 jusqu'en 1815 par un vieux Marseillais.* Marseilles: Olive, 1844.

Lavaud, Martine. *Théophile Gautier: Militant du romantisme.* Paris: Champion, 2001.

Leask, Nigel. *British Romantic Writers and the East: Anxieties of Empire.* Cambridge: Cambridge University Press, 1992.

——. *Curiosity and the Aesthetics of Travel Writing, 1770–1840: "From an Antique Land."* Oxford: Oxford University Press, 2002.

Lebrun, Pierre-Antoine. "Voyages: Voyage dans le Levant en 1817 et 1818 par M. le Comte de Forbin." *La Renommée* 30 (1819): 119–120.

Leff, Lisa Moses. *Sacred Bonds of Solidarity: The Rise of Jewish Internationalism in Nineteenth-Century France.* Stanford, CA: Stanford University Press, 2006.

Lehrmann, Charles. *The Jewish Element in French Literature.* Translated by George Klin. Rutherford, NJ: Fairleigh Dickinson University Press, 1971.

Leroy, Louis. *Artistes et rapins.* Paris: Le Chevalier, 1868.

Levy, Avigdor, ed. *The Jews of the Ottoman Empire.* Princeton, NJ: Darwin Press, 1994.

Lorcin, Patricia, ed. *Algeria and France, 1800–2000: Identity, Memory, Nostalgia.* Syracuse, NY: Syracuse University Press, 2006.

Lowin, Joseph G. "Théophile Gautier et ses juifs." *Revue des études juives* 131 (1972): 411–418.

Löwy, Michael, and Robert Sayre. *Romanticism against the Tide of Modernity.* Translated by Catherine Porter. Durham, NC: Duke University Press, 2001.

Lyons, Martyn. "The Audience for Romanticism: Walter Scott in France, 1815–51." *European History Quarterly* 14, no. 1 (1984): 21–46.

——. *Le Triomphe du livre: Une histoire sociologique de la lecture dans la France du XIXe siècle.* Paris: Promodis, 1987.

Mackenzie, John. *The Orientalism Debate: History, Theory and the Arts.* Manchester, UK: Manchester University Press, 1994.

Malherbe, Raoul de. *L'Orient de 1718 à 1845—histoire, politique, religion et mœurs.* Paris: Gide, 1846.

Marcellus, Marie-Louis-Jean-André-Charles Demartin du Tyrac. *Souvenirs de l'Orient.* Paris: Debucourt, 1839.

Marcil, Yasmine. "'Voyage écrit, voyage vécu?" La Crédibilité du voyageur, du Journal encyclopédique au Magasin encyclopédique." In "Le Siècle du voyage," special issue, *Sociétés et représentations* 21 (April 2006): 25–43.

Marcotte de Quivières, Charles. *Deux ans en Afrique.* Paris: Librairie nouvelle, 1855.

Marmier, Xavier. *Du Rhin au Nil: Souvenirs de voyages.* 2 vols. Paris: Bertrand, 1847.

——. *En Pays lointains.* Paris: Hachette, 1876.

——. *Impressions et souvenirs d'un voyageur chrétien.* Tours: A. Mame et fils, 1873.

Martin, Claude. *Les Israélites algériens de 1830 à 1902.* Paris: Herakles, 1936.

Masson, Paul. "A la veille d'une conquête: Concessions et compagnies d'Afrique (1800–1830)." *Bulletin de géographie historique et descriptive* 24 (1909): 48–124.

——. *Marseille depuis 1789: Etudes historiques.* 2 vols. Paris: Hachette, 1919.

——. *Marseille et la colonisation française: Essai d'histoire coloniale.* Marseilles: Barlatier, 1906.

McMahon, Darrin. *Enemies of the Enlightenment: The French Counter-Enlightenment and the Making of Modernity.* New York: Oxford University Press, 2001.

McMillan, James F. "'Priest Hits Girl': The Front Line of the War of the Two Frances." In *Culture Wars: Secular-Catholic Conflict in Nineteenth-Century Europe*, edited by Christopher Clark and Wolfram Kaiser, 77–101. New York: Cambridge University Press, 2003.

———. "Rediscovering Louis Veuillot: The Politics of Religious Identity in Nineteenth-Century France." In *Visions/Revisions: Essays on Nineteenth-Century French Culture*, edited by Nigel Harkness, Paul Rowe, Tim Unwin, and Jennifer Yee, 305–322. Bern: Peter Lang, 2003.

Meryon, Charles Lewis. *Travels of Lady Hester Stanhope*. 2 vols. London: Henry Colburn, 1846.

Michaud, Joseph-François, and Jean-Joseph-François Poujoulat. *Correspondance d'Orient, 1830–1831*. 7 vols. Paris: Ducollet, 1833–1835.

Michon, Jean-Hippolyte. *Voyage religieux en Orient*. Paris: Vve Comon, 1853.

Mislin, Jacques. *Les Saints Lieux*. 2 vols. Paris: Guyot frères, 1851.

Montesquieu, Charles-Louis de Secondat. *Lettres persanes*. Cologne: Marteau, 1754.

Morot, Jean-Baptiste. *Journal de voyage: Paris à Jérusalem, 1839 et 1840*. Paris: Claye, 1869.

Moxnes, Halvor. "Renan's *Vie de Jésus* as Representation of the Orient." In *Jews, Antiquity, and the Nineteenth-Century Imagination*, edited by Hayim Lapin and Dale B. Martin, 85–108. Bethesda: University Press of Maryland, 2003.

Murphy, Kerry. "Berlioz, Meyerbeer, and the Place of Jewishness in Criticism." In *Berlioz: Past, Present, Future: Bicentenary Essays*, edited by Peter Bloom, 90–104. Rochester, NY: University of Rochester Press, 2003.

Nerval, Gérard de. *Voyage en Orient*. 3rd ed. 2 vols. Paris: Charpentier, 1851.

Nirenberg, David. *Anti-Judaism: The Western Tradition*. New York: Norton, 2013.

Noah, Mordecai M. *Correspondence and Documents Relative to the Attempt to Negotiate for the Release of the American Captives at Algiers*. Washington, DC, 1816.

Nora, Pierre, dir. *Realms of Memory: Rethinking the French Past*. Edited by Lawrence D. Kritzman. Translated by Arthur Goldhammer. New York: Columbia University Press, 1996.

*L'Orient de Théophile Gautier: Colloque international organisé par le Centre d'études romantiques de l'Université Paul Valéry, Montpellier; La Société Théophile Gautier, La Société des amis d'Alexandre Dumas*. 2 vols. Montpellier: Société Théophile Gautier, 1990.

Pagden, Anthony. *European Encounters with the New World: From Renaissance to Romanticism*. New Haven, CT: Yale University Press, 1993.

Paradis, Venture de. "Alger au XVIII siècle." *Revue africaine* 39 (1895): 292–293.

Pardieu, Charles de. *Excursion en Orient: L'Egypte, le Mont-Sinaï, l'Arabie, la Palestine, la Syrie, le Liban*. Paris: Garnier, 1851.

Parfitt, Tudor. *The Jews in Palestine, 1800–1882*. Woodbridge, UK: Boydell Press, 1987.

Pasto, James. "Islam's 'Strange Secret Sharer': Orientalism, Judaism and the Jewish Question." *Comparative Studies of Society and History* 40, no. 3 (1998): 437–474.

Pellissier de Reynaud, Edmond. *Annales algériennes: Nouvelle édition revue, corrigée et continuée jusqu'à la chute d'Abd-el-Kader*. 2 vols. Paris: Dumaine, 1854.

Péricaud, Louis. *Le Théâtre des Funambules, ses mimes, ses acteurs, et ses pantomimes, depuis sa fondation, jusqu'à sa démolition*. Paris: Sapin, 1897.

Peters, Francis E. *The Holy Land in the Eyes of Chroniclers, Visitors, Pilgrims and Prophets.* Princeton, NJ: Princeton University Press, 1985.

Philipp, Thomas. "The Farhi Family and the Changing Position of the Jews in Syria, 1750–1860." *Middle Eastern Studies* 20, no. 4 (1984): 37–52.

Piette, Christine. *Les Juifs de Paris (1805–1840): La Marche vers l'assimilation.* Quebec: Presses de l'Université Laval, 1983.

Plantet, Eugène, ed. *Correspondance des deys d'Alger avec la cour de France, 1579–1833.* 2 vols. Paris: Alcan, 1889.

Poujoulat, Baptistin. *Voyage à Constantinople, dans l'Asie mineure, en Mésopotamie, à Palmyre, et Syrie, en Palestine et en Egypte.* 2 vols. Paris: Ducollet, 1840.

Prakash, Gyan. "Orientalism Now." *History and Theory* 34, no. 3 (1995): 199–212.

Pratt, Mary Louise. *Imperial Eyes: Travel Writing and Transculturation.* 2nd ed. New York: Routledge, 2008.

Privat d'Anglemont, Alexandre. *La Closerie des Lilas: Quadrille en prose.* Paris: Frey, 1848.

Raynal, Paul. *L'Expédition d'Alger (1830): Lettres d'un témoin.* Paris: Société d'éditions géographiques, maritimes et coloniales, 1930.

Regard, Maurice. "Eugène Delacroix et le comte de Mornay au Maroc." *Etudes d'art* 7 (1952): 29–60.

Rémond, René. *The Right Wing in France from 1815 to De Gaulle.* 2nd ed. Translated by James Laux. Philadelphia: University of Pennslyvania Press, 1969.

Renan, Ernest. *Mission de Phénicie.* Paris: Lévy, 1864.

———. *Vie de Jésus.* 13th ed. Paris: Julliard, 1962.

Renoüard de Bussièrre, Baron Marie-Théodore. *Lettres sur l'Orient, écrites pendant les années 1827 et 1828.* 2 vols. Paris: Levrault, 1829.

Richardson, Joanna. *Judith Gautier: A Biography.* London: Quartet, 1986.

———. *Théophile Gautier: His Life and Times.* London: Max Reinhardt, 1958.

Richer, Jean. *Etudes et recherches sur Théophile Gautier, prosateur.* Paris: Nizet, 1981.

Roche, Daniel. "Les Livres de voyage à l'époque moderne, XVIe–XVIIIe siècles." *Dossier: Voyages: Revue de la Bibliothèque nationale de France* 22 (2006): 5–13.

Rosenstock, Morton. "Economic and Social Conditions among the Jews of Algeria: 1790–1848." *Historia Judaica* 18 (1956): 3–26.

———. "The House of Bacri and Busnach: A Chapter from Algeria's Commercial History." *Jewish Social Studies* 14, no. 4 (1952): 343–364.

Rosset de Létourville, Charles-Marie. *Jérusalem: Notes de voyage.* Paris: Amyot, 1856.

Roth, Norman, ed. *Medieval Jewish Civilization: An Encyclopedia.* New York: Routledge, 2003.

Roy, Jules. *Les Chevaux du soleil.* Paris: Grasset, 1967.

Rozet, Claude-Antoine. *Voyage dans la régence d'Alger, ou Description du pays occupé par l'armée française en Afrique; contenant des observations sur la géographie physique, la géologie, la météorologie, l'histoire naturelle, etc. suivies de détails sur le commerce, l'agriculture, les sciences et les arts, les mœurs, les coutumes et les usages des habitans de la régence, de l'histoire de son gouvernement, de la description complète du territoire, d'un plan de colonisation, etc.* 3 vols. Paris: Bertrand, 1833.

Rude, Maxime. *Confidences d'un journaliste.* Paris: Sagnier, 1876.

Said, Edward. *Culture and Imperialism.* New York: Knopf, 1993.

———. *Orientalism.* 1978. Reprint, New York: Vintage, 1994.

Saintine, P.-Gérardy [Xavier Boniface]. *Trois ans en Judée.* Paris: Hachette, 1860.

Samuels, Maurice. *Inventing the Israelite: Jewish Fiction in Nineteenth-Century France.* Stanford, CA: Stanford University Press, 2010.

———. "Philosemitism and the *mission civilisatrice* in Gautier's *La Juive de Constantine.*" *French Forum* 38, no. 1–2 (2013): 19–33.

———. *The Spectacular Past: Popular History and the Novel in Nineteenth-Century France.* Ithaca, NY: Cornell University Press, 2004.

———. "Zola's Philosemitism: From *L'Argent* to *vérité.*" In "Zola," special issue, *Romanic Review* 102, no. 3–4 (2011): 503–519.

Saulcy, Félicien de. *Les Derniers jours de Jérusalem.* Paris: L. Hachette, 1866.

———. *Voyage autour de la Mer morte et dans les terres bibliques, executé de décembre 1850 à avril 1851.* 2 vols. Paris: Gide et J. Baudry, 1853.

Savy, Nicole. *Les Juifs des romantiques: Le Discours de la littérature sur les Juifs de Chateaubriand à Hugo.* Paris: Belin, 2010.

Schechter, Ronald. *Obstinate Hebrews: Representations of Jews in France, 1715–1815.* Berkeley: University of California Press, 2003.

Schreier, Joshua Samuel. *Arabs of the Jewish Faith: The Civilizing Mission in Colonial Algeria.* New Brunswick, NJ: Rutgers University Press, 2010.

Schroeter, Daniel J. "Orientalism and the Jews of the Mediterranean." *Journal of Mediterranean Studies* 4, no. 2 (1994): 183–196.

———. *The Sultan's Jew: Morocco and the Sephardi World.* Stanford, CA: Stanford University Press, 2002.

Schur, Nathan. *Jerusalem in Pilgrims' and Travelers' Accounts: A Thematic Bibliography of Western Christian Itineraries, 1300–1917.* Jerusalem: Ariel, 1980.

———. *Twenty Centuries of Christian Pilgrimage to the Holy Land.* Tel Aviv: Dvir, 1992.

Schwarzfuchs, Simon. *Les Juifs d'Algérie et la France: 1830–1855.* Jerusalem: Institut Ben-Zvi, 1981.

Sellards, John. *Dans le sillage du romantisme: Charles Didier (1805–1864).* Paris: Champion, 1933.

Senninger, Claude-Marie, ed. *Baudelaire par Théophile Gautier.* Paris: Klincksieck, 1986.

———. *Théophile Gautier: Une vie, une oeuvre.* Paris: Sedes, 1994.

Sessions, Jennifer. *By Sword and Plow: France and the Conquest of Algeria.* Ithaca, NY: Cornell University Press, 2011.

Shepherd, Naomi. *The Zealous Intruders: The Western Rediscovery of Palestine.* London: Collins, 1987.

Shurkin, Michael. "French Liberal Governance and the Emancipation of Algeria's Jews." *French Historical Studies* 33, no. 2 (2010): 259–280.

Snell, Robert. *Théophile Gautier: A Romantic Critic of the Visual Arts.* Oxford: Clarendon, 1982.

Spoelberch de Lovenjoul, Charles. *Histoire des oeuvres de Théophile Gautier.* 2 vols. Geneva: Slatkine, 1968.

———. *Les Lundis d'un chercheur.* 2nd ed. Paris: Calmann-Lévy, 1894.

Spurr, David. *The Rhetoric of Empire.* Durham, NC: Duke University Press, 1993.

Stein, Sarah. "Sephardi and Middle Eastern Jewries since 1492." In *The Oxford Handbook of Jewish Studies,* edited by Martin Cohen, Jeremy Goodman, and David Sorkin, 327–362. Oxford: Oxford University Press, 2002.

Talmeyr, Maurice. *Souvenirs d'avant le déluge, 1870–1914.* Paris: Perrin, 1927.

Tasso, Torquato. *Jerusalem Delivered.* Edited and translated by Anthony Esolen. Baltimore: Johns Hopkins University Press, 2000.

Taylor, Isidore Justin Séverin, and Louis Reybaud. *La Syrie, l'Egypte, la Palestine, et la Judée, considérées sous leur aspect historique, archéologique, descriptif et pittoresque.* 2 vols. Paris: Chez l'éditeur, 1839.

Tennant, P. E. *Théophile Gautier.* London: Athlone Press, 1975.

Thompson, C. W. *French Romantic Travel Writing, Chateaubriand to Nerval.* Oxford: Oxford University Press, 2012.

Thompson, Victoria. "'I Went Pale with Pleasure': The Body, Sexuality, and National Identity among French Travelers to Algiers in the Nineteenth Century." In *Algeria and France, 1800–2000: Identity, Memory, Nostalgia,* edited by Patricia Lorcin, 18–32. Syracuse, NY: Syracuse University Press, 2006.

Trivellato, Francesca. *The Familiarity of Strangers: The Sephardic Diaspora, Livorno, and Cross-cultural Trade in the Early Modern Period.* New Haven, CT: Yale University Press, 2009.

Turner, Victor, and Edith Turner. *Image and Pilgrimage in Christian Culture: Anthropological Perspectives.* New York: Columbia University Press, 1978.

Valensi, Lucette. *On the Eve of Colonialism: North Africa before the French Conquest.* Translated by Kenneth J. Perkins. New York: Africana, 1977.

Valman, Nadia. *The Jewess in Nineteenth-Century British Literary Culture.* Cambridge: Cambridge University Press, 2007.

Vidal de Langon. *Jérusalem et la Terre Sainte.* Bordeaux: J. Dupuy, 1846.

Vogüé, Eugène Melchior de. *Syrie, Palestine, Mount Athos: Voyage au pays du passé.* Paris: Plon, 1876.

Voisin, Marcel. "Théophile Gautier et la politique." *Bulletin de la Société Théophile Gautier* 15 (2003): 323–339.

Volney, Constantin-François. *Voyage en Syrie et en Egypte.* Paris: Volland, 1787.

Wakefield, David. *The French Romantics: Literature and the Visual Arts, 1800–1840.* London: Chaucer, 2007.

Waller, Susan S. *The Invention of the Model: Artists and Models in Paris, 1830–1870.* Burlington, VT: Ashgate, 2006.

Wasserstein, Bernard. *Divided Jerusalem: The Struggle for the Holy City.* 3rd ed. New Haven, CT: Yale University Press, 2008.

Weiss, Gillian. *Captives and Corsairs: France and Slavery in the Early Modern Mediterranean.* Stanford, CA: Stanford University Press, 2011.

Werblowsky, R. J. Zwi. "The Meaning of Jerusalem to Jews, Christians, and Muslims." In *Jerusalem in the Mind of the Western World, 1800–1948,* edited by Yehoshua Ben Arieh and Moshe Davis, 7–21. Westport, CT: Praeger, 1997.

Wrobel, David M. "Exceptionalism and Globalism: Travel Writers and the Nineteenth-Century American West." *The Historian* 68, no. 3 (2006): 430–460.

Ziegler, Jean. *Gautier, Baudelaire, un carée de dames.* Paris: Nizet, 1978.

Zytnicki, Colette. *Les Juifs du Maghreb: Naissance d'une historiographie coloniale.* Paris: Presses de l'Université Paris-Sorbonne, 2011.

# Index

Moors, 63, 66
Mornay, Charles de, 55, 67, 135n80
Morocco, 54–55, 59–71
Morot, Jean-Baptiste, 36
Muslims: as counterpoint to Jews, 121; French contact with, 31; in Jerusalem, 22–23, 26–27; and restrictions on Jews, 137n136; as target of Orientalism, 4, 11. *See also* Arabs
Musset, Alfred de, 56
Mustapha, 101, 147n60

Nathan (fictional character), 46–52, 63, 86–88
nationalism: French, 1, 5–6, 64, 119–120; Zionism, 4–5, 11
*Nationalité française* (Didier), 64
Nerval, Gérard de, 43, 54, 56, 62, 135n79
Nirenberg, David, 9, 121
*Noce juive au Maroc* (Delacroix), 73, 75
Nodier, Charles, 46

Orient, the, 1, 10
*Les Orientales* (Hugo), 56, 86
Orientalism: as antisemitism, 4, 123n7; colonial face of, 4–5, 11, 42, 55, 118, 122; French Catholic (*see* pilgrimage); Jew as referent in, 4, 113, 120; overview of, 3–4, 14, 120
Oriental Jews: fantasies of, 9–10, 119–121; French interactions with, 2, 6–9, 13–14, 26–39, 42, 53–74, 130n116; versus French Jews, 40, 68, 72, 75–90, 120; as go-betweens, 31–32, 51, 66–74, 111, 113, 117–118, 121–122, 124n23 (*see also* House of Bacri and Busnach); overview of, 1, 119–122; separation of, 61. *See also specific people*
Orthodox Church, 22, 35–36, 60, 127n47, 130–131n135
Osmin (fictional character), 115
Other, 9–10, 40, 122
Ottoman Empire, 20–22, 103–105

Palestine: Jewish presence in, 19–22; travel to (*see* pilgrimage); Zionism in, 4–5, 11
*La Palestine, ou Une visite aux Lieux-Saints* (Filleul de Petigny), 32
Parfait, Noel, 46, 51
Paris: Jews in, 1, 75; siege of, 86–87
Paris Commune (1870), 86
Party of Order, 15
Pasquier, Baron, 110–111
*La Patrie* (Lamy), 52
patriotism, 49–50, 133n47
*Un Pèlerinage en Terre Sainte* (Delorme), 127n44
Penslar, Derek, 4

petit cénacle, 43, 44
*petit peuple*, 13–14
*Phèdre* (Racine), 78
*Philoméla* (Mendès), 84
philosemitism, 9, 42, 51, 121
pilgrimage, 12–39; Catholicism and, 2, 14–19, 33–38; and encounters with Jews, 2, 13–14, 26–39; to Jerusalem, 22–26; links to Crusades, 12, 17–19, 24–25, 33, 119; overview of, 10, 119, 125n11; Romanticism and, 12, 17–19, 33, 35; travel conditions, 20–22; versus travelers, 36–37; written accounts of, 16–17, 32–39, 119, 126n22 (*see also specific accounts*)
piracy, 98, 107
Pius IX, Pope, 16
Planche, Gustave, 88
Poëri (fictional character), 82–83, 89
Poujoulat, Baptistin, 61, 63, 66, 70–71
Poujoulat, Jean-Joseph, 61, 71
Pratt, Mary Louise, 42
Privat d'Anglemont, Alexandre, 76
*Le Prophète* (Meyerbeer), 88
Protestants, 129n96

Rachel (fictional character), 81, 86
*Rachel* (Foa), 86
Rachel (Rachel Félix), 2, 7, 76–79, 88–89, 120, 141n250
Rachel (sister-in-law of Azencot), 68
Racine, Jean, 78
Ra'hel (fictional character), 82–83, 88
Raynal, Paul, 116
Rebecca (fictional character), 47, 86
Regard, Maurice, 135n80
religion: Catholicism, 2, 14–19, 33–38 (*see also* pilgrimage); Greek Orthodoxy, 22, 35–36, 60, 127n47, 130–131n135; Islam (*see* Muslims); Protestants, 129n96
Renan, Ernest, 36–37
*Revue des deux mondes*, 46, 53
Richardson, Joanna, 80
Rogier, Camille, 43
*Le Roman de la momie* (Gautier), 45, 81–84, 88
Romanelli, Samuel, 136n115
Romanticism: of Gautier, 41–45, 57–58, 65–66, 77–80, 125n3; pilgrimage and, 12, 17–19, 33, 35; in travel writing, 57–58
Rosenstock, Morton, 145–146n25
Rosset de Létourville, Charles-Marie, 17
Rothschild, Gustave de, 38–39
Rothschild, James de, 8, 64, 66, 75, 85, 115–116
Rousier, Abbé, 32

JULIE KALMAN is Associate Professor in the School of Philosophical, Historical and International Studies at Monash University in Melbourne, Australia. She has published extensively on the history of antisemitism and Jewish-Catholic relations in France. Her first book, *Rethinking Antisemitism in Nineteenth-Century France*, was published in 2010.

CPSIA information can be obtained
at www.ICGtesting.com
Printed in the USA
BVOW03s1940190117
473941BV00015B/15/P